MW00777714

Event and World

Series Board

James Bernauer

Drucilla Cornell

Thomas R. Flynn

Kevin Hart

Richard Kearney

Jean-Luc Marion

Adriaan Peperzak

Thomas Sheehan

Hent de Vries

Merold Westphal

Edith Wyschogrod

Michael Zimmerman

John D. Caputo, *series editor*

PERSPECTIVES IN
CONTINENTAL
PHILOSOPHY

CLAUDE ROMANO

Event and World

TRANSLATED BY SHANE MACKINLAY

FORDHAM UNIVERSITY PRESS
New York ▪ 2009

Copyright © 2009 Fordham University Press

All rights reserved. No part of this publication may be reproduced, stored in a retrieval system, or transmitted in any form or by any means—electronic, mechanical, photocopy, recording, or any other—except for brief quotations in printed reviews, without the prior permission of the publisher.

Event and World was first published in French under the title *L'événement et le monde* by Presses Universitaires de France, © 1998 Presses Universitaires de France.

This work has been published with the assistance of the French Ministry of Culture—National Center for the Book.

Ouvrage publié avec le concours du Ministère français chargé de la culture—Centre National du Livre.

Library of Congress Cataloging-in-Publication Data

Romano, Claude, 1967–
    [Événement et le monde, English]
    Event and world / Claude Romano ; translated by Shane Mackinlay.
        p.   cm. — (Perspectives in continental philosophy)
    Includes bibliographical references and index.
    ISBN 978-0-8232-2970-3 (cloth : alk. paper) —
    ISBN 978-0-8232-2971-0 (pbk. : alk. paper)
    1. Events (Philosophy)   2. Phenomenology.   I. Title.
B2433.R663E9413   2008
142′.7—dc22
                                                                                2008043315

Printed in the United States of America
11   10   09   5   4   3   2   1

Contents

Translator's Note

The French text draws heavily on a cluster of words related to *venir* (to come): *advenir* (to happen), *survenir* (to occur), and *devenir* (to become). These words have an etymological connection to "event" that cannot be conveyed in English. *Advenant* is the present participle of *advenir,* used as a noun, and has not been translated, so that the etymological relation to "event" is clear, in at least this instance. Similarly, "advent," "advene," and "adventure" have been used where possible.

The key pair of adjectives *événementiel/événemential* is rendered by "evental/evential." *Événementiel* is the usual French adjective related to "event," while *événemential* is a neologism.

"Significance" has been reserved for the technical phenomenological sense of signifying. It translates *significance,* which in turn refers to Heidegger's *Bedeutsamkeit.*

Due to the lack of an obvious alternative, "receive/reception" has been used to translate both *accueillir/accueil* and *recevoir/réception.* The sense of *accueillir* is not simply passive, but rather it means to receive as one receives a guest. Because this is quite a distinct sense of "receive," it has been marked in the text by including the French original in parentheses.

Neutre has been translated as "impersonal" instead of "neutral."

I wish to thank the Melbourne College of Divinity, which supported this project, and Brett O'Neill, who located the English versions of the various quotations used in the text. The translation owes a great deal to Claude Romano himself, who was actively interested throughout the project and collaborated very closely in its final stages. He carefully reviewed each page and made detailed suggestions for improvements in the text.

Preface

The text that follows is presented as an independent work that can be approached without any preliminaries. However, it is also the first part of a two-volume work, whose second part is entitled *Event and Time* [*L'événement et le temps*]. The human being is not interpreted here as *zōion logon echon*, nor as a Cartesian "*res cogitans*," nor as Dasein, but instead as the one to whom something happens, the one who alone is "capable" of events. This interpretation is completed by a phenomenology of time, where time is understood as what becomes accessible and comprehensible starting from what happens to us, as events "temporalize" it. Thus, the analyses of the present work are taken up and deepened in light of the temporal phenomenon.

The terminology and style of this book call for a brief justification. Philosophy is written in everyday language, but what it tries to bring to light is not necessarily what this language says. In this respect, the limits of language do not coincide with the limits of thought. If there is a point to philosophical research, it is that it aims to think and say more than what is thought or said in everyday language. To do this, it must fashion concepts adequate to the phenomena to be revealed. Events are pure "mobility"—without anything that moves. The vocabulary of classical ontology cannot accomplish the task of describing this anonymous "shifting" in and for itself. Its "static" character condemns it. As the objective of this book is to understand the human individual starting from the differentiated modalities according to which he can happen to himself from what happens to him, it was necessary to be able to describe such a plot in terms that convey something of this mobility of events, rendering it visible in some fashion. First of all, the human being understood and interpreted in light of events is not the one studied by anthropology, sociology, or psychoanalysis. The gap between these disciplines and evential hermeneutics is what separates innerworldly sciences of facts and their causes from an interpretation of meaning in its origin for the human being. Therefore, it was necessary to refer to the latter by a term that made impossible any confusion with either the empirical-factual sciences, which deal with the human being as a fact to study, or with an ontology, even if it is fundamental, that elevates him to the status of exemplary being. With some reserve and without excessive enthusiasm, I have ventured a neologism: the *advenant*. By this present participle used as a noun I am endeavoring to name more an ongoing process than a constituted reality: less a "subject" in the classical sense than diverse modes of subjectivization through which an "I" can come about [*advenir*], responding to what happens to him starting from the kernels of meaning that are for him events. Moreover, this term has the advantage of belonging to a quite rich semantic network of the French language: hence the choice of the word "adventure" for what ontology generally calls "existence," and the term "eventuality" to indicate the properly evential sense of possibility, rather than a contingent possibility that might or might not occur. All these terms are connected to the same root as "event," "advent," "future [*avenir*]": they describe the movement of an arrival inseparable from a transformation. Happily or not, their choice responds to the need for a "technical" vocabulary in philosophy, for terms shifted from their conventional use. It is not owing to pedantry or a liking for paradox—and even less to a kind of idle sophistication that would confine itself to the esoteric—that I have made these innovations: it is because "natural language" in no way exhausts the resources of the thinkable. Nor can it prescribe limits to thought. It is impossible to modify the interpretation of particular phenomena without at the same time modifying the language in which it is expressed. I have endeavored to limit these innovations as much as possible, preferring to redefine the meaning of already existing words (thus, for example, the central notion of "responsibility") rather than invent entirely new words. However, I have not been able to avoid this entirely (thus, terms such as "evential [*événemential*]," "passibility [*passibilité*]," "uncondition [*incondition*]," "*empirie*," etc.). Considerable philosophical problems are created by lexical creations in philosophy, and this is not the place to discuss them. Perhaps the reader will recognize along the way that the innovations in this book respond to rigorous conceptual needs.

᷾

I express my thanks to those whose reading, advice, and support have accompanied the editing of this work, which was, in its first version, a dissertation. Didier Franck's clear-sightedness, friendship, and encouragement have never failed me. The generous and attentive reading of Françoise Dastur and Jean-Luc Marion, along with their penetrating comments at my defense, has allowed me to make substantial improvements. Jean-Louis Chrétien, Catherine Chevalley, and Guy Petitdemange have read my work with friendship and a critical sense that is priceless for a young philosopher. Finally, Jean-François Courtine's advice has been extremely valuable for refining the text in its definitive version. Each of these people well knows what this book and its author owe them.

I would like to address a particular thanks to Jean-Luc Marion for having accepted this book for the collection *Épiméthée*.

Paris, May 1997

Event and World

Introduction: The Problem

> One doesn't say that events are, nor that they are not, but only that they
> happen or occur, appear in disappearing, are born and die in the same
> instant. . . . This occurring—more dazzling than lightning, more brilliant
> and striking than sparks—always comes as a supplement of Being.
> —**Vladimir Jankélévitch**[1]

The world in which we are born and which forms the horizon of all our
human behavior is a world both of things and of events. To endeavor to
describe it, to attempt to state in what sense it is properly a *phenomenon*,
to undertake its *phenomeno-logy*, is to renounce from the outset all no-
menclature having to do with objects, so as to grasp how the world, at
each instant, *configures itself* or *advenes* to itself, "enworlds" itself [*se "mon-
difie"*], the event of its own advent, the "there [*il y a*]" of all that takes
place in it. Any description of our situation in the world is thus inspired
from the outset by the proliferation of *verbs*, which refer to the way
"things" *come to pass, happen*, or *come about*, in turning toward us:

*Outside, it is night. It rains, and the rain steps up its violence, dully ham-
mering the ground, in sad litanies or staccato bursts, at times raging and quer-
ulous, at times pacified and pacifying, smelling like a flower blooming in the
middle of this somber light, far away and yet beside us, submerging everything
in its sweetness. Suddenly, in the time without duration of an instant, lightning flashes: a scrawled flourish of light that is extinguished straightway and*

soon followed by thunder. A window slams and the storm has played itself out:
a blank, inarticulate cry in the electric heat, with its mute warnings, its mad
and impossible calls, the implacable battering of an invisible army on the
march or a torrent that leaves the earth exhausted, worked over, inert.

A "fore-world" or "pre-world" flickers in each of these events; they
bear it and bring it along with them. A rainy and nocturnal world is laid
out and opened as a corollary around the invisible drumming of water, a
world tormented by the storm that announces itself in the eruption of
lightning and thunder. Each time, these events punctuate and accentuate
the advent of the world that opens itself out in them. But what, precisely,
can be said of these events? Does not language fall short here? All that can
be said is that they *happen* or that they *take place*, that they well up like
luminous trails, only to sink immediately into night. Nevertheless, nothing is more familiar to us than what comes to upset the frozen order of
things, introducing "movement." Isn't what we call, maladroitly and for
want of a better term, an "event" simply a change that occurs in the arrangement of things—what the Greeks called *cosmos*—a change that modifies this order without going so far as to overturn it, and that therefore
always happens within the horizon of the world?

This would be satisfactory if we knew what we should understand by
"thing" and by "change," if these two phenomena had not been viewed
in relation to each other since the dawn of Greek thought: in other words,
if change had not always been interpreted within the horizon of a *thing*
that changes and expressed by a noun, such as modification (*alloiosis*) or
mutation (*metabole*), affecting the beingness[2] [*étance*] (*ousia*) of that which
is. But can an event, a pure taking-place, a pure bursting-forth, expressed
grammatically as a *verb*, be apprehended by means of such concepts? Are
we not compelled in a contrary direction, to a profound reform in our
way of thinking, in that "event" is given as "pure change," "*change with-*
out anything that changes," as Bergson puts it,[3] mutation that is in itself
im-mobile if all "mobility" and "movement" in general presuppose a
moved thing, a "mobile," change that is not so much bound up with
Being as it is that which announces itself, freed from all relation to Being,
as the lightning of time—in a sense that is truly apparent only in a resolutely paradoxical phrase, such as Bergson's?

To think events *before anything*: Isn't this an impossible challenge? As
soon as we attempt to grasp an event as it happens in itself, we are almost
immediately absorbed by other things, by "things" precisely, frozen before
our eyes by a Medusa's gaze. We say, "It is night," and straightway ask
ourselves: "What is this 'it' that is night?" We want to look for a cause for
this event, that is, to connect it to *something*. Cause and "arche-thing"

(*Ursache*) say the same thing here. We say, in all innocence, "It's raining," and straightway we want to grasp what "thing" the rain *is*: a thing diffuse and impalpable, obscurely present and pre-possessing, with no limits that can be assigned and no place. We see the lightning flash, and we wonder: "What *is* 'that,' the lightning, which flashes thus?" And we find a cause for it, which we call "fire" or a "strike" or "electricity." We say that the night smells sweet, and we want to know what these blindly launched words actually name or denote. We think that "night" is a certain lack of light, and that "smells sweet" denotes a sensory phenomenon, a type of odor—and so we settle on "the night is full of fragrance" as a synonym, as if it were still a matter of things and causes, and we do not see what thereby *happens, occurs,* or *comes about:* the *impersonal* event of "it's raining," "it is night," "it smells sweet."

However, if we look at things differently and focus on events, what shows itself is quite something else. Nothing is interposed between events and our look; they are an epiphany that anticipates all things, rendered linguistically by a verb, most often in an impersonal form—"it's raining," "it is night"—though sometimes in a personal form: "the storm bursts," "the sun shines," the moon "moons" [*la lune "illunit"*] (Rimbaud). Acting without agent, pure efficacy, change without anything that changes, pure flash of a time without duration, resonating in a verb from which the noun itself appears *derived*, the "moon" being nothing other than that which moons, the "sun" being the substantivized cause of an impersonal efficacy: the sunshine.

Yet what is it about the phenomenality of events, such that they are manifested *before anything*? How can this phenomenality be described in a language without metaphysical presuppositions? Is such an undertaking possible? For the grammatical distinction between verbs and nouns, which guided us at first, proves difficult to handle: is not every verb said, in fact, in connection to a noun? Would not grasping events in themselves therefore free the verbalness of verbs from any noun and understand the essence of nouns from the verbalness of verbs? Verbalness of verbs absorbing nouns, redoubling itself in them to the point of tautology: the sun (*sun*)*shines* [le soleil *ensoleille*], the moon "*moons*" . . . ?

§1 Events Before Anything

Events *before anything:* Nietzsche attempts to make it possible to approach this by denouncing the "metaphysical grammar" that governs ontological propositions, in which events appear from the outset subordinated to beings, folded into them and reduced to one of their properties. Nietzsche affirms that what characterizes an event such as "the lightning flashes," rendered here by a verb, "to flash," is that it radically puts in question the ontological distinctions that affect a being in its beingness:

> If I say: "Lightning flashes," I have posited the flashing once as activity and once as subject, and have thus added on to what happens [*Geschehen*] a being [*Sein*] that is not identical with what happens but that *remains, is,* and does not *"become."—To posit what happens as acting,* and *acting as being*: that is the *twofold* error, or *interpretation,* of which we are guilty. Thus, e.g., "The lightning flashes"— "to flash" is an effect on ourselves [*Zustand an uns*]; but we don't take it to be acting on us. Instead we say: "Something flashing" as an "in-itself" and then look for an author for it—the "lightning."[4]

In this fragment, Nietzsche attacks what he calls a "fundamental belief," the belief that "there are subjects."[5] Indeed, by interpreting every appearance in relation to a *subject*, for example, every "action" in relation to an agent, every "effect" in relation to a "cause," it is implicitly asserted that "everything that happens relates as a predicate to some subject."[6] *Assigning an event to an ontic substrate entails reducing the event to a pure "predicate," which is therefore used in connection with a "subject."* In Nietzsche's example ("the lightning flashes"), the flashing is not understood in its purely verbal sense, as an event that is displayed as such and that manifests itself in and of itself, but as a "predicate," a "property" that manifests *some other thing*, namely its *ontic substrate*, denoted here by the logical subject of the proposition: the lightning. Now, according to Nietzsche, the profound "error" and "mythology" brought about by language resides precisely in this transformation of an event into a predicate; instead of regarding events as "changes in ourselves" we have "invented for them a being in which they inhere, i.e., we have posited the *action as something that acts* and *what acts as a being*."[7] What we call "lightning" is not a "being" that possesses a certain *mode of Being*, for it is *not a being at all* but "is" precisely *nothing else* than the *flashing* itself: it is the "taking-place" of an event that gives a place for the "thing" and not the inverse; it is from the verbalness of the verb that the subject derives, instead of the verb being conceived as that which expresses the "action" of an agent.

What is the import of this Nietzschean critique of metaphysics, which is a critique of the language of metaphysics and of the grammar at work there? In any case, it is decisive for our problem. Indeed, this "fundamental belief," the metaphysical belief par excellence in a "world behind the scenes" populated by substrates and imaginary entities, wipes out the "*there* [il y a]" of an event, as something distinct from the beingness of that which is: an event simply occurs *from itself*, in such a way that, according to the implicit grammar of metaphysics, we cannot distinguish the "flashing" (the event) from *what* flashes (the ontic substrate, the *agent* of the action, the *cause* of the effect). Instead, what flashes, the lightning, is precisely nothing else than the "flashing" itself. Only "the seduction of language"[8] is able to make us think of events, attested to by verbs, as conditioned by ontic substrates, which are expressed in terms of subjects. What is thus wiped out by the influence of grammar and, even more originally, by the logical analysis of propositions as formulated by Aristotle in his theory of syllogisms, are the *phenomenal* characteristics of events themselves.

Analysis of these phenomenal traits will be carried out below, but on its own such analysis does not suffice to resolve the issue of the import of Nietzsche's critique. Indeed, as a preliminary step, it is necessary to determine *what concept of ontology* such a critique presumes when it claims to remove events, in their phenomenality, from ontology. Without a stricter delimitation of the latter's domain and of its leading concepts, the question of determining whether events "are" or "are" not—whether they are or are not thinkable in light of ontological categories—remains futile. Now, there is no doubt that when Nietzsche critiques the reduction of events to the logical categories of subject and predicate and to the ontological categories of being *per se* and being *per accidens*, of beingness and attribute, he is principally thinking of Aristotelian ontology, along with its scholastic and modern heirs. However, is this the only concept of ontology, and does it exhaust the field of the question of being? Assuredly not. Is this critique then void, a dead end? On the contrary!

In any case, it is appropriate to begin with these questions, in order to state clearly the scope of the investigation that follows and to determine its meaning and significance.

§2 The Metaontological Status of Events in Stoicism

For our purposes, what makes ancient Stoicism interesting is its acute consciousness of the impossibility of any *ontology* of events. This word, which is not Greek, must be understood here as meaning a doctrine or science of being qua being (*on hē on*), to which the Stoics, in contrast with Aristotle, always resisted assigning philosophical primacy: they preferred to start with physics, the science of bodies as such—the domain of bodies (*ta sōmata*) being strictly identical to that of beings (*ta onta*), according to their "corporalism." In its own way, Stoicism thus joins and clarifies

Nietzsche's critique of the "metaphysical grammar" that governs ontological propositions, in which events are subordinated to beings, whose Being is first of all indexed as beingness (*ousia*), thus reducing events to an attribute or accident of the latter. Like Nietzsche's critique, that of Stoicism engages the debate principally on the terrain of Aristotle's *Metaphysics*. And, again like Nietzsche, it ends up by removing events from the horizon of ontology.

In their doctrine of "supreme genus [*genikōtaton*]," the Stoics accord a "metaontological" status to events. Unlike Plato in the *Sophist*, who supports the absolute convertibility of a "something" (*ti*) and a being (*on*), by affirming that whatever is "something" is ipso facto a being,[9] the Stoics dissociate the two terms. They not only subordinate beings, which they define as synonymous with bodies, to something in general, but they also subordinate incorporeals (*asōmata*) in the same way, including in their canonical list: the void, place, time, and *lekta*.[10] Even though these incorporeals really are *something*, they are not *beings*:[11] they occur or are encountered as nonbeings (*mē onta*), but, in this ontic nullity of their pure occurring, they are not reduced to *nothing*.

Events or states of affairs signified by propositions (*axiōmata*)—*lekta*, such as "it is daytime" or "Dion is taking a walk"—belong to this latter category of incorporeals. From a logical point of view, such propositions are not analyzed according to the predicative form privileged by Aristotelian logic: "S is P," where the verb "is" plays the role of copula; rather, they are analyzed according to the difference between nouns (*onoma*) and verbs (*rhēma*); more precisely, this difference is expressed in logical terms by the distinction between complete and incomplete *lekta*.[12] Therefore, discourse does not consist fundamentally of "saying something about something [*legein ti kata tinos*]," in Aristotle's famous definition, but of completing a predicate (*katēgorēma*) by means of an inflection (*ptōsis*) expressed by a nominative case. Unlike an Aristotelian attribute, this predicate, or incomplete *lekton*, does not signify a particular ontic property but an *event*. As Emile Bréhier emphasizes:

> Stoic dialectic no longer divides the verb as Aristotle did into a copula and an attribute referring to a general notion; it takes the verb as a whole, as expressing an event. The attribute is only this event, and only events can be objects of discourse (*lekta*). They are not realities; the only reality is being that acts; they are the results of the activity of bodies, "incorporeals." Dialectic is therefore only concerned with events or with a series of events.[13]

The attribute or predicate is no longer a general concept under which the subject is subsumed, with the copula signifying the relation of inherence that unites them; the *logos* no longer consists in the connection of two terms by means of the verb "to be," each referring to a class of objects, in a demonstrative proposition (*apophansis*) that can be true or false. Instead, the Stoic determination of the *logos* moves away from the fundamental concepts of *sunthesis* and *diairesis*, which govern Aristotle's analysis.[14] They define the *logos* as an utterance that is "articulated and issues from thought [*phōnē sēmantikē apo dianoias ekpempomenē*],"[15] such as "it is daytime." Stoic semantics is thus able to move away from the copula. They no longer consider the verb, or the incomplete predicate, as a noun that refers to a property of a subject,[16] but establish a radical heterogeneity between subject and predicate, which Frege will later reestablish in his *Begriffschrift*.

Stoic logic is thus able to move beyond the copula. It is more inclined to formulate the proposition "the tree is green" in the form "the tree greens." It no longer conceives the predicate as a property occurring to a subject, or as an accident (*sumbebēkos*) affecting a beingness (*ousia*), but as an incorporeal event, which is neither a being nor of the order of beings, which names nothing, but is said about something. To express this paradoxical nonbeing of events, the Stoics have recourse to a specific vocabulary: they do not say that a signified incorporeal event (*lekton*) "is" (*esti*), but that it occurs, happens, or, more rigorously, that it "is encountered [*huparchei*]."[17] For an event, in itself, is precisely *nothing* ontic, ungraspable in the frame of beings, and consequently also irreducible to the *Being* of beings, unable to be assimilated to their beingness.

This is what appears in the second "place" (*topos*) where the Stoics thematize the metaontological status of events: no longer in the logical doctrine of propositions, but in the physical doctrine of causality. This doctrine follows entirely from their calling into question ontology's status as the most universal doctrine, since the domain of beings, the *bodily*, is interrupted on its margins by this obscure limit of *asōmata*, which no longer refer to ontology but rather exempt themselves from it and assign an exteriority to it: something in general (*ti*). Indeed, the Stoics make a distinction between the "category"[18] of quality, a bodily, active, and pneumatic principle that resides in all matter, and the incorporeal predicate, which refers to an event. Quality (understood as individualizing quality: *idiōs poion*) is expressed by an epithet; the predicate by a verb. Here again, physics is nourished by logical and grammatical distinctions. But how are these distinctions to be articulated? Consider any event whatsoever: for instance, a knife cutting meat. This event is characterized in relation to many terms. First, it puts a cause (i.e., a being) into play: a knife, which has the property of sharpness, by which it is the active cause of the meat's being-cut. As well, it puts a passive cause in play: the meat, which has at least the property of being able to be cut and which is that without which the being-cut, the event described here, could not happen. The being-from-which (the knife), as an active cause, and the being-without-which (passive cause: the meat) produce an effect by their coming together: the being-cut of the meat (the event). Both causes referred to here are *bodies*: the knife and its quality (sharpness), the meat and its quality (being able to be cut, tenderness). By contrast, the effect is not a body but an accident or an attribute that occurs to a body. This attribute is an "expressible," an incorporeal *lekton*: "Zeno says that a cause [*aition*] is 'that because of which' [*di ho*], while that of which it is the cause is an accident [*sumbebēkos*]. The cause is a body, while that of which it is a cause is an attribute [*katēgorēma*]."[19]

In the first sentence, an effect is defined as an "accident," while in the second it is an "attribute." Is this confused? Not at all. A cause attributes a new property to a body: the meat is *cut*. However, more radically, rather than an effect being described as the addition of a new property or accident to a thing, it should be described as an attribute that befalls it: *being-cut*. This difference is specified by another of Sextus' texts: "The Stoics say that every cause is a body which becomes the cause to the body of something incorporeal. For instance the knife, a body, becomes the cause to the meat, a body, of the incorporeal predicate 'being cut.' And again, the fire, a body, becomes the cause to the wood, a body, of the incorporeal predicate 'being burnt.'"[20] By reducing all cause to action, the Stoics set themselves against Aristotle's theory of the four causes: every cause is efficient,[21] even if some are principal, and others are simply "auxiliary."[22] How, then, should the action of an efficient cause be analyzed? Sextus reports that a cause is a body acting on another body to produce an effect, which is not itself a body but rather an incorporeal attribute. What is particular to this attribute is precisely that it *is expressed by a verb and not by a noun or an epithet*: "Hence," writes Clement of Alexandria,

> becoming, and being cut—that of which the cause is a cause—since they are activities, are incorporeal. It can be said, to make the same point, that causes are causes of predicates, or, as some say, of sayables [*lekta*]—for Cleanthes and Archedemus call predicates "sayables." Or else, and preferably, that some are causes of predicates, for example of "is cut," whose cause [i.e., substantival form] is "being cut," but others of propositions, for example of "a ship is built," whose cause this time is "a ship's being built."[23]

All causality is expressed first by verbs, which indicate an *activity*. For the Stoics, there is no passive cause, like Aristotle's matter. The example of a knife cutting meat illustrates this well. We have two active causes, expressed by two *verbs*, in the active and passive voices respectively, such that it can be said indifferently that "the knife is the cause to the meat of being cut, while the meat is the cause to the knife of cutting."[24] Thus, for the Stoics, *causes are causes of the fact that a predicate (expressed by a verb) is true of something.* Clement opposes this conception to that of Aristotle, who "thinks that causes are causes of appellations [*prosēgoriai*], i.e. of items of the following sort: a house, a ship, a burning [*kausis*], a cut [*tomē*]."[25] There is, therefore, a difference here between a cut and the fact that something is cut (*temnesthai*), or again between a boat and the fact that something becomes a boat (*gignesthai naun*): in the first case, it is a matter of the class of words that are called "appellatives" in Greek grammar and that comprise both our nouns and our adjectives; in the second, it is a matter of predicates or verbs, since the Stoics sometimes use *katēgorēma* as a synonym for *rhēma*.

Thus, the Stoics distinguish between a process, a coming-to-be, which is an event ("becoming a boat"), and the being that becomes this or that. As subtle and Sibylline as this distinction might appear, we shall see that it is based in the things themselves. For the Stoics, who in this respect are opposed to Aristotle, "beings are not causes of each other, but causes of particular things for each other."[26] From this, it follows that an effect itself causes nothing, as it is incorporeal and inactive. An effect is certainly the effect of a cause, but it is not itself the cause of an effect. Émile Bréhier comments on this very accurately:

> These results of the action of beings [the *katēgorēmata*], which the Stoics were perhaps the first to consider in this way, are what we would call today facts or events: a bastard concept that is neither that of a being, nor of one of its properties, but is what is said or affirmed about Being. . . . An incorporeal fact is in a way at the limit of the action of bodies. . . . The act of cutting adds nothing to the nature and essence of a scalpel. The Stoics . . . in one sense are as far as possible from a conception like Hume's or Mill's, which reduces the universe to facts or events. In another sense, however, they make such a conception possible, by radically separating two levels of Being, which nobody before them had done: on the one hand, deep and real Being, force; on the other, the level of facts, which play on the surface of Being and constitute an unconnected and endless multiplicity of incorporeal beings.

So, "causes are substantial realities, while effects are events; causes are bodies, effects are incorporeals, *lekta*, whose entire essence consists only in being able to be expressed by a verb."[27]

However, by making of events that which "plays on the surface of being," to use Bréhier's expression, by according them a *metaontological* status, do not the Stoic analyses point, first and foremost, to the limitations of an *ousiological* ontology such as Aristotle's? And, in this case, mustn't we reconsider the problem entirely and assert that an ontological thematization of events can only be possible on condition of a radical reform of ontology? Isn't it, then, appropriate to turn to Heidegger's fundamental ontology and the subsequent developments of his elaboration of the question of Being rather than to Aristotle's ontology?

§3 Events from the Perspective of Heideggerian "Ontology"

If traditional ontology manifestly falls short of according events the place they deserve in the general economy of Being, how are things placed with the breakthrough beyond classic ontology in Heidegger's *Being and Time* and later works? This question seems even more justified since, as we will see, from *Being and Time* onward, Heidegger's fresh approach to the question of Being tends to confer a wholly *evental* sense on Being, contrary to the primarily predicative sense that classic ontology gives it. But is this opposition between an attributive sense of Being and an evental sense really pertinent for thinking Heidegger's reformulation? I need to briefly show that it is.

Levinas was the first to draw attention to what he considered to be the major innovation of *Being and Time*: the fact that "Being" receives the verbal or transitive sense of a way of Being or a *mode of Being*:

> I think that the new philosophical "thrill" that comes from Heidegger's philosophy consists in making the distinction between *Being* [*être*] and *being* [*étant*] and carrying into Being the relation, motion, efficacy that until then resided in the existent [*existant*]. Existentialism [a term Levinas uses for Heidegger's thought as a whole, without thereby reducing it to anthropology] *is feeling and thinking existence—the being-verb* [*l'être-verbe*]—*as event*. . . . In short, there are no more copulas in existential philosophy. Copulas express the very event of Being.[28]

It is because "Being" denotes the very event of being, and not *what is*, that Being is not to be found in the realm of beings, as one being among others: Being *is* not; only beings "are." What Heidegger calls the "ontological difference" is located in this discrepancy. Now, to bring this difference to light presumes that *logos*—interpreted as "saying something about something [*legein ti kata tinos*]," following a predicative structure where "being" plays the role of copula—is no longer taken as the guiding concept for responding to the question of the meaning of Being. The only possible starting point is a *being*—an exemplary one, to be sure—for which Being is indexed in a singular way because, in its Being, what is at stake is this very Being. In other words, it is necessary to start with the only being for whom an understanding of Being belongs essentially to its Being, the being that is ontologically ontological. We *are* ourselves this being, *Dasein*.

What is particular to this being is that it is not *this or that* in the sense that one could attribute it such-and-such a property; it does not have an "essence" in the traditional sense, since, on the contrary, its ontological constitution demands that it determine itself ontically on each occasion by existing its possibilities, that is, by making them possible. By existing, it has to decide *who* it is: its lack of definite ontic characteristics is a definite ontological characteristic. In other words, its possibilities do not lend themselves to being enclosed and delimited by a defining essence, since it *is* its possibilities and determines them only by existing. It *is* ("essentially") nothing other than the *event* of existing its possibilities—or, as Heidegger writes: "*The 'essence'* [das "Wesen"] *of Dasein lies in its existence.*"[29] And because such a being does not have an essence, in the medieval sense of *essentia*, since such an "essence" is inconsistent with its ontological constitution, neither should its "existence" be understood in the scholastic sense of *existentia*. Unlike beings that are merely present-at-hand (*vorhanden*), Dasein is not simply there. Rather, it *is* (transitively) its There, in that it exists it. It is not merely "there" alongside other beings; it is *the* fundamental There for the manifestation of Being, from which beings themselves become manifest and encounterable as such. Thus, Heidegger proposes the expression "being-the-There [*être-le-Là*]" for translating Da-sein into French. But what matters first of all for understanding this expression is being careful not to miss the verbal sense of Da-sein in opposition to *Daseiendes*. It is because Dasein exists its Being transitively, because Being is not a property or trait of its essence, that Dasein *is* there. For Dasein, Being can only have the transitive sense of *existing*. As Levinas rightly emphasizes, this verbal form "expresses the fact that each element of man's essence is a mode of existing, of being situated there."[30]

But what exactly does "exist" mean here for Dasein, if existence is no longer that which answers the question "*an sit?*" in contrast with the question about essence "*quid sit?*" if it is no longer the *quodditas* that contrasts with the *quidditas*? To exist is a *way of Being* of a being, Dasein, which is characterized by being its Being transitively, in that it exists it in the first person. For such a being to understand Being is to relate itself to Being as its own; in other words, for itself to be at stake in its Being. Affirming the mineness (*Jemeinigkeit*) of Being therefore merely develops the seemingly obscure formula according to which, for this being, in its very Being, that Being is an issue for it. In understanding Being (by existing), this being also understands *who* it is. For Dasein "cannot at all be *interrogated* as such by the question *What* is this? We gain access to this being only if we ask: *Who* is it? The Dasein is not constituted by whatness but—if I may coin the expression—by *whoness*."[31] The question that is addressed to Dasein and that requires it to answer in such a way that it thereby answers for its Being is the question: *Who* are you?—for *Jemeinigkeit* belongs to Dasein's Being fundamentally. This mineness should not be understood in a naïvely "subjectivist" sense, as if affirming that "Being is in each case mine [*je meines*]" made Being itself something "subjective." Rather, "subjectivity" itself—being oneself, *Selbstheit*—is an *ontological* trait of Dasein. As Heidegger makes clear in *Introduction to Metaphysics*, "Dasein is 'in each case mine'; this means neither that it is posited by me nor that it is confined to an isolated ego. Dasein is *itself* by virtue of its essential *relation to* Being in general. That is what the oft-repeated sentence in *Being and Time* means: 'the understanding of Being belongs to Dasein.' "[32]

This is why, just as the verbal sense of existence indicates the event of transcendence by which Dasein understands and relates itself to Being in order to uncover Being and thus discover beings in general, including the being that it itself is, so "understanding" denotes an *event* by which Being itself becomes manifest and is uncovered for Dasein. Understanding does not mean some theoretical comportment of a subject to an object, a kind of knowledge in the traditional sense: it is a mode of existing, a way of Being, the fundamental event of Dasein's transcendence, in which Being is uncovered and, in this uncovering, the being is brought to openness. To understand is to bring about the uncovering of Being by existing (it).

The profound upheaval that Heidegger introduces into ontology thus becomes apparent: existence, understanding, truth come into view as events that happen to Dasein and thereby to Being as such. Understanding is a *work of truth;* truth is *uncovering*. These existentials denote, in some way, the very event of Being [*l'événement même de l'être*], which is inseparable from the event of being [*l'événement d'être*] and for which Dasein is, consequently, the "site." For, strictly speaking, there would be nothing such as Being unless Dasein understood it and unless truth happened with Dasein. In a deeply thoughtful commentary, Levinas writes: "The essence of the human being is in this work of truth; the human being is therefore not a noun, but firstly a verb: he is part of the economy of Being, the 'self-revealing' of Being."[33] Henceforth, it is only insofar as truth is an existential, the event of Dasein existing itself, insofar as Dasein *is truth* (transitively) by existing, that an onto-*logy* in the traditional sense is possible—an ontology that is built on categories of the predicative *logos* in its truth-asserting or "apophantic" function. This is why the categories of assertion (in particular the distinction between subject and predicate), on which traditional ontology is structured, are ultimately grounded in Dasein's existentials and especially in understanding. It is only because Dasein exists in the mode of Being-in-the-world that an entity is uncovered to it *by* its existence, in such a way that the uncovered entity can be made the subject of an enunciation. Thus it becomes possible to *derive* traditional ontology, whose guiding concepts are *logos* and its predicative structure, from Dasein's ontology, which alone is *fundamental.* Truth in an ontic sense, as accordance (*homoiōsis*) or adequation of the assertion and the thing, is ultimately grounded on the disclosedness (*Erschlossenheit*) of Being; that is, on truth in an ontological sense. This ontological truth is identical with the very openness that Being-in-the-world *is* by existing.

Thus, because, from *Being and Time* on, Being has been interrogated from the outset in its verbal and transitive—evental—sense, with Dasein as the guiding concept, it has become possible to derive and dismantle onto-logy, which, as ousiology, has been governed since Aristotle by the primacy of the predicative structure. In short, from *Being and Time* onward, Heidegger no longer thinks Being "logically" in its meaning as copula (with its various significations: existential, "the tree is"; essential, "the tree is a plant"; accidental, "the tree is green"; truth-asserting, "the tree *is* green"; etc.), but more originarily as Event. It is only on this condition that time can be determined to be the horizon for the understanding of Being.

What is referred to as the "*Kehre* [turn]" largely consists of deepening this thought about Being in terms of event. Dasein becomes what is in play (Heidegger plays here on the word *Bei-spiel* [example], which he earlier used to refer to the "exemplary" being) in the play of concealing and unconcealing, which belongs to Being itself. It is certainly not by chance that, in *The Onto-theo-logical Constitution of Metaphysics*, which is crucial in more than one respect and in which Heidegger sets out to think Being itself starting from Difference (Being-beings), Being is described as "the unconcealing overwhelming [*die entbergende Überkommnis*]" that, as such, covers itself over in a being's "arrival that keeps itself concealed [*sich bergende Ankunft*]."[34] Here, the eventness of Being, or its "mobility," as

Levinas would say, is made visible by the particularly paradoxical affirmation that "the Being of beings means Being which is beings."[35] But doesn't the ontological difference specify that Being "is" not, and that only beings "are"? How, then, can one hold an affirmation such as "Being is beings"? Actually, this formulation of the ontological difference contradicts the more customary statement only if "is" is understood in the sense of *identity:* Being is obviously not identical to beings and is certainly not itself a being. However, it is quite different if "is" is understood here in the sense of the inherent mobility of Being itself, with which Being advenes and, in this occurring, withdraws, in making beings happen—if "is" is understood as Heidegger specifies it, in the sense of a "transition" or a "passage [*Übergang*]": "The 'is' here speaks transitively, in transition. Being here becomes present in the manner of a transition to beings."[36] Not that Being "leaves its domain," so to speak, to rejoin the beings from which it is separated. Being's movement is instead the very event by which Being comes over the being that it uncovers: "Being transits (that), comes unconcealingly over (that) which arrives [*ankommt*] as something of itself unconcealed only by that coming-over [*Überkommnis*]."[37] Hence, Being shows itself as the unconcealing overwhelming according to which a being itself appears in the mode of an arrival that conceals itself in unconcealment (*Unverborgenheit*). Thus, Being and beings are deployed starting from the dimension (*Unter-schied*) of their differentiation, in which the overwhelming and the arrival are "held toward one another, are borne away from and toward each other."[38] This dimension, which correlates unconcealing overwhelming (Being) to concealing arrival (beings), is that in which Being, by unconcealing beings, conceals itself in the unconcealment of beings, *is* beings, and covers itself over in them; this dimension is "the unconcealing keeping in concealment [*der entbergend-bergende Austrag*]" that governs the between (*das Zwischen*) of the two: Being and beings.[39]

But this twofold deployment of Being and beings as unconcealing overwhelming and concealing arrival, this movement of difference that is difference itself in movement, *differentiation* of the two, has the consequence that it is not only Being, as passage "toward" beings, which is thought eventually; it is also beings that are understood and characterized according to the drama of Being's self-differentiation. Therefore, it is not only Being but also beings themselves, conceived in terms of the more profound "mobility" of truth as *Unverborgenheit,* that are characterized as the event of their own uncovering, insofar as Being is concealed and obfuscated there. Consequently, however multiple its resonances might be, it seems that *Ereignis,* that from which Being *is given,* the *Es* of "*Es gibt*

(*Sein*)," cannot be deprived of the sense of "event," even if its meaning is neither reduced to this nor exhausted by it. Or, rather: though "event" is undoubtedly an inadequate translation of this key term of Heidegger's later thought,[40] "appropriation" or "enowning," which are most often preferred to it and emphasize the root *eigen* [own], are just as unsatisfactory. Indeed, as Wolfgang Brokmeier emphasizes in his study "*Heidegger und wir*,"[41] *Ereignis* only apparently derives from *eigen*, in the sense of "own"; the actual construction of the word is *Er-äug-nis*, which derives from the verb *äugen* (to look), formerly written *eugen* or *eigen*. Thus, as François Fédier rightly states, "to understand *Ereignis* faithfully to its etymology is, above all, not to lose sight of the ostensive aspect which is evident in it. *Ereignis* must be understood as the movement which leads to visibility, makes a view possible, makes appear, and thus makes a standing-out."[42] Apart from considerations bearing on translation, the import of these comments consists in their making apparent something about the very thing that Heidegger has in mind. If this originally ostensive sense of *Ereignis* is primary, its sense as "event" derives from it. It is because a showing-forth takes place with *Ereignis* that it can then have the sense of that which, by its standing-out, makes an event. So Fédier can conclude: "If we look carefully, *Ereignis* does not name an event, *but that which makes way for an event:* the appearing that takes place first of all . . . so that an event can appear."[43] *Ereignis* is therefore that which makes something like Being possible and, more precisely, it is that from which Being itself can be shown and appear (come into view, according to the root *Er-äugen*) *as event*. It is the hidden and nevertheless essential dimension by which the very eventness of Being can be shown, and thereby the co-belonging of Being and time. To this extent, *Ereignis* is clearly that from which the position of the question of Being itself becomes intelligible but which, apart from the paths traced by such thought about Being, is reduced to an empty word. In other words, Heidegger's *Ereignis* cannot be used to object to attempts to elaborate an autonomous phenomenology of events, as if *Ereignis* could be separated from the very position of the question of Being, whose originality I have attempted to sketch out. *Ereignis* is the "condition" for the manifestation of Being as event. We must therefore return once again to Being, in order to formulate our question one last time: Does thought about Being do justice to the way events show themselves from themselves, to their phenomenality? Can they be understood in terms of "ontology," even one that is extensively reworked, such as the fundamental ontology of Dasein?

In the end, it seems that the decisive alternative is this: Does Heidegger think Being itself as *an* event?—in which case an evential hermeneutics seems to be a methodological prerequisite for all ontology, even "fundamental"; or: are events thinkable only on the horizon of *the* Event of Being? But this alternative is obviously too rigid for a simple response, *a fortiori* in the restricted context of an introduction. If we are to hope for even an initial answer at this stage, we need an extra step. We need to ask a question that clearly transcends any history of philosophy in the traditional sense and any factual enquiry into what Heidegger did or didn't think—consequently, a question that presumes a genuine orientation toward the *phenomena* that Heidegger is concerned with and endeavors to make visible: What place does Heideggerian "ontology" give to events in their irreducible plurality, and how does it give an account of their characteristic phenomenality in light of its existentials?

At this point, a constitutive paradox of Heidegger's thought becomes evident, a paradox that, far from being accidental, is rooted in the "thing itself." To the extent that this thought defines Dasein as its own event, the event of being or existing (in the verbal sense), which is at the same time the event of Being or the uncovering of Being in understanding (*Verstehen*), *no event*, apart from the event that it itself "is," *can happen to such an existence*. The existential analytic is thus limited to setting forth in its diverse modalities the *single event that Dasein is itself, the event of its being*. The existentials are these diverse modalities of one single event of being. Not only does the ontological constitution of existence have no relation to events (*Ereignisse*), but Dasein, by its very constitution, is closed to any event. This is why, as far as can be said now before the fuller consideration below,[44] each time that the question of events arises in Heidegger's fundamental ontology, they are in the domain of Dasein's inauthentic (*uneigentliche*) understanding of itself: especially in the existential analytic's crucial moments of Being-toward-death and the call of conscience.

The whole analytic of Being-toward-death rests on the assertion that only an understanding that fails to recognize the fundamental *Eigentlichkeit* of one's own death, of death as *my* death, can transform this possible impossibility of authentic Being, which is still a mode of authentically being its Being, into the mere "certain fact [*gewissen Tatsache*]"[45] of an "empirical certainty," or again into a mere "event which one encounters in one's environment [*umweltlich begegnendes Ereignis*]."[46] A rarely appreciated consequence of this is that in *Being and Time* Heidegger always understands events in the sense of *innerworldly facts*, whose mode of Being is subsistence (*Vorhandenheit*).[47] Thus, only an inauthentic understanding of Dasein allows dying, originally uncovered by anxiety, to be leveled out in a way that perverts its meaning, by understanding it as "an event of public occurrence [*ein öffentlich vorkommendes Ereignis*]."[48] In such an event, Dasein is no longer at stake in its selfhood; death, transformed into demise, becomes a mere fact, an incident or accident, which no longer provokes anxiety, but fear instead: "The 'they' concerns itself with transforming this anxiety into fear in the face of an oncoming event [*Furcht vor einem ankommenden Ereignis*]."[49] But this fear is itself flight and evasion, a "carefreeness with which it [the public] concerns itself [*besorgten Sorglosigkeit*],"[50] which only arises because inauthentic Dasein no longer has the heart or the courage (*Mut*) to be anxious. This demise, which I expect and for which I prepare myself as for a worldly event, is therefore only the covering-over of my being-able-to-die, which is the irrevocable and inalienable possibility of my Being. "Death *is* just one's own"—and Heidegger emphasizes the "is": this is the very last word of an ontology of death.[51] To this extent, demise—the event of an expected death, the chronicle of a death foretold—is necessarily founded in dying, in the chronology of an anticipated death.

The call of conscience could be analyzed in an analogous way. At this central point of the existential analytic, since what is at stake is Dasein's testimony (*Bezeugung*) to its own potentiality-for-Being, we find that the same reduction of events is indispensable for bringing to light the ontological sense of conscience (*Gewissen*). On the one hand, indeed, "neither the call, nor the deed which has happened, nor the guilt with which one is laden, is an occurrence [*Vorkommnisse*] with the character of something present-at-hand which runs its course";[52] on the other hand, and above all, conscience "gives no information about world-events [*Weltereignisse*]"[53] and imputes Dasein with no particular fault of which it would be culpable. It is the "they," and it alone, that understands the call as a "fact" or an "event" coming from a foreign (*fremde*) voice, and it is because the call is neither a fact nor an event that it can be this silent request that Dasein addresses to itself from the uncanniness (*Unheimlichkeit*) of its Being-in-the-world. The call is nothing other than anxious care calling itself from the unable-to-be-overcome potentiality-for-Being of death, so as to assume its factical Being-guilty (*Schuldigsein*). Therefore, it is formally identical to the phenomenon of resolution and provides selfhood with its existential ground. Here again, it is the phenomenological reduction of the call and its subordination to the possibility that Dasein itself is, in its resolute anticipation of death, which makes possible an authentic understanding of its ontological structures.

Thus, Heidegger establishes his fundamental ontology on reducing events to the rank of mere innerworldly facts, so as to bring to light the singular meaning of possibility that Dasein itself *is* by *existing*. Such a reduction should not be surprising. How could it be otherwise, when Dasein's ontological constitution conserves the prerogatives conferred on the modern subject since Descartes? When Dasein remains the measure of all phenomenality by its understanding of Being, which as hearing or listening only apparently decenters it? With such a primacy, everything that happens to the existent is conditioned by its very existence: the possibilities that are offered to it are themselves *made possible* by the fundamental possibility that Dasein itself is as *finite* potentiality-for-Being—and thus also by death, as the possible impossibility of its existence—by the possibility of existing for the sake of this very existence (care) that death alone delivers (and at the same time delivers us from). How, then, could events be envisaged as themselves, and thus *comprehended*, when Dasein's understanding of Being remains an *ontological-formal condition of possibility* for all that can present itself to it as event? For an event is in principle what *itself opens the playing field where it can occur*, the unconditioned "condition" of its own occurrence, that whose an-archic welling up abolishes all prior condition, or even that which occurs *before being possible*.

We can therefore also understand the primacy Heidegger confers on death in his fundamental ontology: not death as a factical event, which he dismisses with the term "demise [*Ableben*]," but death as always mine (*je meines*), the possible impossibility of all existence, a possibility that remains, by this very fact, a *modality of this existence*. Rigorously understood, death is here a mode of *Being* of Dasein, in which it is related, through the ordeal of anxiety, to the uttermost possibility of the impossibility of the possibilities in which it is thrown from the outset of its existence. A modality of authentic existence and the uttermost possibility of that existence, death *is* just as much as existence *is*, it is the very possibility of existing. Finitude that Dasein already carries in itself solely by the fact of existing, finitude that does not *happen* to existence from outside but is as inseparable from it as shadow from light. Death without adversity, without mystery, where nothing of ourselves is actually broken, where nothing alien awaits us, since by existing we have already been existing it from the outset. To be is nothing other than transitively existing that death in which we are thrown as soon as we are, so much so that nothingness, or rather the *nihilating* that is at play in the "not" of the ontological difference—Being is *not* beings—still remains a guise of Being itself. Dying is existing authentically by understanding authentically this existence, and thus existing, in its authentic sense, is dying. Death is no more a foreigner to Dasein than Dasein is to itself.

Completely torn away from any idea of event by being ontologized, death, a mode of existence uncovered in anxiety, Dasein's *mode of being its possibilities against the background of impossibility*, resolution, appears to

Dasein not only as its most authentic possibility, but as the possibility of authenticity as such, the origin of all self-authenticity and selfhood. And since, by existing, we are thrown (toward death), the authenticity of existence is There with Da-sein as soon as it exists. Hence the ontological primacy of death: it alone removes Dasein from the *impersonality* of events, of which it is not itself the origin. Death alone allows the constitutive *mineness* of existence to be affirmed.

However, there is a price for reducing events so as to bring existence to light: there is no place for birth in this existence, because birth refers to *the original nonoriginarity of existence and mineness with respect to the impersonal event that is their condition.* More exactly: what we are compelled to think about by birth, the complex phenomenon to which it refers, and whose meaning is, in a fashion, the sole object of this book, is *the original disparity between the originary and the original* that on its own introduces a rupture in the origin, a hiatus, an opening, a fissure that will never be filled. To be born is to be a self originally, but not originarily; it is to be free originally, but not originarily; it is to understand the meaning of one's adventure originally, but not originarily. This gap between the original and the originary precludes any attempt to think Being itself as origin. At the same time, because it is itself original, the gap fundamentally modifies Dasein's existentials and urges us to think differently about the very meaning of its existence.

But what is birth if not an event? Is it not both in fact and by right the first event of our mortal adventure, in light of which all other events must be characterized and understood? Birth is eminently an event, since being born *is precisely not being the measure of the occurring of this event that happens to us without prior measure and that alone* gives *us the possibility of receiving* [accueillir] *other events, by initially having us as its destination and thereby conferring a destiny on us.* If Dasein—to keep calling it that—is that from which birth can appear, this cannot be any longer in the sense of a condition, but must rather be as *un-condition*; that is, as the "condition of possibility" for what is in principle exempt from all prior conditions, a "condition" that is inverted and ends up to the favor of what it conditions: the event that is, in itself, its own measure and condition. In this respect, birth cannot be identified with any facticity, that is, with that which determines the ontological constitution of Dasein as care, since by right birth precedes both pro-ject (*Ent-wurf*) and being-thrown (*Geworfenheit*): Dasein's principal existentials. Birth is rather the (originally impersonal) event from which Being *ad-venes*; consequently, it is that which *radically forbids a simple identification of Being itself and event.*

That Being itself is given to us, handed over to us, conferred on us by the event of birth not only introduces a fundamental heteronomy into existence, thus breaching Dasein's existential "Self-subsistence";[54] in addition, and this is the essential point, identifying the event of Being (ontological understanding) with the event of being (birth) is thereby precluded—an identification on which the whole ontology of Dasein ultimately relies. "Earlier" than Being is the event by which it *occurs*. Having priority by right over Being, which it establishes, and of which it alone is the condition, such an event "is" not. Even if Being can indeed be thought in Heidegger's fashion as an event, not every event is an event of being (existence). Preceding my existence is the impersonal event "one is born." This governs any understanding of the human adventure, as an opening to events by which "Dasein"—let us call it thus for the final time—*advenes* to itself and has a history.

And if Being itself is something that *ad-venes* in its turn, it can no longer be considered as *originary*. Henceforth, a hermeneutic of the *advenant* is prior to a hermeneutic of Dasein. I use *advenant* to refer to that which comes before Dasein and which is in some sense the condition of possibility for Dasein. *Advenant* is the term for the human being as constitutively open to events, insofar as humanity is the capacity to be oneself in the face of what happens to us. An *advenant* therefore happens to his possibilities only from an even greater *possibility* with respect to the events that punctuate his adventure and thus give him a history. Rigorously understood, this ad-venture signifies an *advenant*'s opening to what happens to him.

A phenomenological hermeneutics of the *advenant* is the aim of this book. Up to this point, I have limited myself to tracing briefly what is at stake and to outlining the question that governs the development that follows below. In doing this, I have merely anticipated what will need to be set out and justified *in concreto* through a series of phenomenological analyses. Before engaging in this, let us return one last time to the principal moments that articulate this project. It can be summed up in five theses. Thus far, we have seen that:

1. The question of the phenomenological status of events demands a critical confrontation with ontology, not only with classical ontology but also with the ontology of Dasein, since only the latter gives a full account of the former.

2. Fundamental ontology thinks Being primordially as event.

3. Far from contradicting this characterization of Being, Heidegger's *Ereignis* is rather that from which Being comes into view as its own event.

4. Birth is the event according to which Being itself is given or ad-venes. Being is itself something that happens to Dasein: the event of Being and the event of being are not identical.

5. The impersonal event of birth, preceding by right and in fact the event of Being as existence, opens the possibility of a hermeneutics of the human adventure with event as the guiding concept.

Advenant is the term for the human being insofar as something hap-pens to him and insofar as by his very ad-venture, he is open to events. Consequently, birth authorizes us and urges us to think the human adven-ture on some other "ground" than the analytic of Dasein. I will refer to this interpretation of an *advenant*, in which event is the guiding concept, as "evential hermeneutics."

PART $\boxed{1}$

Events

> A Mystery are those of pure origin.
> —Hölderlin, *The Rhine*[1]

§4 Events as Innerworldly Facts

How do events show themselves from themselves? In what sense are they properly *phenomena*? Do events have a single mode of appearing, or is their phenomenality indexed across multiple modes? These are the first questions that must be addressed by a phenomenology that, because it takes appearances themselves as the source for description by right, without preempting the meaning of these appearances, must shed light on the diverse guises in which events declare themselves on each occasion.

It is not easy to specify what can be called an "event" from a phenomenological point of view. Those who have attempted to establish a semantic of action phrases in which events are expressed have unhesitatingly asserted that events depend conceptually on the logical subject to which they are related. For a logician like Strawson, this assertion is based on the fact that we generally conceive events as changes occurring in more or less permanent substances.[2] This thesis rests on the idea that we can formalize every expression of our natural language that bears on events by specifying it not in terms of events but in terms of substances: instead of saying "it's raining," we can always say "the rain is falling," and so on. But even without considering the purely logical difficulties to which this thesis might

23

give rise, we can wonder whether it doesn't fall prey from the outset to the grammatical—and thus metaphysical—illusions that Nietzsche denounces. All the logico-semantic debate on this point by authors like Davidson confirms such an interpretation. Indeed, the crucial point for them is the question of whether events can be considered as "entities" in their own right, on which a quantification can be performed and which would consequently belong to the minimal "ontology" that is needed by a coherent semantics—to what Russell terms "the fundamental furniture of the world." Thus it is in a completely naïve manner that the logico-semantic debate is engaged with the question of whether events should be admitted to the status of "entities" listed in an "ontology," for in this debate both these latter notions remain entirely indeterminate. Further insights: that events do not have the same status as beings at all (or, at least, as a logician's "entities," which belong to a formal ontology), that the mode of phenomenality of events differs entirely from that of beings, and that these attempts only prolong the metaphysical illusion denounced by Nietzsche, by making events into quasi-subjects—all this is apparent only to a *phenomenology* that, beginning from "things" as they give themselves, enquires into the mode of appearing of events as such.

Consider Nietzsche's example of a lightning flash. Here, the event is what shows itself in and of itself as a luminous trail streaking across the sky and disappearing straight away. What happens is certainly a *change* that occurs within the world, but can this change be *attributed* to a particular being as an intrasubstance modification? In other words: *to whom* or *to what* does this "occurrence" occur, this "taking-place" that we call an "event"? Is the event "something" *of* the lightning flash and not rather the lightning flash itself? There is no doubt here: the event cannot be assigned an ontic substratum that would be proper to it; it is not a modification occurring within a being, since the only being that *is*, the lightning flash, is only another name for its *event*: the "flashing."

But this description remains insufficient until it takes into account a phenomenal characteristic of every event: simply to be able to *manifest itself*, all change, even if it is not necessarily a change *of something*—in the sense that this "something," determinable as a being, would have an existence independent of the change itself, since in the case of lightning, the "being" in question "is" only this fleeting flash of its own "taking place" as event—must at least be a change that happens *to something*. The lightning marks out its bright flourish in the sky, lighting up clouds and also the whole countryside; thus, it can be seen by the fretful walker, caught by the storm on the exposed slopes. Consequently, in the case of the lightning, the ontic "subject" of assignation *to whom* or *which* the event happens *remains fundamentally indeterminate, because multiply determinable.* The event just as much "affects" the whole sky, the earth, some cloud whose silhouette it marks out, the lake in which it is reflected, the walker *to whom* it appears and whom it scares or dazzles.

The case of lightning makes clear the following two phenomenological characteristics. (1) The event is not a change occurring within a "subject" with some particular mode of Being, since the "being" in question, the lightning, *is* nothing other than its sudden flash, the event of its own occurrence. (2) Nevertheless, the event can *appear* as such only by happening *to something* or *someone*—consequently, by having an ontic support of assignation. But assigning the event in this way seems problematic and even impossible, for the event does not occur to a being *in particular* but rather to an open plurality of beings: the sky, the lake, the countryside, the walker and his dog, etc.

These two elementary phenomenological characteristics are found in any number of events that are expressed impersonally: "it's raining," "it's snowing," "it is day," "it is night," etc. For example, to what privileged being could we assign the banal event of "it's snowing"? This event is a change that happens of itself and that happens inseparably to the sky, which becomes gloomy, to the surrounding air, which chills, to the whole countryside, which is blanketed with snow, or even to me, who watches the twirling flakes from my window, feels the change in temperature, and shivers. . . . And the same holds for the rain's silky rustling or sudden hammering, of this immense fusion of water and light, of the sky and earth whose raw fragrance suddenly wafts up, a purely atmospheric phenomenon, as elusive as the wind. Rain and snow are pure events whose impersonal occurrence coincides with the impossibility of any univocal ontic assignation.

Now, this impossibility of univocally assigning events to an ontic subject as one of their phenomenological features not only concerns that category of events we have been considering to this point, namely events where the change does not occur within a subject, since this "subject"—lightning, rain—is nothing other than its own event. It concerns just as much a category of facts, processes, or states of affairs, in which events at first glance appear to be "connected" to some particular being, occupying the place of the grammatical or logical subject: the *train* arrives at the station, the *apple* falls from the tree, etc.

Does not this latter category of events in fact hide itself away from what could be phenomenologically accurate in the preceding analyses? Isn't the apple the real "subject" of the event of falling, not only in the grammatical sense but also as the "subject" of ontic assignation? Or the train, in the same way, of the event of arriving at the station? Are not events reduced in these cases, and others analogous to them, to simple modifications happening to a *thing*? To respond to these questions, it is necessary to reconsider the two phenomenal characteristics of events set out above:

(1) Clearly, these phenomena differ from the earlier ones in that the train in question cannot be reduced to the fact of its arrival at the station. It possesses its own ontic features: it is "a means of transport," and from this angle it has what can be called a "history," in a broad sense; it was constructed at such and such a time, belongs to such and such a series, is this or that model, transports this many passengers, has traveled from such and such a place, etc. The same is true for the apple, which, as a being, cannot be reduced to the event of its falling.

(2) Nevertheless, when we ask: "To whom or what do these events happen?", the first response, no matter how "obvious" it may be ("to the train," "to the apple"), is radically insufficient. The event of falling does not happen only to the apple, which as the logical "subject" receives new characteristics by means of a change of its predicates: it is a "ripe" apple that has "fallen to the ground," whereas it was previously a "green" apple on its branch. On the contrary, the event of falling can be described equally well as happening to the tree (the apple tree loses its fruit), to the observer of this fall (Newton sees an apple fall), or to the orchard as a whole (one more apple is strewn on the orchard). It is exactly the same with the event of the train's arrival, which clearly happens to the train itself, but also to the passengers, to those who await the passengers on the platform, previously deserted and now full of people, to the platform itself, and to the station as a whole.

These extremely simple analyses reveal the following phenomenological traits.

1. An event, considered in itself, is not of the order of beings nor can it be assigned to a univocally determinable being. It happens to an open plurality of beings. In this respect, there is no being that can be characterized in its Being as the support for its assignation. An event "is" not (a property or an ontic attribute), but simply "happens": it is the pure fact of occurring, which is made evident only when it has taken place and in which *nothing* takes place other than the "taking-place" itself: the event in the strict sense.

2. The absence of any determinate ontic support for assignation distinguishes two types of events: innerworldly facts, on the one hand, and events in the properly *evential* sense, on the other.

3. There is a positive counterpart to the ontic subject of attribution for innerworldly facts being fundamentally indeterminate: facts do not

have a univocal ontic assignation, but rather an *evental context*, in relation to which alone they have meaning. In every innerworldly event there already glimmers a "world."

Let us examine these two latter characteristics successively (sections 5 and 6).

§5 Innerworldly Facts and Events in the *Evential* Sense

The first phenomenal trait of events that has become apparent to us is the impossibility of assigning them a univocal ontic support. But what is the exact status of this characteristic? Is it a characteristic of *every* event? Are there not events to which it does not apply?

The impossibility of making a univocal ontic assignation for innerworldly facts became apparent in analyses that were explicitly characterized as still naïve and unilateral, in other words, *preliminary*. This feature pertains *only* to those "events" that happen *to nobody*, or rather to nobody *in particular*, and to which alone I will henceforth refer as "innerworldly facts": lightning, rain, the train's arrival at the station, and so on. "Personal" events, whose "subject" of assignation is *univocally determinable*, have a completely different character: they happen to me myself, or to you, and they never happen *simply on their own*. But do such events "exist"? And, if so, to what extent do they differ from the former type?

Innerworldly facts range from events that can be sensed (I hear the telephone ring), to decisions that I take, to thoughts that occur to me, to actions that I undertake. As events, all of them enter *into* the world, which consequently forms the horizon of their *meaning*. And, in truth, it was only by a misunderstanding of this assignation *to a given person* that I could earlier assert, for instance about the rain, that it happens "to nobody" in particular. Even if it happens *simply on its own* and occurs for the sake of its occurrence without being addressed to anyone, the event of rain, its sweet freshness and vast pattering, could not be "there" if it were strictly *for nobody*, if I weren't there at least to *hear* this impersonal and indefinitely multiple spattering, or to *observe* through the bay window the interminable streaming of the sky. Therefore, it was only by an abstraction—that was, nevertheless, necessary—that I could assert that innerworldly facts such as rain and lightning are deprived of a univocal subject of assignation: for events can appear, and happen thus on the horizon of a world, only if at least *somebody* is there to grasp them. This merely asserts the extremely simple phenomenological observation that every phenomenon—and events must be able to *appear* if they are to be the object of a "phenomenology"—is a phenomenon *for* . . . a "subject," a person, who allows it to appear, to show itself in and of itself. However, this assertion is trivial only as long as it says nothing further on *the mode of appearance of events in the midst of the world.* This is the decisive question that we must leave in suspense for the moment, foreshadowing later analyses.

The question we are concerned with can therefore be articulated in the following way: Innerworldly facts are *also* "personal" events, but are personal events necessarily also *innerworldly facts*?

The thesis of the plurivocally determinable character of the "subject" of assignation for any innerworldly fact has not been shown to be false from a phenomenological point of view, but rather only "naïve" and "unilateral." This naivety and this unilateralness taken on by preliminary phenomenological descriptions will presently reveal their meaning. For if it is true, strictly speaking, that there is no event, not even a "natural" one, without a minimal assignation, no lightning in the sky without an observer *to whom* at least the *fact* of observing happens, it is no less true that the *meaning* of such an assignation differs profoundly according to the type of event being considered. In the case of a fact that occurs of itself and of which I am merely the observer—the flashing of lightning—this fact undeniably brings about modifications in the world and changes in my own perception. All the same, it will be useful to make a careful distinction here between three things:

(1) The fact that an event happens as such, with its own innerworldly modifications: and, to put it more rigorously, *as* these very modifications.

(2) The necessity, in order for this event to happen as such, for it to happen *to somebody,* that a "subject" be there to grasp it. The being in question, the subject of ontic assignation of an innerworldly fact, is not a being like other beings, but has a particular characteristic: it is able *to make appear that which occurs in and of itself,* without actually having to intervene or "do" anything whatever. It is only by virtue of the presence of such a being that an event can burst forth with the "independence" that is proper to it in respect of any properly human "doing," that it can occur in and of itself and thus appear as it has taken place as itself. It is only thus that it can be, strictly speaking, a "phenomenon," if a phenomenon is that which shows itself in and of itself, *as itself,* that for which German has the word *Erscheinung*—which distinguishes a "phenomenon" from *Schein,* an appearance—and for which French, if it wants to avoid all equivocity,[3] perhaps has to resort to a word invented by a poet, which is not at all a "technical" word: *montrance* [showing-forth].[4] "*Montrance*" is an admirable name for the "flashing" proper to lightning, the manifestation proper to the event, inasmuch as this manifestation is a

pure "occurring" in and of itself, which makes no presumption of a "subject" other than itself "behind it." It is not by chance that Claudel speaks of "*montrance*" precisely in reference to events or processes that *occur only of themselves and "open" only to themselves*; he describes the occasional breaks in an overcast sky, its fugitive sunny openings, as "the alternation of the sun's showing-forth and its disappearing [*la montrance alternative du soleil et son occultation*]." Such a display pertains to what German says with its word *Erscheinung*, as Hegel's famous definition in *Phenomenology of Spirit* attests: "Appearance [*Erscheinung, montrance*] is the arising and passing away that does not itself arise and pass away."[5]

Consequently, innerworldly facts do indeed have a *privileged* subject of ontic assignation, who alone can make them appear as showing themselves in and of themselves—and who I will call *advenant*—even if they do not *in general* have a univocal subject of assignation (the lightning happens *just as much* to the sky that it lights up as it does to the walker who observes it); it will be quite a different matter with those events that happen *unsubstitutably* to me, by completely upending my essential possibilities articulated among themselves in a world and so upsetting my own adventure: events in the properly evential sense, on whose meaning I will shortly expand.

(3) However, before this, it is useful to distinguish a third point, namely the meaning of an *advenant*'s privileged ontic assignation, which varies according to the type of event in question; also, the relations that enter into play here between events, *advenant*, and world. Innerworldly facts do indeed have a privileged "subject" of assignation: they necessarily happen to *me*, to the extent that they could not *appear* in their bursting forth in and of themselves, and in their radical independence with respect to any "subject," without manifesting themselves *to somebody* in general, but, in the case of such events, I—as this "somebody"—*am not myself put in play, in my selfhood*, by that which "happens to me" in this way: I am a "pure spectator," no doubt implicated in the display and perhaps even struck by it, but not at all to the point of *understanding myself starting from the event that has happened*. Strictly speaking, this lightning flash could be seen *indifferently* by any other or by me, without its phenomenal meaning-character [*teneur de sens*] being altered in the least. It could not occur as such without somebody *in general* grasping it, but this doesn't necessarily have to be *me* in particular. Furthermore, my seeing it does not overtake me so much as to completely upend my world and compel me to understand myself differently, starting from the fissure that the event opens in my adventure by reconfiguring my intrinsic possibilities.

It is a different matter with events in the properly evential sense, insofar as they are distinguished from simple facts. While innerworldly facts are not addressed to anybody in particular and occur indifferently for every witness, an event is always *addressed*, in such a way that *the one to whom it happens is himself implicated in what happens to him*. Consequently, to understand the meaning-character of an event is never to relate oneself to it in the impersonal mode of a pure observer, as one does with an "objective" fact in the world. An event is never "objective" in the way a fact can be; it does not lend itself to impartial observation. Anyone who understands what happens to him as happening to him precisely *as himself* is ipso facto engaged in what he understands, so that it is the same thing to understand an event and to undergo it unsubstitutably, that is, to undergo it as destined for oneself and no other. Here, *the one* who understands is strictly implicated in the very act of understanding: I can understand an event as being addressed to me only if I am myself in play in the possibilities it assigns to me [*me destine*] and through which it makes history by opening a destiny for me.

In other words, innerworldly facts happen *to me*, but they do not put me in play *myself*, in my unsubstitutable selfhood. It is quite a different matter with those events that will serve here as the guiding thread for interpreting the human *advenant*, according to the historic plot of his or her own adventure. This evential hermeneutics of the human adventure, in light of events in the properly *evential* sense, constitutes the primary and ultimate task of a phenomenology of events.

Thus, while innerworldly facts happen, strictly speaking, *for nobody*, it is quite different for events that occur in the human adventure befalling me *in particular*. These are "events" in the "proper" sense, since "event" derives etymologically from the Latin *evenire*, which not only signifies "happen," "occur," "come about," and "ensue," but also "*befall*": *alicui, to somebody*. A bereavement, a meeting, an illness are all events that occur incomparably for each person and thus render each one incomparable to all others, giving him or her a history. Of course, an event is *impersonal* in itself: it is appropriate to say *it* occurs, or rather *that* occurs, so as to distinguish precisely between what occurs and *the one to whom* it occurs. Consider the event of the death of a loved one and the bereavement that I undergo: another's death as an "objective fact" is obviously not identical to the bereavement intimately suffered by those who remain. But, "between these two," where is the event situated? Clearly, it is not a second fact, situated in some way "alongside" the first. Even less is it a mere "subjective experience" pertaining to a region of psychological interiority. On the contrary, it is the fact itself that is an event for me, to the extent that the loss of a cherished being, by striking me to the heart, upends the totality of possibilities that are articulated for me in a world. There is no objective fact *first*, which *in a second stage* upends my possibilities: *an event is nothing other than this impersonal reconfiguration of my possibilities and of the world—a reconfiguration that occurs in a fact and by which the event opens a fissure in my own adventure.* Transformation of myself and of the world is therefore inseparable from the experience I undergo of it. Thus, while the innerworldly fact of death is the same for anybody, *the event* of this death and the bereavement I undergo will not have the same *meaning* for myself and for another. Bereavement is incomparable for each person, even when it is bereavement of one and the same person, and even, at the limit, when it is bereavement that is common to us all, that we *"share"* in suffering: for it is always *my* suffering and *yours*, which are incomparable with each other, because they always put into play our unsubstitutable selfhood. Thus, as with every genuine event, the loss of a loved one leaves me *alone*, and irremediably so: alone in face of an event that befalls me *in person* and that is assigned first hand [*en propre*][6] only to me; alone, even if I am able to communicate my distress and share it with others. As soon as there is bereavement, it is not bereavement "in general" but bereavement *for me*, uniquely; I feel the event "in my flesh," and nothing can take away this suffering that I feel, nor can anyone undergo it in my place. If others are bereaved of the same person, *strictly speaking it is not the same bereavement*, for it occurs as a unique event, to me as unique, *unsubstitutably*.

Thus, on the one hand, events in themselves are impersonal, since they occur in fact, in a fact, but, on the other hand, by their very meaning, they are inseparable from their being addressed or assigned. The impersonality of events can be reconciled here with their addressed character, which differentiates them from innerworldly facts. Although an event is *impersonal* with respect to me, unlike a fact it can never be an *ob-ject* (understood etymologically as pure vis-à-vis *Gegen-stand*): I am implicated in it *myself*, as soon as I understand it precisely *as such*.

But though this difference is the greatest there can be, is it, for all that, the sole one? Does it not condition a whole series of distinctions that need to be expanded on? What is to be said of the third characteristic of innerworldly facts, namely, that the positive counterpart of their lack of a determinate ontic assignation is the evental context in which they appear and in relation to which they take on meaning—what I have called, in an as yet obscure way, their "world"?

§6 The Phenomenological Problem of the "World": Fact, Context, and Interpretation

If we reconsider the events that have guided our analyses to this point—for example, the first of them, the "flashing" of the lightning—we are led to the following conclusion: this event cannot be understood and characterized as this particular meteorological phenomenon *without being previously given in the midst of a world* from which it is inseparable. In the middle of the night, on the seashore, I recognize the flash of lightning, and I distinguish it from the furtive beam of a lighthouse suddenly piercing the shadows, by the dryness and electric heat that generally precede a storm, by the somber piling up of clouds that has progressively covered over the moon and the stars, by the clap of thunder that follows straight after it. All these concomitant phenomena do not merely add fortuitously to the event of the lightning, they are themselves atmospheric events with an essential relation to the lightning, in that they envelop it in a context that gives it *meaning*; without such a signifying context, the lightning could not, strictly speaking, flash for me *as* lightning, it could not be understood, which is to say interpreted, as this "meteorological" event that accompanies a multitude of other spectacles: the wind suddenly stronger, intensifying, the ravaged circle of clouds, and then, suddenly, like a liberation of so much accumulated violence, the powerful attack of the rain, not single but multiple, full of light and water, of which Claudel says admirably: "I hear with both ears the rain coming down *immensely*," comparing its monotonous sound to the "neutral and numberless intonation of the psalm."[7]

Therefore, the lightning can only *appear* as this particular meteorological phenomenon by declaring itself on the horizon of a world. But what should be understood here by the "world" of an event? How does the world occur in each innerworldly fact? How is the world "enworlded" as the "there [*il y a*]" of all that takes place under the innerworldly aspect of *facts*? All these questions are directed at the *mode of display* of innerworldly facts; they ask about their *montrance*. The lightning's eventual context is never merely a spatiotemporal "setting" for such a phenomenon; *it refers to an articulated unity of meaning, from which this event can be understood, which is to say interpreted, on a unitary horizon.* An event's context is not merely a sum of phenomena, but the understandable articulated unity of their *meaning*. This is why causality intervenes here in a privileged way, since it is from their causes that facts are articulated with respect to one another on a context's horizon of meaning. Every cause is a fact, a thing, or a state of affairs, from which one of the world's preexisting possibilities is actualized; the *world*, then, is the totality of these preexisting possibilities, from which all that happens happens and is open, consequently, to *explanation*. This characterization of "world" will be referred to in what follows as purely *evental*, by contrast with its *evential* characterization, which rests on a completely different concept of "possibility." Thus, explaining an event always means understanding it in the light of preexisting possibilities, which prescribe its meaning in the world, necessarily understanding it as an *inner*worldly fact, precisely by relating it to these possibilities. Lightning happens *because* such and such known and recognized meteorological phenomena have taken place, and they explain its triggering: the coming together of air masses, condensation, electromagnetic phenomena, and so on. This connection by "*because*," which governs the linking together of innerworldly facts on the horizon of a world, bringing them together in a single signifying context by relating them in understanding to preexisting possibilities, is what I call "causality."

Hence, since the world of an event is a matter of an articulated unity of *meaning* and not merely a spatial or temporal juxtaposition, *by right* it can extend to the most remote causes of the event. From this the world's *historicity* ensues. Going back to another example that has already been analyzed, the train's arrival at the station is an event that is inscribed in the context of rail transport's development, technical evolution, and the increase in commercial trade; it can also be the herald of a modification in artistic "sensibility," by becoming the theme of a painting by Turner or Monet: in every instance, even if all these significations are not expressly present for the one who understands the *event* of the train's arrival at the station, they nonetheless confer its meaning within its historical world, a world of a given epoch and culture. Without the signifying context of such a world, in which other events occur—the invention of the steam engine, its development and technical application as the steam locomotive, then the discovery of electricity, etc.—the event of the train's arrival at the station would be, strictly speaking, incomprehensible, just as the event of lightning would be incomprehensible for someone who had never known a storm and did not know how to recognize its warning signs. Even "natural" events have their explanatory etiology subordinated to a historical horizon: the Greeks of Homer's time did not interpret lightning as a meteorological fact but, instead, in a mythological perspective, as the expression of Zeus's anger.

However, this a priori characterization of innerworldly facts, as being able to appear as such only within a given context and as open to an etiology that is at least possible, does not mean de facto that their context is immediately comprehensible for anyone who is contemporary with them.

Rather, what is primary here is a certain incomprehension, in that this context, without which their meaning cannot appear at all, be understood, be received in an interpretation, is most often lacking for their contemporaries or only displays itself through its gaps. This is what William Faulkner describes in his novel *The Reivers*, recounting the appearance of the first car in Jefferson, a small town in the American South. Bought by the narrator's grandfather, the vehicle appears one fine day in the midst of the carts, wagons, buggies, and other carriages in which the townsfolk traveled at that time:

> My grandfather didn't want an automobile at all; he was forced to buy one . . . he believed then and right on to his death many years afterward, by which time everybody else even in Yoknapatawpha County had realized that the automobile had come to stay, that the automobile was an insolvent phenomenon like last night's toadstool and, like the fungus, would vanish with tomorrow's sun.[8]

Neither an understanding of the economic and commercial context nor an anticipation of technical evolution accounts for the purchase of this car; in the backward South, which Faulkner contrasts with the commercial and industrial North, the event of this futuristic machine's appearance is a kind of hapax, eluding understanding, because it is cut off from the historical and cultural context in which such an event can take on meaning. Unsuited to the roads and promptly exchanged for a racehorse by one of the black workers, the car is reduced to an object that crystallizes and exacerbates all the social tensions, encapsulating the drama of an impoverished and insular South, with wraithlike beings wrangling over it, while their very existence is already under threat, and they are destined soon to be carted away and crushed by the inexorable march of Progress.

It is always within a world, embedded in a causal framework, that an event is able to appear with its own meaning, interpreted and understood in light of other events that determine its specific meaning; but event and world can sit uneasily with each other, like that purchase of a car at the beginning of the twentieth century in the American South; most often, incomprehension precedes any explicit understanding of an event in its context. But what does such a "context" signify? I have initially characterized it as a particular *unity of meaning* in light of which events become comprehensible in their mutual articulation, a horizon of meaning from which they are illuminated—that is, as a thoroughly *hermeneutic* structure. But how should "meaning" be understood here? How can such a "horizon" be understood phenomenologically?

There is *meaning* only for an understanding. Understanding and interpreting are comportments of an *advenant*. As such, they constitute fundamental modalities of its adventure, or eventials. Understanding can be characterized more precisely as *projection*, a way for an *advenant* to relate to interpretative possibilities, a projection that is always carried out according to a particular *orientation*. Insofar as an *advenant* relates himself to interpretative possibilities according to some particular orientation, all projections of understanding are directed to a *meaning* that can be defined as the projection's *aim*. Consequently, understanding generally has three aspects: (1) the phenomenon to be understood (text, thing, event), (2) the orientation of understanding according to which the interpretative projection is carried out, and (3) the meaning of understanding, which is what the interpretative projection aims to bring to light. Thus, all understanding is a projection that is directed at something, for the sake of bringing a meaning to light, according to some particular prior orientation.[9]

But what gives this projection of understanding a horizon of possibilities, from which it can be put into action and aim at some particular meaning according to a specific orientation? That which to this point I have called "world." Here, "world" refers to the horizon of meaning for all understanding, the totality of possibilities articulated among themselves from which an interpretation is possible, the totality of interpretative possibilities that prescribe a horizon in advance for understanding, from which alone it can be put into action and brought about. It is itself a hermeneutic structure and thus refers to the totality of possibilities from which a meaning can come to light as such.

Now, if "world" refers to the totality of interpretative possibilities articulated among themselves, from which all that happens can appear as endowed with meaning, we find among these possibilities not only those prior possibilities *from* which all that happens happens (i.e., causes) but also those possibilities that depend solely on an *advenant*'s projections and *for the sake of which* certain events occur: acts. I call those possibilities *in view of which* an *advenant* acts "ends." He alone is able to project them, and his action in the world takes on a *meaning* in relation to them. In their turn, these ends (mine as much as those of others) enter into the world's horizon of meaning, and there determine all understanding. But how do the ends of our acts contribute, in the same way as the causes of an innerworldly fact, to the eventral characterization of its world? More exactly: how is the hermeneutic unity of the worldly context, from and in which every innerworldly fact is able to show itself in itself, conjointly determined by the system of ends that an *advenant* projects on the world, insofar as he is capable of bringing things about there?

Even events regarded as "natural" announce themselves for me as endowed with a meaning within their worldly context, in being conditioned by the ends that I alone project. An example will make this clear. This innerworldly fact I straightforwardly call "rain" actually encompasses an open multiplicity of concomitant events, which no enumeration will ever run through to the end: an innumerable tumble, sometimes muted by the vegetation and lost in a diffuse murmur, sometimes echoing on the iron roof, as on a makeshift musical instrument, the "rearing clouds" that "begin to neigh a whole universe of auricular cities,"[10] but also the languorous warmth that swathes the summer rain, the shifting and uncertain light, the sudden resurgence of smells—so many phenomena, which can be grasped and unitarily referred to as "rain" only on condition of their being related to an action that is at least virtual.

There could never be any such thing for me as this innerworldly fact of "it's raining" unless I was able to "meet" this phenomenon in the unitary mode of a certain adversity or, inversely, with a kind of connivance: whether I go out and face the rain, or, staying home and meditating at the window, I soak in the sound of its refrain. Rain is never "rain" for me unless, meaning to go out, I open the window and realize that it is raining. This apparently trivial observation has phenomenological import: the event of "it's raining," which in itself is multiple, acquires meaning and unity for me only if it "enters" the sphere of my action and is characterized in terms of the system of ends that articulate this sphere; it can *appear* as this innerworldly fact, with the meaning that belongs to it, only in relation to other innerworldly facts I alone can make happen and that thus serve as the ground of its signifying revelation: my acts. Of course, "acts" should not be understood here simply as physical behavior such as getting up, opening the window, and picking up an umbrella; this generic term refers here to the ensemble of behaviors that take shape as events in the human adventure—or, to remain strictly within the limits of the current analysis, as innerworldly facts—whether their occurrence depends on me or not. Wishes and decisions are acts, as can be refusals, renunciations, or abandoning oneself to contemplation: acts in whose light the world, the articulated totality of events, acquires its significance. For, in general, events mean something only if events mean something *for* each other— and this "*for . . .* " structure is precisely what I call "finality." Consequently, the world's significance, the totality of meaning of the events that is accessible for an understanding within a unitary horizon, is not characterized only by the series of cause and effect that orders events *in relation to* one another according to prior possibilities, in light of which they are explained; it is also characterized by the system of ends that orders events *for the sake of* one another, according to possibilities that also preexist in their own way but that can only be projected by an *advenant* who is capable of an action which realizes them.

Thus events appear in the world only as articulated among themselves on a single horizon, according to a causal framework, on the one hand, and an organized complex of ends, on the other. The articulated totality of my projections, the complex structure of ends from which my action is possible, introduces an order and coherence in events, allowing me to understand them in light of a context and to act according to this context, thereby modifying it. However, as an innerworldly fact, for such action to appear as meaningful, it must be inscribed in a context in turn. Consequently, it must be given within a causal framework. For example, it is *because* the house is in flames that I race to the car *in order to* summon help. Granted, the "because . . . " here does not refer to a physical cause but rather a motive, which therefore depends on a particular end and conditions this end only insofar as the latter is already given—that is, freely put forward or projected by an *advenant*. Nevertheless, this "cause" that I myself put forward for my action, this motive (the fire), takes on meaning here in light of my goal (saving the building and its occupants) only because it is itself announced in a causal fabric from which it is inseparable. The act of running to the car strikes me as something "to be done" only to the extent that the innerworldly fact of the fire is originally displayed to me as embedded in an inexorable network of cause and effect: first, the cause of its catching alight, whether known or unknown, then its likely consequences, which I understand immediately without any theoretical reflection and that resolve me to act without delay. It is only when an action is itself inserted in an evental context that it can truly modify this context, affecting it and its meaning.

Thus, whether we consider the series of causes or the complex of ends from which the world takes on its signifying configuration, the question is posed of knowing what makes the unity of such a world: what I have just above been calling its significance. The world refers to the horizon of possibilities on which an interpretation can draw as it strives to bring the *meaning* of an innerworldly fact to light. To understand a fact as innerworldly is nothing other than subordinating it to a universe of prior possibilities from which its factical arising becomes explicable. This *universum* of possibilities opens the dimensionality according to which an innerworldly fact can appear, become a phenomenon, and which thus furnishes this fact with the measure of its phenomenality. It includes those possibilities that precede such a fact on the horizon of the world—or, rather, those possibilities that are contextually articulated as "world"—its *causes*, and at the same time those projections by which an *advenant* anticipates future possibilities by giving himself goals to realize: *ends.* In both respects, this horizon of possibilities appears as already given and precedes the interpretation of the fact for which it forms the context. What is decisive here is that the contextual and explicative understanding of a fact is limited to receiving its interpretative possibilities from this *universum* of possibilities (the world); it assigns meaning to an event only by relating it to this *universum.* In such an explicative grasp of an event's meaning in light of its context, the only "meaning" is that which articulates events in relation to each other on the unified horizon of the world. The world is that in light of which events enter into relation and are significatively articulated on a single horizon, according to the double polarity of "*because . . .* " and "*for . . .* ": the world's worldliness is its *significance.*

But is all understanding of events limited to explaining them by grasping their meaning in light of a prior context? This would undoubtedly be the case were it not for events that radically upend their context and, far from being submitted to a horizon of prior meaning, are themselves the origin of meaning for any interpretation, in that they can be understood less from the world that precedes them than from the posterity to which they give rise. Isn't this precisely the situation in the case of events in the *evential* sense?

In other words, if the world is the ultimate horizon of meaning for every event that an *advenant* can understand, if every event is announced in a context that is governed by an ascending series of causes and by the organized totality of ends that determines the *sui generis* events of our singular actions (whether mine or those of others), then the question is posed of knowing whether or not there are events that, far from being subordinated to a horizon of prior meaning, burst forth and upend from top to bottom what I have been referring to as "world." Bursting-forth that is necessarily an-archic, since it eludes any antecedent causality and is announced, freed from any relation to a preexisting possibility, as *its own origin.*

Indeed, an event, in the evential sense, illuminates its own context, rather than in any way receiving its meaning from it. It is not a consequence of this context that could be explained in light of preexisting possibilities, but it reconfigures the possibilities that precede it and signals the advent of a new world for an *advenant.* This is not to say that the former world entirely disappears as such, but that its *meaning* is so radically modified, the totality of projections and finalities that dwelled in it and conferred a signifying structure on it are so altered, that strictly speaking it is no longer the *same* world: the occurring of such an event renders the former world insignificant, since this event can no longer be understood in light of that world's context. And, when the world is insignificant, it loses the fundamental phenomenological trait that precisely determines it as context: its significance. It is *abolished* as world. Going beyond every forecast and anticipation, this event has reconfigured my intrinsic possibilities articulated among themselves—my world—it has opened a new world in and by its bursting forth. However, does "world" have the same meaning here as previously, when it was characterized as the context of meaning for all *innerworldly* facts? For the event that arises on its own horizon obliges us to characterize the world in another way, as that which can be altered and reconfigured by it. This possibility can take concrete form only if we learn to distinguish between two phenomena of the world and, consequently, two phenomenological concepts of the world: an event*al* concept, related to innerworldly facts, which can be understood and acquire meaning only within a given context, and an event*ial* concept, related to events in that they escape any horizon of prior meaning and, in their an-archic bursting forth, make themselves manifest with their meaning only *on their own horizon*. As they occur beyond any measure of prior possibilities—of a "world" in the first sense—events in the evential sense become *world-establishing* for the *advenant*.

But before we can come to this second concept of "world," we need to spell out the sense in which an event can be set free from all contextual explanation and removed, by its own bursting forth, as much from the causal chain that governs every fact's appearance in the world as from the organized complex of ends that illuminates every innerworldly fact. To do this, it is necessary to show, first, in what sense an event can be said to be an-archic, or in other words set free from all antecedent causality (see section 7, below), and second, the extent to which, by reconfiguring my essential possibilities, an event upends my projections and therefore transcends the system of ends starting from which every innerworldly fact becomes interpretable as such. This latter characteristic will have to be elucidated later, because it presupposes a recharacterization of "possible" (see section 14, below). In any case, it is solely on this double condition that my assertion—that an event in the evential sense is not inscribed *in* the world but instead *opens a world* for an *advenant*—can be given meaning and that its phenomenological justifications can be set out.

§7 Causality and Origin

Every innerworldly fact, as something that is announced on the horizon of the world, must be able to be causally explained. Just as every action that is performed possesses a *finality*, referring to the totality of actual or possible ends of a given individual, so every event that occurs must have its causes, which themselves refer to other causes, linked to each other in a signifying context. The question of a first cause, an *arche*, a principle, is not at play here, any more than is the question of an ultimate end for human action. For the question of causality is always posed for us starting from a particular event, not as a question of principle—which is the form it takes on, for example, in the *Critique of Pure Reason*'s "transcendental dialectic," namely: is there or is there not a *first* cause for what happens, one that does not in its turn, according to a law of nature, presuppose an antecedent causality?[11]—but as a question of fact: every singular event, precisely as singular, can be identified only within a context; it does not have one single cause, but an indefinite number of causes, which depend on the multiplicity of events that articulate this context, and thus its causality appears inexhaustible *in fact*, even if it can be recounted *in principle*, in its infinite ramifications. Consider the particular event of an apple falling. Stating that the cause of this event is the universal law of gravitation is insufficient, for this law holds identically for every event subject to its jurisdiction; the apple's fall, as *this* particular event, is just as much caused by the ripening of the fruit, which depends on the sun shining on the orchard where this apple tree grows, on the mildness of this Indian summer, on the variety of apple, etc., but also on the atmospheric conditions: was the wind blowing on that day, and how strongly? It is clear from this example that, even though a causal explanation for every innerworldly fact is always possible *in principle*, it remains inexhaustible *in fact*, because a multiplicity of causes play a part and it is impossible to encompass their infinity. From this perspective, Leibniz is correct when he asserts that the causal arche-ology of a contingent fact only reaches its end by recounting the totality of causes, as they stand in the complete and primitive notion of the world for a creator's understanding; any causal enquiry can be exhaustive only if it attains this first and last *ratio* for the world, which by definition remains inaccessible to a finite understanding.

This is why classical science can isolate *the* sole pertinent cause of the fall of bodies *in general* only by disregarding in advance the events that surround this particular fact in its context and its inexhaustible causal framework. It is only at the price of such methodic abstraction that a "general law of the fall of bodies" can be discovered. This abstraction entails restricting the *context* in which the event has appeared, a restriction by methodic experimentation that allows the elimination of variables not pertinent to the calculation of a physical law: the apple's ripening, the wind's speed, etc. In other words, to meet the requirements of its method, science surrenders itself to *de-worlding innerworldly facts*, eliminating from their causal frame all the nonpertinent causes, which interfere, in the theory, with the calculation of the only law that is explanatory in scientific terms. But no matter how valuable the results of such a step might be, they should not conceal the process of de-worlding, which alone gives universal validity to these methodic enterprises. Inversely, an irreducible feature of every event's phenomenality is the inexhaustibility of its causal framework, envisaged in its innerworldly context.

Nevertheless, even if an innerworldly fact's causal framework is inexhaustible in principle, it still lends itself to an explanatory arche-ology, albeit partial and incomplete. But does the same hold for events in an evential sense? Are they able to be causally explained as well? And, if so, does such an explanatory arche-ology do justice to their eventness?

Pure beginning from nothing, an event, in its an-archic bursting forth, is absolved from all antecedent causality. This doesn't mean that nothing prepares for or prefigures events, that they have no anchor point in a history, and that they burst forth mysteriously, with no relation to that history. On the contrary, one can say that an event has causes, just like an innerworldly fact, but its causes do not explain it, or rather, if they "explain" it, what they give a reason for is *only ever* the fact and not the *event* in its evential sense. For example, it is always possible to enquire about the causes of an encounter: it happened one evening at the home of friends common to them both, or at a political meeting, or in their youth at university where they were enrolled in the same course, etc. Not only is the meeting physically possible only if two beings are put in each other's presence in the same place, but a "psychological" background parallels this purely physical causality, and one could endeavor to *explain* this background in turn. Does not having friends or intellectual interests in common constitute a "sufficient reason" to account for their mutual attraction? Their youth, for example, or their belonging to the same social circle: so many reasons that, even if they do not "entirely" account for the event of the encounter, nevertheless seem to constitute the beginning of an explanation.

Such "reasons" would undoubtedly be explanatory if the event of the encounter were reduced to its *actualization as a fact*, for there is sense in enquiring about the causes of a fact, even if these causes are *in fact* inexhaustible. However, in the case of an event, no causal archeology can solve the riddle, nor can it exhaust the *meaning*, as it is "meaningless" to look for the cause of something that is itself the origin of meaning for human adventure. An encounter does not have its character as *event* conferred on it simply by happening as a *fact:* it becomes an event by radically transcending its own actualization, reconfiguring my possibilities articulated in a world, and introducing into my adventure a radically new *meaning* that shakes it, upends it from top to bottom, and thus modifies all my previous projections. After this encounter, which I neither sought out nor decided on, the very meaning of my adventure is decided for me. If it is not utterly pointless to enquire about the "physical," "psychological," or "sociological" causes of an encounter, this is only insofar as the encounter is envisaged here as a mere fact and not as an *event.* With an event, one can only say one thing: it has its cause in itself; that is, strictly speaking, it has none: "If you press me to say why I loved him, I feel that it can only be expressed by replying: 'Because it was him: because it was me.'"[12] Every explanatory archeology necessarily opens on this inexplicable. An event has no cause because *it is its own origin,* and it is precisely here that its real *meaning* for a human adventure resides.

An event is marked off from all prior facts by its very arising—coming about from itself, free of any horizon of meaning and any prior condition. An event advenes only on its own horizon. It is a pure bursting forth from and in itself, unforeseeable in its radical novelty, and retrospectively establishing a rupture with the entire past: it will never again be the same world, with its possibilities and impossibilities articulated among themselves, for by lighting up its own path and happening beyond any prior measure, an event *reconfigures* the world for the one to whom it happens. While every thing is encountered against a horizon and every fact announces itself against the background of its own context, an event is never encountered on a horizon. Rather, it is the horizon of its encounter. While every fact and every being can be encountered in the world, in that they occur in the openness of their *montrance, an event opens to itself, gives access to itself, and, far from being subjected to a prior condition, provides the condition of its own occurring.*

That an event is thus absolved from all antecedent causality and originates in itself can only really be understood in light of an analysis of its temporality. It is not that we cannot enquire about causes for it; rather, these do not explain it, precisely to the extent that they do not match its extent. I have said that a cause is a fact, or a thing, or a state of affairs, by which a preexisting possibility comes to be actualized on the horizon of the world. By contrast, an event's eventness is not a matter of its innerworldly actualization, which could even give rise to an explanatory etiology, but of *the cargo of possibilities that it carries in itself and brings with it,* and that prevents it from being reduced to a fact in the world. For an event does not bring about a prior possibility but makes possible the possible and upends its own context by its an-archic bursting forth. Literally *eventum*, that which comes about [*advient*], it presents something irreducibly excessive with respect to every *factum*, that is (etymologically), with respect to everything that is "already made [*tout fait*]," brought about, and finished; this excess comes from the cargo of possibilities held in reserve by every genuine event and that makes these events something that upends the world by reconfiguring it. In this respect, an event does not belong to a fact's *actuality* but to its *possibility*, or better, to the possibility of making possible, to *possibilization*. Distinct from a fact, which occurs merely in a completed and definitive present, it is what holds itself in reserve in every fact and every actualization by giving the latter its cargo of possibilities and, consequently, its cargo of a future. It is what retransfigures my world to the point of introducing into it an excess of meaning inaccessible to any *explanation*. For the multiply determinable causes of an encounter explain nothing about the encounter as *event*, nor about its evential meaning-character; they explain nothing about what it is in this encounter that upends me forever[13]—that by which an event irreducibly transcends the causal framework in which it is nonetheless inscribed as a fact.

If events thus transcend their own actualization, not bringing about a prior possibility but rather making possible the possible in their an-archic bursting forth, this is so in that they *originate* in themselves and in that their meaning can be understood only on the horizon they have themselves opened by their arising. An origin—*origo*, *Ursprung*—is what arises (*orior*) and lifts itself by a leap (*Ur-sprung*) that breaks with all provenance, a living source, a pure bursting forth, distinct from any cause (*Ur-sache*), for causes always refer to another thing (*Sache*) from which the rest would follow. If events thus uproot the causal framework, this is because the context in which they are inserted—the "world," in the evential sense—does not explain them; on the contrary, they illuminate their own context, by conferring a meaning on it that was in no way prefigured. For if the world is the totality of interpretative possibilities from which facts become understandable in their mutual articulation and take on *meaning* for an *advenant*, an event is precisely that which, by breaking the horizon of prior possibilities and introducing into it a meaning that cannot be understood in light of any causal explanation, brings its own horizon of intelligibility with it, obliging an *advenant* to understand both himself and his world differently.

Breaking with the order of facts and actuality, events are therefore what introduces into the human adventure a meaning that is inaccessible to any etiology: *after* an event's bursting forth, things will never again be the same as *before*; it will never again be the same world, with its open possibilities, but the event's very arising, by opening new possibilities and, correlatively, closing others, upends an *advenant*'s world from top to bottom. But how is this last assertion to be understood? Is it not only some *particular* possibilities, and not all, that an event upends in its an-archic occurring? Does not an illness solely affect my relation to my body, or a bereavement solely the history that connects me to the other, and so on? Not at all. For there are no such things for an *advenant* as detached possibilities. By radically reconfiguring some *particular* possibilities, an event always upends the possible *in totality*. The world is not a *tally* of independent possibilities but rather the structural and hierarchical totality that articulates them and that articulates all understanding and all projection of meaning in general. Thus, the illness that afflicts me is not only a matter of something that alters my relation to my body; rather, it comes and upends the whole of my tasks, activities, and projections, to the point that their very meaning is modified. It is indeed such a world that an event deploys, by introducing into my adventure a hiatus and rupture that will never be filled. It is indeed the world that it transfigures through and through, by making the world's possibilities possible otherwise, by transforming these possibilities' relations and upending their hierarchies. However, the meaning of such a reconfiguration of the world can only be made clear if we first elucidate what we should understand here by "possibility."

Nevertheless, proposing that, in their very *meaning*, events are freed from all causality, since causality can only be established between facts, and that they transcend all actuality, being of a different order from a mere state of affairs, proposing that events, in their properly evential sense, project a world for an *advenant* by rearticulating his or her possibilities—in the end, does this not amount to excluding thought of any "relation" whatsoever between events, any causal "linking-up," any "history"? This objection, which seems to be legitimate, only holds if history itself has been defined in advance as a succession or linking-up of events. But it is not history that is a linking-up of events; rather, every genuine event, as such, has its history, *opens* a history, which can later be closed in its turn when the new possibilities given rise to by the event have been "exhausted," when other events have arisen without relation to this history. History can be conceived in this way only if the internal constitution of time is first of all brought to light; that is, the radical bursting open of times in their ab-solute character, cut off from one another, radically diachronic and nonsynchronizable.[14] What concept of "history" will do justice to the concept of event that we are trying to determine here? This question is one that we have to leave open for the moment.

But the problem of the temporality of events only becomes more cru-cial and more urgent in the framework of these preliminary analyses. Even if all that can be provided here is a mere sketch of analyses that will have to be taken up again and deepened, we need to try to specify the temporal meaning of events by contrast with that of innerworldly facts. We will thus obtain the fourth distinctive trait for differentiating between these two types of phenomenon.

§8 The Impossibility of Dating Events, and Their "Unexperienceable" Character

The first three phenomenological differences I have pointed out between events in the sense of innerworldly facts and events in their evential sense are:

(1) While innerworldy facts appear without any univocal substratum of ontic assignation, events are always able to have a determinate assigna-tion: they happen to me, to you, etc.; they never simply happen.

(2) Lacking a univocal substratum of ontic assignation, innerworldly facts necessarily always show themselves within a context that confers a sense on them; that is, on the horizon of a world. On the other hand, events in the evential sense light up their own context instead of being reduced to it; in this respect, and strictly speaking, they signify the advent of a new world for those who experience them. Of course, it is not the same "world" that is at stake in these two assertions; shifting from the first to the second, the very "meaning" of "world" has changed: in the first case, "world"—in the evental sense—refers to the signifying context of each fact in the horizon from which it draws its meaning and in light of which it is explained; in the second sense, "world" refers to that which comes about in each event, an *advenant*'s totality of possibilities articu-lated among themselves, which an event reconfigures in its an-archic bursting forth. "World" in the evential sense is therefore the horizon of meaning *that an event itself opens for the human adventure*, inasmuch as this event advenes only on its own horizon. We will see shortly how a "transition" from the first sense of "world" to the second is possible (see section 12, below).

(3) Facts are limited to bringing about preexisting possibilities, which are already prefigured on the horizon of the world. In this respect, they are subject to a causal explanation. It is a completely different matter with events, which appear without being reducible to their context. By tran-scending its own actualization as a fact, an event is freed of all prior causal-ity and declares itself, unconnected to any condition, as its own origin.

Inaccessible by any explanation, an event opens itself only to an understanding that grasps its *meaning*. This meaning can only be understood from the horizon that the event itself has opened; it is accessible only starting from its own posterity, according to a structural "delay," whose sense we will have to elucidate further.

A fourth principal phenomenological difference remains to be grasped. While a fact is brought about in a datable present, a definitive present in which everything is accomplished—precisely as a *fait accompli*—events are not datable: they are not so much inscribed *in* time, as they are what *opens* time or *temporalizes* it. Their *unexperienceable* character follows from this, in light of the empiricist concept of "experience." We must now elaborate on this final characteristic of events.

Overflowing in its essence the present of its actualization, an event is never brought about in the present, never *presented* on a temporal horizon: it opens an entirely new future and is given wholly in the movement of this *futurition* by which possibilities come about, these latter appearing utterly impossible from the view of the present and the past. Thus, an event introduces a fissure between the past and the future, from which time itself wells up in the diachrony of its radically burst open and nonsynchronizable times. We have seen that this excessive character of events with respect to the present in which they occur as facts—a present in which facts are brought about and completed by being actualized—this temporal suspense and overhang, derives from the cargo of possibilities that events carry in themselves, bring with them, and by which they upend the world, the present, and the *advenant*. As Proust writes in *The Prisoner*, "it seems that events are larger than the moment in which they occur and cannot be entirely contained in it."[15] But where does this overflow come from and how is it to be described?

It is apparent first of all in the impossibility of *dating* events as such. *When* exactly does an event happen? This question does not ask about an event in its factical actualization, but about an event as it occurs on the margin of its actualization, an event in its eventness as impersonal reconfiguration of the world. Consider, for example, an encounter, which cannot be reduced to the actual and innerworldly bringing into each other's presence of two particular *advenants*. The dimension of surprise, ecstasy, and enrapture that an encounter introduces "into the world" is as such inseparable from an upending of this world: anxiety, agitation, and timidity are assuredly essential phenomena of any encounter, in the way it shatters all familiarity with the world and suspends all "settledness" and assurance, by exposing me to the risk of a radical otherness that is screened from any mastery or foresight. Upending of the world itself, because, as an event, an encounter is not inscribed in a prior world, in *my* world, in this "*Welt*" that is always mine (*je meines*) and that Heidegger declares is one of Dasein's ontological constituents, but it introduces in this world that is always "mine" the strangeness of an incomparably "other" world, the world of an *other*, thus transforming my world through and through: where there is a genuine encounter, the event itself gives me access to something I could never have accessed by myself, the world of another, allowing me to "see" my own world and to "see" myself starting from it. By shattering an *advenant*'s solitary world and thus introducing possibilities that were not sketched out in it at all, an encounter constitutes a *metamorphosis of the world* for an *advenant*. In a letter to Milena, Kafka writes of his encounter with her:

> What's happening [*was geschieht*] is incredible [*Ungeheurliches*; literally: immense, terrifying]—my world is collapsing, my world is rebuilding itself [*meine Welt stürtz ein, meine Welt baut sich auf*] . . . I'm not lamenting the falling apart, it was already in a state of collapse, what I'm lamenting is the rebuilding, I lament my waning strength, I lament being born, I lament the light of the sun.[16]

Metamorphosis of the world that is, however, impossible to date, in contrast to the *fact* of their actual meeting, because it never appears to one who experiences it until it has already taken place, so that the first moment, the beginning of a love, the start of a friendship, are always already "lost": once an event "is brought about," it is already too late; we are never contemporaries of its actualization and can only experience it when it has already taken place, and this is why an event, in its eventness, happens only according to the secret of its latency. An encounter is not the datable fact of the meeting of two beings but rather that which lies in reserve in this meeting and which gives it its future-loading: it is the silent upending that the other introduces into my own world, reconfiguring my possibilities from the outside, before any projection of an autonomous potentiality-for-Being.

Paradoxical as it may seem, what is true here for the extreme "passivity" of an encounter where another has the sole initiative in approaching me and where I, for my part, could never anticipate this or prepare to receive it [*l'accueil*], is just as true for behaviors that show, by contrast, will, power, or mastery. While in every encounter, according to Levinas' penetrating formulation, "the other strikes me with powerlessness," in a decision, on the contrary, I demonstrate a power that is proper to me, a liberty and autonomy that belong to me alone. Nevertheless, major decisions, which transform us and are inscribed in our lives as genuine *events*, are brought about in us in such a way that we are never contemporary with their origin: not because, as Sartre thought, we have always already decided, which would amount to hypostasizing human freedom and conferring on free choice an unconditioned and strictly demiurgic power (deliberation would be only a "charade" that one plays out with oneself, when in fact the dice are already cast), but because every genuine decision, if it is genuinely a decision, is heralded long before it is declared. In a passage of *The Grass*, Claude Simon describes this impossibility of *dating* a decision, which belongs to its eventness:

> But she didn't answer, and, after a moment, he appeared: she could see him later the way he stood there, and she would wonder then if it wasn't at that moment that she made up her mind, although, she would think bitterly, it was about as futile to try to know the moment when a decision was reached and the reasons for that decision as to know the moment (and the reasons why) one catches a cold, the only possible certitude in the one case or the other (the decision or the cold) being when the one or the other reveals itself, and by then they have already been established for a long time.[17]

An event is precisely that which anonymously reconfigures my possibilities (here, my amorous possibilities) in such a way that, when it is brought about as an actual decision in the datable present of its actualization, when a decision transpires or, more accurately, "breaks out," the event has already taken place "long before"—this "already" should not be understood in terms of a linear temporal succession but in terms of the fissure that the event itself has carved out between a past and a future that are irremediably separated, a fissure from which time itself wells up, gaping beyond measure—in the impersonal mode.[18] In the end, by the time a decision is made, the event has already taken place long before, and as much as the event's actualization might be noisy and spectacular, its occurring, its advent, is silent and invisible. The epigraph from Pasternak in Claude Simon's novel encapsulates this unfathomable gap between a fact that can be experienced, on the one hand, and an event in its unexperienceable occurring, in its eventness, on the other, whose occurring I can undergo only *after the fact* (and therefore nonempirically), in the *essential a posteriori* of necessary retrospection: "No one makes history, no one sees it happen, no one sees the grass grow." This is not because we are restricted to a limited point of view on history, but because an event, an anonymous reconfiguration of the world, always happens *on the margin* of its actualization, silently and imperceptibly, coming "on the feet of doves":[19] it declares itself only much later, when it is already long settled.

When an event becomes visible in its actualization, it has *already* happened, and that is why, as Nietzsche writes: "The greatest events and thoughts . . . are the last to be comprehended: generations that are their contemporaries do not *experience* these sorts of events,—they live right past them."[20] This delay is not at all contingent and accidental, but necessary: if I can never be contemporary with an event, live it, or experience it, this is because the very meaning of an event is given only in terms of an *essential a posteriori*—a "transcendental" *a posteriori*, one could even say, in virtue of which the *experience* of the event qua impersonal reconfiguration of the world escapes any "*empirie*"[21] and any empiricism in the traditional sense.

This delay, this latency, this temporal deferral are not characteristics of an event that are "added," so to speak, to it from outside. An event, as such, is *nothing other* than this imperceptible deferral and silent latency, by which and according to which it upends or, rather, has already upended who we were. What cannot be experienced can yet, by this very disparity, this intimate being out of step, come and touch us, wound us, and, by addressing itself to us, by prescribing that we undergo it, give us the possibility of receiving it [*l'accueillir*] by being transformed.

§9 The Task of an Evential Hermeneutics: Elucidating the Meaning of the Human Adventure Using Events as the Guiding Thread; The *Advenant* and His Eventials; Temporality

We have seen four phenomenological traits of events: (1) their univocal assignation, by which, in every event, I am in play *myself* in my selfhood; (2) their character as world-establishing for an *advenant*; (3) their constitutive an-archy, according to which, although inexplicable, they nevertheless make *sense* in a human adventure; and (4) the impossibility of any dating, such that they do not happen in time but rather open time or temporalize it.

Henceforth, these four fundamental characteristics will serve as a guiding thread for shedding light on the meaning of the human adventure. I call such a shedding of light, which is *interpretation* through and through, evential hermeneutics. This hermeneutics is, first, a phenomenology; second, an interpretation of the *advenant*, who is decisively distinguished from the classic concept of the "subject"; and third, a hermeneutics of temporality. To conclude this first part, let us now turn to these final three points.

First: To what extent do events lend themselves to a phenomenology? As we have already seen, in contrast to mere facts, events are not possible before being actual; neither are they foreseeable according to a causal regime, nor can they be anticipated in the mode of a projection. They occur, strictly speaking, *before being possible*,[22] and thus are set free of their own conditions. They do not have "conditions of possibility," which would be somehow rooted in a "subject," as a particular "passivity" that prepares to receive them [*l'accueil*]. In their radical unpreparedness, they are the sole condition (without conditions) of their own advent. Indeed, their own occurring opens the playing field and space where they can occur. Their arising is its own measure; it reaches us *outside any measure from ourselves* and is not subjected to any prior condition, any ontological a priori, for instance, which would give a measure for their manifestation. Consequently, if a fundamental requirement of phenomenology is that it takes appearances as being the source for description by right, without presuming in advance about the meaning of these appearances, then the first phenomenon, the one that is primary by right, is precisely the one that is the source of all meaning and right for itself (and hence also for us), the one that illuminates itself and is brought about in light of its own manifestation: the pure *montrance* of events.

Of course, this primary assertion solves none of the problems that a phenomenology of events raises *in concreto*. It suffices for the moment to establish the primacy of events and their "inalienable" right to become phenomena for a phenomenology.

How does it stand, then, with the second of our assertions? In what way can this phenomenological analysis of events according to the diverse modes of their *montrance* serve as a guiding thread for a hermeneutic of the *advenant*? And, in addition, does it allow us to radically differentiate the *advenant* from the "subject" in the classic sense? A response to such a question would still need to determine what should be understood by the traditional "subject." Without such a prior characterization, it becomes impossible to grasp what taking events as a guiding thread *makes us see* about ourselves—which the traditional subject by contrast conceals. The modern characterization of the "subject" since Descartes is inseparable from the conventional translation of Aristotle's beingness (*ousia*) as *substantia*:[23] that which *lies at the base* and *continues underneath* the various attributes or accidents, their permanent *substratum* (*hupo-keimenon*). It is not very difficult to see how such a characterization of the modern "subject," by reducing events to mere attributes or properties of a substance, fundamentally excludes defining the subject as *the one to whom something happens*. On the contrary: determining the human being as "subject" precludes from the outset that anything like an event could touch him; this characterization thinks of a human being as the one who always continues underneath what happens (to him) (*sub-jectum*), who exercises so great a mastery and control over events that he relegates them to simple attributes, the one who is identical with himself even in his alterations. This characterization fundamentally excludes that a human being could be touched by something like an event, upended or transformed by it. Indeed, as Levinas writes, the subject is "a power of endless stepping back, an ability always to find oneself behind what happens to one."[24] To be a subject is always to be able to find and rediscover oneself "behind" or "underneath" what comes to pass, "of relating to events while still being able to not be caught up in them."[25] It is to be one to whom every event is related as a predicate, attribute, or accident, and thereby subordinated and reduced to a downgraded regime of being. Hence, to be a subject is to be one who, by subordinating events to oneself, reduces them to one's own status.

It is still too early to judge the extent to which thinking that explicitly sets out to leave behind the horizon of the subject's metaphysics nonetheless still moves in its orbit and still adopts, surreptitiously but firmly, a characterization of the subject as "a power of endless stepping back." In particular, it is too early to judge the extent to which, despite the decisive step outside metaphysics accomplished by *Being and Time*, Heidegger's Dasein still remains on the horizon of such a concept of sub-jectivity. For if the "subject" is precisely one to whom every event is ordered as a predicate, *on the one hand*, access to Dasein presumes the destruction of the traditional "subject," since "there are no more copulas"[26] in the existential analytic. *On the other hand*, however, it could be that Dasein is established as an ontological instance only by a phenomenological reduction of events.[27] Now, if Dasein is secured in its Being by a reduction of events (*to* Being or *as* Being), it remains an open question whether the "subject" is not reborn here in the wake of its destruction by fundamental ontology and whether it is not necessary *also* to destroy Dasein so as to reach the *advenant*, who alone is "capable" of events. But how is this latter radically distinguished from any "subject" or "subjectivity"? How does the *advenant* escape from, or rather rebuff, all thinking in terms of "subject"?

Advenant is the term for describing the event that is constantly underway of my own advent to myself from the events that happen to me [*m'adviennent*] and that, by addressing themselves to me, give me a destiny: adventure without return. It refers to neither a privileged being nor an ontological instance but rather the very opening to events in general, that is, the evential "condition" (or rather, as we shall see, *un-condition*) of all history. As such, the *advenant* is therefore the dimension from which events become visible, in and of themselves, and he is this in two respects.

First, the *advenant* is the one *to whom* events occur. In this sense, *and in this sense alone*, he can rightly be called "subject" if one wishes, in that he is the sole and unique ontic substratum of assignation *necessarily* implied for any innerworldly fact to be able to show itself from itself, as it happens as itself. The necessity for such an assignation results from the fact that events in their primary sense (i.e., innerworldly facts) can appear *only* for a "subject" who is capable of *understanding* them, that is, of grasping their *meaning* in an interpretative scheme, in accordance with a particular evential *context*.

However, this first aspect is immediately reinforced by a second and more fundamental one. The *advenant* is *the one* to whom events happen, *in that he is himself implicated in what happens to him*, that is, in that it belongs to him to understand *himself* in what happens to him in this way. The event in play here in such an understanding is no longer an innerworldly fact but an event in its properly evential sense, such that it *happens to me, unsubstitutably*, and thus brings me to understand myself starting from the reconfigured possibilities that the event itself has made to arise. *Advenant* is the evential term for describing *this implication itself*, that is, the implication of myself in what happens to me and makes history for me in my own adventure. In other words, it is the term for selfhood, understood and interpreted in its evential sense, as the capacity to face and relate myself to events by unsubstitutably undergoing them.

Hence, *advenant* is the most original characterization of the human being, in that the latter is the one *to whom* something can happen *only* if he is implicated himself in what happens to him. To be implicated oneself in what happens (to us) is to be capable of *experience* in the most fundamental sense, which does not refer to a modality of theoretical knowledge understood as the way a subject and object face each other, but rather an undergoing and passage from self to self, which is inseparable from a constitutive alteration. The *advenant* is the one who, because he is capable of experience, of unsubstitutably undergoing an event in which he is himself altered with no way back, has the possibility of understanding *himself* in his selfhood starting from the possibilities articulated in a world that the event has pushed forth, and, consequently, to advene himself precisely as *the one* to whom what happens happens.

Thus, the *advenant* is not first a "subject," who would subsequently be capable of events: for to think of him as "subject" would from the outset take away the ground from which and on which thinking about events can be constructed. The *advenant* is rather the one who bars thought about a subject and begins by declaring its end. Indeed, the *advenant* is not primarily a "subject," in that he is the one *to whom* something happens (the "subject" of an event's assignation) only *inasmuch as* and *to the extent that* he is first and more originally *the one* to whom events befall and who is able to understand himself starting from them—that is, strictly speaking, able to advene to himself as himself by way of an experience. An *advenant*'s characteristic as an event's "subject" (of assignation) presumes a more original characteristic of his selfhood, as capacity to undergo the experience of what happens to him, such that the first of these characteristics *derives* from the second and does not direct it in advance. Any claim to conceive events beginning from the subject trips up on this necessarily derived character of its starting point. And it may well be that Dasein, whose selfhood is ontologically and *formally* defined without any reference to events, does not escape this fate.

Now, if the *advenant* is the phenomenological ground of the appearing of any "subject," this necessarily implies in turn that the "subject" itself is something that *advenes*; it must be understood eventially. Hence the peculiar inversion that takes place in the very way of formulating the question of "subjectivity" or, more accurately, of selfhood. It is no longer a matter of conceiving events as what happens "from outside" to a subject who is autonomous, autarchic, and free of any implication in what happens to it, but, inversely, of conceiving "subjectivity" itself, divested of its role as ontological instance and, consequently, stripped of the privileges of the "subject," as that which *occurs* only from events. Such a conception demands commitment to describing the diverse phenomenological modes (or "eventials") according to which an *advenant* advenes to himself *as himself*. These are not the modes of Being of an exemplary entity but rather *processes of "subjectivation."* How does an *advenant* advene to himself from events that are themselves differentiated—and hence differentiating—such as bereavement, encounters, decisions? As we shall see, to consider the processes of subjectivation in this way, "before" any subjectivity, is also to go back prior to any given subject, toward its origin in the *impersonal*. For an *advenant* can be implicated in this way in what happens to him and, subsequently, endowed with selfhood, only starting from the *impersonal* event of birth, which courses through his adventure from one end to the other and which is accessible only to a phenomenology of the presubjective.

This structural liaison between the evential meaning of events and the original characterization of the *advenant*, according to which the latter can be the one *to whom* something happens only if he is, more originally, the one *to which* something happens, and if, consequently, he is *himself* implicated in what happens to him; this connection that can be formulated in other terms by stating that events are addressed to me (an *advenant*) unsubstitutably only insofar as I can understand them by understanding *myself* in my selfhood starting from the possibilities opened by them; or, to put it differently again, this phenomenological implication of an *advenant* in what happens to him, such that he can undergo an event as befalling him *singularly* only by *singularizing* himself through this experience and thus becoming the incomparable in his unsubstitutable undergoing of the unique—this implication of an *advenant* in events is rooted in the following phenomenological characteristic: events, in the eventful sense, *are precisely nothing other* than this reconfiguration of my possibilities, in which I am given the capacity to understand myself differently, by letting myself declare *who* I am through events.

Therefore, *advenant* is the term for selfhood itself in its *advening*, the event that is always on the way of my own advent to myself from the events that happen to me [*m'adviennent*] and through which I become. Or again: *advenant* is the term for the human being as constitutively open to events, insofar as humanity is the "capacity" to undergo unsubstitutably what happens to us. The humanity of the human being means being open to events in a way that allows one to understand them and to understand oneself starting from them as *advenant*. The human being's adventure strictly signifies openness to what happens [*advient*]. This ad-venture, which must be understood here, like the *advenant*, in a transitive and verbal—eventual—sense, signifies the event of my own advent to myself, inasmuch as it is constantly on the way, inasmuch as it is, strictly speaking, *time*. The openness of the human adventure is therefore temporality. This is why an *advenant* is never a *terminus a quo* but rather a *terminus ad quem*. In itself, it "is" only the event always already happened and yet deferred of its own adventure.

From this unfolds, finally, the third thesis I announced earlier: eventful hermeneutics is a hermeneutics of temporality. Indeed, the human adventure can no longer be brought to light phenomenologically by orienting oneself on the form of the ontological or, rather, ousiological question "what is that?" It is neither essences nor existentials that are being sought here, but *modalities* of the adventure, or eventials, that is, the ways in which the *advenant* advenes to himself. The leading question for our interpretation would rather be "what is happening with . . . ? [*Qu'en advient-il de . . . ?*]" or even "how is he (the *advenant*) advening?" Of course, these are not merely to do with grammatical modifications, unless "grammar" is understood in a far more profound sense than usual, in the sense of a true "grammar of philosophical questions" that would orient every hermeneutic projection. An *advenant* "is" nothing other than what *comes to light, happens, or occurs* from events; he "is" simply the process of his own "subjectivation," a process that is continually on the way. "Eventials" are therefore the phenomenologically diverse modes according to which this "subjectivation" is brought about.

Now, such processes of subjectivation are already *temporal* through and through. Or rather: for an *advenant* to happen to himself in this way is already to open himself to time, and to open time as such. On the one hand, time is not something that is, so to speak, "added" to an event as a simple property. Rather, an event can only occur temporally; it "is" intrinsically time. On the other hand, if human adventure is simply the event of my own advent to myself, which event is constantly on the way, the human adventure is itself indexed temporally: from the outset, time is its essential plot. Because of this, the question of the procedures according to which an *advenant* advenes to himself, or the modalities of his adventure (evential hermeneutics), can open in a second moment on the question of the phenomenological meaning of time itself. Thus it will no longer be a matter of understanding the temporality of events on the horizon of an interpretation of the *advenant* in his adventure but rather of grasping the *evential meaning of time itself*, by freeing the temporal phenomenon from the formal frameworks to which it is limited by its metaphysical understanding. This is the task of the second volume of this study: *Event and Time*.[28]

PART ☐2

The *Advenant*

The I, really, is nobody, is the anonymous; it must be so . . . in order to be the Operator, or the one to whom all this occurs.
—**Merleau-Ponty,** *The Visible and the Invisible*[1]

§10 Evential Hermeneutics and Its Delimitation from Psychology or Anthropology

"Evential hermeneutics" is the name I have given to the interpretation undertaken here of the human adventure in light of events. The adjective "evential" has been coined so as to avoid any possible confusion with a conception of the human adventure as a succession of "events" occurring in a world, as a succession of facts or biography. "Evential," which refers to events in their proper sense, is therefore distinguished in principle from "evental," which qualifies anything to do with events in the sense of innerworldly facts. However, does not such an evential hermeneutics risk being a simple repetition or facsimile of analyses that could equally be classified as psychology or philosophical anthropology? Could not analyses of bereavement, despair, encounters, decisions, and so on be located just as well in these other disciplines? And, if this is not the case, where exactly is the boundary between evential hermeneutics and these other disciplines? Can we establish a *difference in principle* between their various modes of access to an *advenant*?

In the course of our preliminary analyses, we have been led to ask ourselves about the essential phenomenological difference that separates a cause from an origin. Consider Kant's assertion in the *Prolegomena*: "everything of which experience teaches me that it happens must have a cause."[2] This assertion has a universal validity that admits of no exception; it is true, to be sure, for every event, *except for events in an evential sense*. This is not to suggest that these latter "float" around without a cause, but rather to say that the causes that condition them operate at a completely different level from their phenomenological *meaning*-character. Of course, an event also occurs as a *fact*, and as such it has causes. However, it is an *event* only because it transcends its causes, which are always necessarily linked together on the horizon of a world, understood as the horizon of preexisting possibilities. Consequently, the only thing that can be said about an event is that it happens "because it happens," just as an encounter could be said to take place "because it was him, because it was her." In both cases, the word "because," which generally has the function of introducing something else that is understood as the reason or the cause of what one is trying to explain, is detached from any explanatory function. It is an empty gesture that says nothing and that nevertheless says everything there is to say about an event and its causes. An event is "without a why"; it escapes in principle from the principle of reason. Even if an event is always able to be causally explained, no matter how incompletely and imperfectly, in its actualization as a fact, in its eventness, it entirely eludes all explanatory etiology. Strictly speaking, it is *meaningless* to attempt an explanation of *the very origin of meaning* for the human adventure. An illness, for instance, as an innerworldly fact, has epidemiological and genetic causes, whose interlinked sequence could be traced back, at least ideally. But the *event* of an illness, as it happens unsubstitutably to an *advenant* by reconfiguring his essential possibilities, his world, and by bringing him to *understand himself* differently, is rigorously *without a why*, and *happens "because it happens."* It is itself its own *origin*.

But how can these considerations put us on the way to a response to the question formulated above of the difference *in principle* between disciplines like psychology or anthropology and evential hermeneutics? Precisely in that this difference is itself that which separates innerworldly "sciences," on the one hand, disciplines that operate at the level of facts and their causes, endeavoring to understand the former in light of the latter, and, on the other hand, a "discipline" that aims only at illuminating events as origin, which asks about the *origin of meaning* as it comes about in the human adventure starting from events. For understood in this sense, "origin" is not a principle or first cause; it eludes any explanatory arche-ology. It arises only from itself, has no cause on which it depends, and is not the cause of anything else; still less is it *causa sui*: it escapes entirely from the reign of cause and effect, which governs the interlinking of facts in the world. "Origin" in this sense is a modality of *meaning* as it wells up in and through events.

Thus, an event is this irreducible meaning, which wells up in a human adventure as its own origin and which can be *understood* in its properly eventful tenor but not explained. This distinction between "understanding" and "explanation" should not be confused with its homonym, which Dilthey uses to draw a line between natural and human sciences: the former governed by the principle of a strict causality and the latter drawing only on the concepts of "motives" and "drives" to understand the meaning of a historical action, for example. Granted, a motive is not a cause, in that it is connected with a goal: it is always necessarily *for the sake of* some project that a motive acquires its determining value. Sartre's version of this classical definition highlights this intrinsic connection between motives and goals well: "We shall therefore use the term *motive* for the objective apprehension of a determined situation as this situation is revealed in the light of a certain end as being able to serve as the means for attaining this goal."[3] Drives, by contrast, refer to the dimension of "irrationality" and contingency that is attached to human actions and that belongs not to the will and conscious choice but to emotions, passions, and affectivity in general. While a historical action can *sometimes* be understood in light of motives and *sometimes* in light of drives, understanding in terms of motives will, as often as possible, prevail and get the better of that in terms of drives, to the extent that the former alone is "rational."

Now, whatever the phenomenological pertinence of this distinction between motives and drives might be—a question I cannot broach here—what has been called "understanding," following Dilthey, belongs instead, with some nuances, to what I have thus far called "explanation." For what such understanding aims at is nothing other than *explaining* the *why* of human acts—not in terms of "causes," to be sure, but in terms of motives and drives, which are, in the human world, the *analogue* of natural causes—thus, in a way that is certainly distinct from what applies to natural regularities. Such an explanatory "understanding" of human acts operates entirely within the "world," with its causal chains and its goals articulated among themselves in a signifying context, and from the outset falls short of the dimension of events as, strictly speaking, *origin of the world*: as far as their very *meaning* resides precisely in that they are, in their arising *without a why*, world-establishing.

And so psychology and anthropology, like sociology or ethnology, are innerworldly sciences of facts and their causes—regardless of whether these are analyzed more closely in terms of "motives" and "drives"—and are situated on a completely different plane from that of evential analysis: the former progress entirely on the horizon of the world, and "understand" still means "explain" for them, even if their explanations proceed according to modalities distinct from those that govern the natural sciences; the latter asks about *the very origin of the world as it arises from and with events.* The understanding that is in play here is what addresses itself to these kernels of meaning that events are, not for investigating their causes or motives, but for determining the extent to which they *make history* for me, the extent to which the world will never again be the same for me after their occurring. Nodes of an adventure, and crises for it, in which an *advenant* is exposed to the peril of a transformation at the risk of himself, unless he succumbs into an anonymity that takes different guises in the experiences of despair, terror, or traumatism.[4]

Consider the event of a fundamental decision, which engages an individual entirely. The difference between a purely psychological or anthropological approach, still causal-explanatory, and an approach that is evential through and through will appear clearly. The first will ask about the *why* for such a decision and will explore reasons and drives, comparing their respective importance. It will examine the decision starting from the preexisting possibilities of a "world" in which it is inscribed and that forms the past or the "passive" from which it is inseparable. Such an explanation will proceed under the regime of a complete *relativity*, for motives and drives, essentially inexhaustible, push an explanation always further back, without ever providing it with a *final* reason, even if this remains necessarily in the background, constantly demanded and yet never provided; a condition that is necessary but impossible to display. The second, by contrast, will be limited to *understanding the intrinsic meaning of this event*, in that it *makes history* in a human adventure; in other words, in that the one who decides is himself wholly in play in his selfhood in this very decision.

Thus, to investigate the causes (motives, drives) of a decision is to miss its meaning from the outset, for it is its own origin. The radical, "in principle" and insurmountable difference that separates an evential analytic from any anthropology, psychology, and even psychoanalysis[5] is tied to the fundamental difference between explaining by causes and understanding meaning. It is this difference that must now be brought to light for its own sake.

§11 Understanding as Evential

"Understanding" is the most fundamental characteristic of the relation between an *advenant* and the world. An *advenant*'s adventure consists wholly in understanding what happens to him—his adventure is itself hermeneutic. A "world" (in the evental sense) belongs to him only insofar as he is able to interpret facts in light of their context, trace their causes, identify what they result from, and project goals in light of which the "world" itself takes on an aspect and countenance. However, this primacy of understanding does not exclude, and in fact implies, that most of the time an *advenant* may lack understanding and may even have the deepest incomprehension with respect to what "occurs."

Before being a gnoseological act, a modality of the theoretical meeting of "subject" and "object," understanding is a modality of adventure, an evential, a way for an *advenant* to advene to himself starting from these pure preludes to adventure that are its crucial or critical moments. In this respect, understanding does not demand a privileged attitude, by which an *advenant* would withdraw himself from his own adventure, so to speak, nor a theoretical or reflexive stepping back, by which an *advenant's theoria* would be set free from his *praxis*, even if only "for a while"; it is not a "reflexive" attitude that is split off from the "practical demands of life." On the contrary, understanding is the primary attitude, prior to any other, in which an *advenant* constantly holds himself and by which he always relates to all that happens to him: a prereflexive and pretheoretical comportment that is inseparable from the way in which an *advenant* ceaselessly advenes to himself, and that is the sole ground on which every explicit theory can be built up. Hence, such understanding, which is pre-linguistic and preconceptual, even if it is only accomplished in and as speech,[6] precedes every thematic formulation and conceptual elaboration of the meaning of the phenomena to which it is directed. Thanks to this understanding, an *advenant* can, prior to any intellectual "reflection," encounter what happens to him doubly, both as an innerworldly fact and as an event in the proper sense.

Nevertheless, there are essential distinctions in understanding these two phenomena, and it is helpful to set these distinctions out clearly here. To what extent is understanding arrayed differently, depending on whether it is relating to a fact or an event? What differences follow from this for the evential sense of understanding itself?

As we have seen,[7] the articulation of this evential encompasses several moments: (1) the phenomenon that is to be understood; (2) the prior orientation according to which the projection of understanding is brought about; (3) the phenomenon of the meaning, as what a projection is directed toward; and (4), the *universum* of possibilities from which the projection of understanding can set off toward its meaning and thus be put into action with a specific orientation. Thus, understanding can be specified as a projection directed toward something, for the sake of bringing a meaning to light, according to a particular prior orientation, in conformity with a horizon of interpretative possibilities or context. The question that arises at this point is the following: if to understand a fact in a prior context is always to explain it, to grasp its meaning in light of causes or ends that preexist it in the world, what is it to understand an event, which appears without being reducible to its context and which is announced as its own origin, without any connection to a causal condition? Correlatively: how are we to conceive of the meaning of an event, if it appears as necessarily irreducible to any worldly explanation?

These questions lead us to set out the concept of understanding at greater depth and to distinguish between (1) a simple explanatory grasp of a fact in light of its context—understanding in an evental sense—and (2) an interpretation of an event that can no longer be carried out in conformity with a horizon of prior meaning since, strictly speaking, an event is its own prelude, freed from all horizons, and only comprehensible in conformity with a meaning that wells up with it and is one with this very welling up: understanding in an evential sense. If the former has, for the most part, already been analyzed, it remains to bring to light the phenomenological meaning-character of the latter. Indeed, in the case of *events*, interpretation can no longer be set out on the horizon of a prior context (of causes and ends). Instead, an event itself prescribes the possibilities from which the projection of understanding can be carried out, by upending its context and shedding a new light on it, one that burst forth with it. To understand is no longer to aim at a meaning, according to a prior orientation and in conformity with a given context. Rather, it is to appropriate a meaning that is irreducible to its own context, according to the structural delay with which a projection is carried out after its interpretative possibilities. This is the case, for instance, with a work of art, which cannot really be understood in its singularity except from the posterity to which it gives rise, the refashioning it brings about in the forms, themes, and techniques of its period. A work of art cannot be understood within the artistic context in which it is born, which it necessarily transcends if it is an original work. In this respect, every interpretation of an event must draw on interpretative possibilities in the event itself: an event alone provides the key for its own deciphering. And this is the case for every event in an *advenant*'s singular adventure: each event can be understood solely starting from the upheavals that it triggers, from the posterity that it opens by occurring. For example, a decision is never free from a context that to a certain extent explains its arising as a fact: as much from a "historical" context, in a broad sense, as from an *advenant*'s motivations, the ends freely posited by him, which refer in their turn to other ends articulated to one another on a single horizon: the global practical projection that belongs singularly to this particular *advenant*. Nevertheless, even if the decision is in some way foreseeable as a fact (and, consequently, explicable in retrospect), this decision, when it occurs, introduces such a radical upheaval of an adventure and its possibilities that the world itself shudders. This is the way Joseph Conrad's novel *The End of the Tether* reveals the meaning of a decision taken by an aging captain about selling his sailing ship, which is now competing with and being made obsolete by steamboats:

> What to the other parties was merely the sale of a ship was to him a momentous event involving a radically new view of existence. He knew that after this ship there would be no other; and the hopes of his youth, the exercise of his abilities, every feeling and achievement of his manhood, had been indissolubly connected with ships. He had served ships; he had owned ships; and even the years of his actual retirement from the sea had been made bearable by the idea that he had only to stretch out his hand full of money to get a ship. He had been at liberty to feel as though he were the owner of all the ships in the world. The selling of this one was weary work; but when she passed from him at last, when he signed the last receipt, it was as though all the ships had gone out of the world together, leaving him on the shore of inaccessible oceans with seven hundred pounds in his hands.[8]

As much as it might have been somehow anticipated, as much as its context—in economic and technical history—might be able to explain it, to understand what happens with this event is to understand the way the decision, once taken, triggers the collapse of a world that is henceforth completely buried under the debris of a dead past. *Singular and unindexable meaning* that this decision possesses, opened solely to a first-person understanding and consequently inseparable from an experience. Meaning that is, therefore, indecipherable in conformity with a worldly context, revealing itself to an interpretation that is necessarily retrospective and, as such, unable to be definitive.

Indeed, "understanding" can no longer mean simply projecting oneself toward a meaning in conformity with a context, since a prior context from which it might be illuminated is precisely what is lacking to an event as such. If understanding is still necessarily characterized as projection, what such a projection aims at is precisely that which exceeds in principle all my projections by removing itself from a prior horizon of meaning. This is a paradox, but a necessary one, for the projection of understanding is always an anticipation that presumes as such a horizon of interpretative possibilities from which alone it can reach the meaning of the phenomenon that is to be understood. However, when this phenomenon is an *event* in the strict sense, the projection of understanding finds itself always preceded by the interpretative possibilities that the event makes possible, such that it reaches the meaning of the phenomenon in question only by first understanding to what extent it is inexplicable, to what extent it transcends the context with which the projection of understanding normally conforms. Hence, to understand an event is always to aim at it according to an interpretative projection that is no longer laid out from a horizon of prior possibilities but is instead governed, in reaching its meaning, by the possibilities that the event alone has pushed forth. Such a projection can therefore reach its meaning only retrospectively, since what it aims to bring to light is actually that by which the event spills over every projection and every horizon of prior possibilities: *its meaning*. Necessarily delayed, exceeded from the outset by the interpretative possibilities that an event opens by occurring, such an understanding is retrospective precisely to the extent that the event itself is *prospective*, precedes itself, and is accessible solely from its future.

And since evential understanding is no longer an explanatory grasp, which relies on a context and is limited to bringing to light a meaning that is already declared in the world, with it the primary relation between an *advenant* and the world is profoundly changed. Indeed, the meaning of an event is strictly *in-comprehensible* within the worldly context that explains it. This incomprehensibility does not reflect a mere shortcoming of understanding; it has a *positive* signification. The horizon of meaning, within which any interpretative projection is possible, is in this case no longer the world as context: *the significance of the world appears instead to be insignificant for understanding the meaning of a genuine event.* The sole horizon of interpretative possibilities from which a projection of understanding can be carried out is the horizon that the event *has opened* by opening possibilities that are in no way prefigured in the world, or that only an essentially retrospective understanding can ascertain there, once an event has appeared. The *world* with which an *advenant* is concerned is thus the one that arises from the event, in that it declares itself to be its own origin, freed from its context. This world, which happens with and through an event, is what I have called world in its *evential* sense. Only such a concept of world articulates the understanding that we are presently considering.

Thus, there is an understanding that is not of the order of an explanatory grasping of meaning since, by contrast with explanation, it does not deal with what may or may not be endowed with meaning—the fact—but concentrates *on meaning itself at its origin*: in an event. At this point, the advent of a world and the event of meaning are one and the same. Evential understanding operates in the interplay between two worlds, in the between-world that an event has opened and from which alone what is meaningful for human adventure can be brought to light. Moreover, this understanding can operate there only according to a delay that belongs to it constitutively. But whence exactly comes this "delay" that is consubstantial with understanding in its original meaning? In other words: on what conditions can understanding, in its evential sense, receive its projective possibilities from an event, instead of from the "world" as context? Solely on the condition that an event itself makes a world [*fasse monde*], or, to put it differently, that before any projection of his own, an *advenant* is originally exposed to possibilities that exceed him, and of which he is not himself the measure. Only the precursor event of birth will allow us to bring this "condition" to light and thus to reach the primary sense of this adventure.

Thus, the following questions will guide our analyses: (1) What should be understood here, phenomenologically, by "world"? How does the transition happen between the eventyal and the evential senses of world? (See section 12, below.) (2) How does the world originate in the precursor event of birth? What is the original evential meaning of birth? (See section 13, below.)

§12 The Evential Concept of World: Event as "Phenomenological Transition"

What is the relation between events and world? How does the phenomenological meaning of the world come to be "seen" from the perspective of events? Writing of the arising of the new in his *Phenomenology of Spirit*, Hegel describes it as "a shaking [*Wanken*] of the world," and compares an event to "a sunburst which, in one flash [*ein Blitz*], traces the features of the new world [*das Gebilde der neuen Welt hinstellt*]."[9] But how are we to describe this shaking and establishing? If it is one and the same world that trembles on its foundations, that both collapses and is built up, is it not the *very meaning of world* that is modified through this trembling?

With an event's arising, the world collapses as context. The signifying horizon within which every innerworldly fact can be displayed as such, and set in the infinite framework of its causes and the articulated complex of ends in light of which an *advenant* understands it—this horizon is suddenly exposed as *insignificant* with respect to what is declared. In upending the world from end to end, an event removes its *significance* from the hermeneutic context in light of which every fact is explained. For the one who understands it, an event signifies the advent of a new world. However, this description of events as the irruption of a new world-configuration, altering the former one irrevocably, remains insufficient. For through this metamorphosis of the world, *one sense of the "world" shifts over to another:* the evental sense shifts over to the evential one. The world no longer appears as the factual context for any innerworldly understanding, but as the articulated totality of possibilities from which an *advenant* shapes himself in the course of his adventure. Consequently, this sense of "world" is a modality of this adventure, or an "evential." But how does the world as an evential, an a priori of the human adventure, in that the latter is essentially structured by its "relation" to events, differ from the "world" as *context?* What phenomenological difference is marked out between these two phenomena?

The signifying context, in light of which every innerworldly fact becomes interpretable, is constituted by a multiplicity of concomitant facts, known or unknown, to which this fact refers as its circumstances. In this respect, there is never any such thing as an isolated fact. But what is the precise relation between an innerworldly fact and its context? By contrast with events, a fact lacks specific assignation: in it there is no issue of an *advenant* in his selfhood. It bears an "objective" profile in the world and puts itself forward for whoever might witness it, as a pure vis-à-vis (*Gegenstand*) of an experience. And so, the worldly context that explains it stands out for whoever might consider it in an interpretation. Here, "world" is the swarm of circumstances that illuminate the fact itself *without thereby being a part of it*, the "ambience" that envelops it as its hermeneutic context, the signifying horizon on which it is distinguished, including the unbounded multiplicity of other facts that enter into relation with it according to the double modality of "causes" and "ends": such an *ambient world* (*Umwelt*) thus appears as *an intrinsically incomplete "totality," an open-ended multiplicity or whole*, since new facts can always be added to it, and since an explanatory etiology can, in principle, always go further, by aiming at a more exhaustive account. The worldly context therefore refers to a factual whole *that can always grow* to give an account of a given event's meaning.

It is quite a different matter with the second sense of "world," to which we gain access from events in their *evential* sense. By contrast with mere facts, which occur in the world by modifying *particular* possibilities but which nevertheless lend themselves to explanation starting from a prior causal horizon, events, by modifying particular possibilities, always upend the possible *as a whole*. The "whole" in question here is not an indefinite multiplicity of facts in light of which events might be explicable, nor is it a collection of separate possibilities; it is the structural, hierarchic, and signifying unity that confers meaning on them. For example, by striking me in my physical integrity, an illness does not modify only some particular possibilities of mine; it strikes at the very root of the possible: it inverts the order of priorities, makes the likelihood of a journey more remote, ruins intellectual or affective projects, places an insurmountable obstacle between me and the world. In ruining projects and upending hierarchies, it also always produces new constellations of meaning. Perhaps I will realize only later that, without it, many of the decisions and acts that seem today to be inseparable from my own destiny and, so to speak, consubstantial with me as a person would probably have been impossible. In any case, the world in the evential sense is not a collection of independent possibilities but the structural and hierarchic whole that integrates them. Each possibility takes on a meaning only in its relation to the whole. An event is precisely what exposes this *cohesion of possibilities*: the *world*. Solely on this condition can an event reconfigure the world *as a whole*, by introducing novel possibilities in the former world and by altering its meaning *through and through*. The "whole" that is in play here in the evential phenomenon of world is thus a whole that preexists its parts, an articulated unity of possibilities that cannot be detached from one another nor understood in isolation. The whole of the world (*Welt*) is no longer the "ambience" (*Umwelt*) of an explanatory context as an unbounded multiplicity of facts or a swarm of circumstances that can always be enlarged; it is a globality that *absolutely* precedes any given multiplicity, an indivisible but nevertheless articulated unity preceding any addition or summation of possibilities. This all-encompassing unity of meaning is an a priori for understanding that is only exposed as such in the a posteriori of the event and in the lighting that the latter projects on it.

Consequently, the world is not really distinct here from the event as such but is rather an a priori for it. While a context is by definition independent from the fact that is presented in it—and relies on this independence if it is to provide an *explanation*, since any explanatory account presumes circumstances that are distinct from the fact that is to be explained—with the fact putting itself "forward," standing out for whoever might consider it, and the "world" holding "back" as the signifying background against which the fact is distinguished—by contrast an event always appears *interdependent* and in solidarity with the world in an evential sense. Not only does the world originate in an event, but also, strictly speaking, it does not differ from the latter. For, on the one hand, an event "is" precisely nothing other than a metamorphosis of the world and its meaning, and, on the other hand, the world "is" only the event of its own advent, which happens or enworlds through this metamorphosis of the possible—the event in its pure sense. It is because an event is *a modulation of the world* that it can reveal the world as such, as the articulated totality of possibility for an *advenant*, and thus disclose the Open in its presubjective and preobjective emptiness: as that from which an *advenant* himself takes place, the very event in which he originates. An event is then, strictly, what gives access to the Open of the world that opens in it, to the possibility of the possible that it makes possible.

Thus, the world in an evential sense is neither objective nor subjective. Not objective, by contrast with any factual context, and not subjective, since it does not refer to the structure of a "subject," a characteristic of "subjectivity in its proper ontological sense" (Dasein as Being-in-the-world). Rather, as will be shown shortly by analyzing birth, the world in this evential sense is that from which the "subject's subjectivity" itself *advenes*, in a mode that we have yet to describe. By contrast with any empirical fact, events are the transcendental for any "subject," the condition without condition from which the very "subjectivity" of the "subject" *is constituted* in the disparity between self and self that is constitutive of the "Self" itself, as delayed response to what happens to us, "responsibility,"[10] in which alone lies the selfhood of an *advenant*. The world in an evential sense is thus impersonal, presubjective, and preindividual, since rooted from the outset in the event's impersonality. In short, by contrast with the factual context that governs *any* interpretation for any *advenant*, the world taken in its original sense concerns each *advenant* in his unindexable selfhood, since it is that from which such an *advenant* can occur as himself in his singularity, by appropriating the possibilities the world articulates.

Hence, an event not only brings about a shift from one world to another, but also a *phenomenological transition* from one meaning of "world" to the other. "World" in the evental sense of an explanatory context gives way to world as the *universum* of possibilities from which an *advenant* has to understand himself. In a sense, the *advenant* "is born" in this mutation of meaning. For it is only to the extent that an event takes place that there is also an *advenant*. In face of what happens to me beyond my measure, I discover myself deprived of settledness; the gap in the "world," the collapse of any interpretative settledness, are what gives an event its specific traits. To this extent, the transition from one phenomenon of "world" to the other is not the result of a subjective procedure such as the phenomenological reduction in its diverse modalities and varieties (Husserl's transcendental *epoché*, of course, but also the "phenomenological reduction" Heidegger refers to in *The Basic Problems of Phenomenology* as a "leading back or re-duction of investigative vision" from beings to their Being).[11] In *Being and Time*, even though the move from *Umwelt*, structured by *Bedeutsamkeit*, to *Welt*, originally uncovered by anxiety, is not the result of an act of will, it still depends on a Dasein who is anxious. Here, by contrast, the transition from one sense of world to the other is not something carried out by a "subject," even involuntarily. Nor does this transition "succeed" an event or "proceed" from it. *In its eventness, an event "is" itself this transition.* This is why, in an evential hermeneutics, there is no longer a reduction. An event is this metamorphosis of the world in which *the very meaning of the world is in play.* Metamorphosis through which, in the world's collapse as context, the world glimmers as *evential.* World as horizon of all possible meaning, which originates as such in events and is assigned to each *advenant* as to no other, allowing him to understand himself: not only to interpret what happens to him in light of its posterity, but to understand *the one* to whom that happens as precisely himself.

Thus, it is only on the occasion of an event—a bereavement, an encounter, an accident, an illness—in the shipwreck of the possibilities that gave shape to the world, that the evential meaning of the world can be revealed to me. It is this *universum* of possibilities that are redrawn by an event, from which I advene to myself, and which thus confer on me the meaning of "*advenant.*" This mutation of meaning is decisive in this regard: it is that from which an *advenant* becomes thinkable in his adventure. Inseparable from an event and an addressing, the world opens only *for* an *advenant*, who advenes to himself only *through and from* the world, takes place only where an event wells up, is the "place" for the taking-place of the world as such. The "there" of the world takes place only if there is an *advenant*, and there is an *advenant* only if the world takes place: the two phenomena are inextricable.

But the evential concept of world can be completely elucidated only by a phenomenological analysis of birth. This is the singular and inaugurating event from which the meaning of an *advenant* and his world is determined. How does the world happen from an inaugural first event? In what mode is an *advenant* himself in play in this event?

§13 The Evential Meaning of Birth

Only an *advenant* is born. Birth is not a contingent feature of his adventure. Rather, at the core of this adventure it sets up a gaping fissure that will never again be closed. Both by right and in fact, birth is the first event of any evential hermeneutics; it is the original and inaugural event from which and in light of which all other events can in turn be characterized. It is this primary event—which is also the first event—that opens an *advenant*'s world for the first time and that alone gives rise to all the events that come after it. For the world must first be opened if other events, through their joyous or painful breakings in, are to reconfigure it in their turn. The event of my advent into the world is thus not merely one event "among others." Not only is it the original event, the *Ur-ereignis*, but it also introduces in the origin a hiatus that will never again be filled: for the fact that an *advenant*'s adventure is itself something whose possibility ultimately rests in the event of birth means that one is never oneself the origin of one's own adventure nor of the possibilities that it articulates. The impersonal event of birth always comes before an *advenant*, and it is through birth that he is given the possibility of advening himself— precisely as *advenant*. Before any of his projections and before any understanding, this event makes possible all his possibilities and the world. Hence, birth is the complex phenomenon according to which an *advenant* is not originarily what he nevertheless is originally. To be born is to be a self originally but not originarily, it is to be free originally but not originarily, it is to understand the meaning of one's adventure originally but not originarily, it is to make possible the possible (by projecting it) originally but not originarily, etc. *This original disparity* [décalage] *between originary and original characterizes the primary evential meaning of birth*. It introduces a deferral in the origin itself, such that the origin never declares itself until after the fact, nonoriginally, according to a constitutive delay and a nonempirical a posteriori that nevertheless belongs to its character as origin. *This original nonoriginarity of the origin* is what opens for an *advenant* as the abyss of his own birth, and opens his adventure itself to events, according to a prior and radical exposure that is beyond measure.

The hermeneutics of birth is articulated in three principal stages, which can be formulated as three sets of questions.

1. What does the world-establishing character of this event mean? What is the result of this for understanding the relation of an *advenant* and the world? In other words, in what sense is birth a properly *evential* characteristic of an *advenant* and not merely something that belongs to his "facticity"?

2. To whom does the event of birth happen? Is it to the *advenant himself* in his selfhood? In what sense can this *advenant* relate in the *first person* to what is at stake in the event of birth?

3. To what extent does the origin's original delay, which pervades the human adventure to its depths, affect the meaning of the principal eventials? How is the intrinsically retrospective character of all evential understanding to be interpreted starting from this delay? What is the result of this for the phenomenological meaning of the possible?

Let us endeavor to develop these three stages of the analysis successively.

The event of birth opens the world for the first time; it is that from which the world itself advenes to itself and is configured, event of its own advent—conjointly with the *advenant*. Consequently, in the event of birth the "birth" of the world itself is in play. An *advenant*, whose whole adventure is arrayed by this first event, cannot be formally characterized first as "Being-in-the-world" such that being born would be a fortuitous and contingent characterization;[12] he advenes to himself as such only commencing with birth, in that it is starting from birth that a world is first *opened* to him. He is *in the world* only inasmuch as the world *befalls* him as his lot. He is in the world only inasmuch as he is *born* into it [*Il n'est au monde que pour autant qu'il* naît *au monde*].[13]

This is why this original event, which is also the origin of every other event, appears to be strictly inconceivable in terms of *facticity*. For facticity, as analyzed by Heidegger among others, is a moment of Being-in-the-world that is opposed to existentiality; the former rests on thrown-ness (*Ge-worfenheit*) as an ontological characteristic of Dasein, while the latter is rooted in pro-jection (*Ent-wurf*). But birth cannot be an ontological structure of Being-in-the-world; rather, what is in play in it is the very *eventness of the world*. To understand birth is to reach the world in its very origin, that is, to understand that the world as such cannot be an ontological structure of Dasein, indifferent to the question of knowing whether Dasein, formally characterized by Being-in-the-world and the various moments that articulate the latter (facticity, existentiality, fallenness), factically (*faktisch*) exists or not. If an *advenant* is in the world only by being born there, the evential of the world, this a priori of his adventure, characterized as the totality of possibilities, articulated among themselves, from which he is able to understand himself and advene as himself, is something that *is conferred on him*—therefore a posteriori—by the event of birth. Here already emerges the original disparity of the originary and the original by which the origin is always split from itself, originally delayed in relation to itself. This disparity characterizes the phenomenon of birth and consequently pervades the whole human adventure and structures it through and through. According to such a disparity, the world's a priori itself appears only a posteriori, according to an "a-posterity" that intrinsically belongs to the meaning-character of its a-priority. This a-priority is made possible in its turn by an *event*, since birth alone is the source of its possibility and meaning. Only in this respect is the world an *evential*. Behind the paradox of these contentions, one must grasp their deeper necessity. Could it not be objected that an *advenant* must already be ontologically "Being-in-the-world" in order to be able to grasp the world as opened by an event? To be sure. But this necessity says nothing in favor of an a priori–ontological characteristic of the world, for this a priori necessity is *made possible* in its turn by an event. Thus, one must already be in the world to be able to grasp the a priori of the world as conditioned in its turn by an event—and, consequently, as a posteriori. What could appear as a condition (Being-in-the-world) is here conditioned in turn. The formal a priori condition of an understanding of birth as event is inverted by the very movement of understanding into an *un-condition*: a "condition" that is conditioned in turn, and more originally, by what it conditions. Being-(already)-in-the-world is thus the uncondition of the understanding of the world as it occurs through the event of birth. This means that the world is an evential: an a posteriori belongs a priori to this a priori of adventure and roots it originally in the very event of birth.

Thus, the opening of the world by which an *advenant* is related to his possibilities by understanding them is something that *is opened to him* through an inaugural event. It is not of the order of a possibility that an *advenant* would make possible by means of an original projection. It is not possibility but rather *passibility*: being exposed beyond measure to events in a way that cannot be expressed in terms of passivity but precedes the distinction between active and passive. This passibility cannot be conceived as a prior structure "in the subject," preparing the reception [*accueil*] of events, since events in their radical unpreparedness constitutively escape any structure of reception [*accueil*]. It is thus the very concept of "subjectivity" that is insufficient for grasping passibility's meaning. Passibility is instead a characteristic of events themselves, in that it is only by its own prevenient initiative that an event reaches an *advenant*, opening the playing field where it can occur, and inversely in that an *advenant* can advene to himself in his selfhood only out of events. This is why an *advenant* can neither constitute nor make possible this opening, which is instead opened to him by the event of birth—this passibility that is irreducible to any passivity and that hence holds itself "prior" to the latter.

Now, precisely because it precedes any "anticipatory making-possible" and any pro-jection, the world's opening is irreducible to any facticity, as we have just noted. For facticity, which is inseparable from existentiality, is precisely what must be *taken over*, and thus caught up in a particular pro-jection. Thus, for Heidegger, who still considers birth on the ontological horizon of *Geworfenheit*, birth can be caught up and "taken over"[14] by Dasein, that is, literally, repeated, in the self-transparency (*Durchsichtigkeit*) of authentic existence: "Its 'birth' is *caught up* [*eingeholt*] *into its existence* in coming back from the possibility of death (the possibility which is not to be outstripped), if only so that this existence may accept the thrownness of its own 'there' in a way which is more free from illusion."[15] But is not birth precisely that which *cannot be taken over*, if taking over means "taking in charge," "taking on oneself," "not leaving forgotten"? What exactly is this "Self" that can take being born on itself? Such a taking in charge would presume, after all, that it was *me* in an existential sense, who was born—a "Self" capable, in anticipatory resolution toward death, of reaching its total potentiality-for-Being and taking over its thrownness as a moment of its destiny. But "we were children before we were men" (Descartes). And thus I can assert only one thing about birth: "I was born," in both its past and passive senses, or rather, "there was birth"; birth is first an event that befalls me impersonally, before I can take charge of it in the first person. It is an event that makes possible all my possibilities, and consequently it cannot be inherited as one of my factical possibilities, since it founds any possibility of inheritance. Birth, as an impersonal event that cannot be taken over, radically transcends my thrownness and therefore also my own potentiality-for-Being; it is not an inherited possibility that I would be able to take over, but that by which I inherit myself and all my possibilities, consequently situated *prior to* these.

Thus, by contrast with Dasein's Being-guilty, resolutely open from the anticipation of death, birth in its evential sense, as the opening of possibility in general, and of the world, can no longer be conceived as a "groundless ground" (which still remains a *ground*, since although delivered to Dasein, it can be *taken over* by Dasein) but must be conceived as an absolute nonground (*Ungrund*), to use Schelling's expression. To be born is to be handed over to the nonground of a radical powerlessness with respect to this primary *event*, which as such cannot be taken over, which runs through an adventure as projection and, by coursing through it from end to end, opens it beyond its capacity, to the impossible as well: to events *in general*. The nonground of birth is thus that according to which every condition topples over and inverts into uncondition.

With this question of birth's character as unable to be taken over, we already broach the second question posed at the start of this section: If birth is an event, *to whom* does it happen? In one sense, it is, indeed, necessarily me who is born. But what exactly does this assertion mean? At the moment of being born, I am able neither to say "I" nor understand myself starting from this event, by appropriating the possibilities that it opens and by taking them over as such in a free projection; even less can I understand its meaning. What comes to pass here literally passes beyond my comprehension. Granted, the event of being born is assigned and addressed *to me* (in the dative), according to the heteronomy of a gift, the gift of a world, that radically overhangs me and precedes me and that I can therefore in no way anticipate or prepare to welcome, a gift that is therefore addressed to me prior to any capacity to appropriate this event, that is, prior to any self-ownership and any *selfhood*. Even though the event of birth may well be assigned to me as a de facto ego, even though I may be its "subject" (of assignation) or, rather, may *be subject to it*, in the sense of a genuine *subjection* to what happens to me beyond any measure of myself, it is not true that I am its "subject" in the sense of being able to relate to it in the first person, that is, in the sense of being able to hold *myself* (in my unsubstitutable selfhood) in the possibility of being exposed beyond measure to what happens to me. Selfhood, as an *advenant*'s capacity to hold himself open to what happens to him and to be free *for* what happens to him, by advening freely to himself, is not originarily implicated in birth, which in this respect happens more as a *neutral* and impersonal event preceding any possibility of an *advenant*'s appropriation or self-ownership. Thus, in the passibility of this original event, I am aimed at and assigned, without being able to grasp the possibility of holding myself facing what exceeds me from the outset.

Therefore, this event being addressed to me, happening *to me* in the dative, and my being literally "subject" there in no way means that I am already capable of holding *myself* before what happens to me. The assigned and addressed character of the event, which befalls each *advenant as no other*, does not imply that this *advenant* can appropriate it as his own by relating to it in the first person and understanding it as such. For this reason, it is helpful to distinguish between the *advenant*'s "egoity," his status as the unchanging "subject" of what happens to him, which is inseparable from the event's addressed character, and his selfhood, which implies the possibility of relating to this event first hand, in the first person, which is manifestly lacking in the case of birth. While it is of course *me* to whom *that* happens, nevertheless *I* cannot recognize myself as such (as "*myself*") in this event, nor can I understand myself in my selfhood from the totality of possibilities it configures. It is in this sense that the event of birth is, strictly speaking, unable to be taken over by the one who undergoes the ordeal. As the gift of the world, it radically exceeds any power of appropriation.

However, even if taking over charge of this event is not possible "at the time," cannot birth at least be taken over "later" by the one to whom it happens? What, then, could it mean to "take over" one's birth? One possibility is for "take over" to have a weak sense here, without denoting a positive attitude and meaning nothing more for an *advenant* than persevering in one's own adventure and, consequently, abstaining from suicide. In this case, "take over" loses its entire meaning of taking charge of a possibility that is in each case *specific*, in a projection of oneself. Alternatively, "take over" can be understood in its strong sense, in fact its only possible sense, with "taking over birth" meaning taking charge of specific possibilities, but, in this case, it appears that the possibilities in question are at first the possibilities *of nobody:* they circumscribe and invest my adventure from the outset, by putting me in relation to an immemorial history older than *my* history, and one that is properly that *of others.* "Taking over" my birth, if it is a matter of a positive attitude, would thus be taking over all the prepersonal anonymous factical possibilities that are assigned to me in the event of birth, and thus taking over the history of others: that of my parents first and also by degrees that of *every* other, since it is precisely this opening to a past *other* than mine that is unveiled as such in the event of birth. Birth is, in itself, opening to a past that is "older" than any past that can be taken over, a past that has never been present for the *advenant.* His finitude resides in being always already thrown outside his origin, never able to coincide with it, and thus receiving his meaning from beyond his adventure, and to this extent being handed over to a *destiny.* "Taking over" such a past, in a positive sense, would then mean being responsible for everything, for the whole. However, supposing that such a universal responsibility were possible, would it not be a flight from my own inalienable responsibility, from what I alone can take over, from taking charge of *my* unsubstitutable possibilities? If "taking over my birth" means, in any case, taking over impersonal possibilities that precede, in universal history, my own potentiality-for-Being, then such a Promethean task is both impossible and absurd: if I am responsible for everything, I am no longer responsible for anything. As the event of a gift that surpasses me, my birth is not something for which I either can or should be responsible. Therefore, birth happens *to me* according to a total *innocence.* That in it which, strictly speaking, cannot be taken over is my "destiny." Or, rather, the very possibility of something like a "destiny": this powerlessness, which lies in the depths of temporalization and gives me the impression of always "coming after" my possibilities, can arise from birth alone.

We rediscover here a figure of that original disparity between the originary and the original, whose provenance we have learned to recognize. Even if it is true that an *advenant* is originally himself, in the mode of an essential capacity to face what happens to him—for if ipseity in this sense were not original, an *advenant* certainly couldn't acquire it after the fact—he is not himself originarily. In front of his originary undergoing of his origin, in front of the event of birth itself, an *advenant* is not *himself*. This original nonoriginarity of selfhood is inscribed in the evential character of birth. It is why, even though selfhood is *original*, this originality is laid out only in the delayed movement of its temporalization; that is, necessarily after the fact, such that this "delay" belongs to the origin in its evential sense. Selfhood advenes to itself only with this original delay after the origin—a delay that is inscribed in the very meaning of origin such that this origin never coincides with itself and is accessible only after the fact, according to a necessary retrospection. Consequently, selfhood can only grasp itself starting from this impersonal event and, rather than opening to this event, it is originally anticipated and exceeded by it.

Therefore, birth is that which makes evident the phenomenological difference between selfhood, as a capacity to relate oneself first hand to events and respond to them,[16] a capacity that alone is original, and egoity, as subjection to events in singular assignation. Birth is assigned to me prior to any selfhood, in that there I am "subject" prior to being myself. As we have already noted, this difference is inseparable from a particular hierarchy of the two terms: where egoity can be conceived on the basis of selfhood, the contrary is not the case. I am the one *to whom* an event happens only if I am *the one* to whom it happens, the one who can understand myself in my selfhood from the possibilities that it (re)configures. In light of the phenomenon of birth, it is apparent that I can originally be *the one* to whom it happens (the Self of selfhood) only retrospectively, while I am *first* (originarily) only the one *to whom* it occurs. *If selfhood is original, it encompasses the original disparity of originary and original—a disparity that belongs intrinsically to the origin in its evential sense.* Selfhood only happens after the fact, starting from a primary and original neutrality; consequently, it is constitutively deferred and out of phase. For, if selfhood means the capacity to appropriate to myself first hand what happens to me, birth is that which I can never entirely appropriate, that which makes the appropriation of my own an unachievable task.

This is why the anonymity of birth escapes the authentic/inauthentic demarcation that governs Dasein-ontology through and through. Birth's anonymity is irreducible to the inauthenticity of the "they" in the existential analytic, which merely means the factical concealing, understood as ontological "fallenness [*Verfallen*]," of an authenticity that is necessarily primary, original, and unindexable, since it is already contained in outline in the initial assertion that Dasein is "in each case mine [*je meines*]." From an evential point of view, however, the impersonal character of the human adventure is *irreducible*: because of this impersonality, an *advenant* can understand himself, in his selfhood, only according to a constitutive delay on himself—according to the disparity of the originary and the original, which is itself a structure of the origin and, consequently, an *original* characteristic of the *advenant*. As he is not contemporary with his coming into the world and can neither receive it [*accueillir*] first hand nor entirely appropriate it, the *advenant*'s appropriation of his own, his singularization, is revealed to him as a task to be taken on: his very singularity is arrayed as history.

Moreover, since I can *never* experience this event of birth *myself*, its meaning differs fundamentally from that of other events. Thus, it withdraws from any experience in the proper sense, as one's own experience and experience *of* one's own, inseparable from a particular appropriation by the *advenant* of the meaning of what happens to him; consequently, it also withdraws from any genuine memory, if this eventially signifies the undergoing of the past as concluded in itself. In this respect, birth is strictly *immemorial*. There is never any such thing as one's own first-hand experience of this "first time" of birth, which is only arrayed in the "second time" of an essentially retrospective understanding, which, because an *advenant* is never contemporary to his coming into the world, is necessarily open to an inexhaustible meaning.

Thus we come to the third question formulated above. The intrinsically retrospective and delayed character of all evential understanding is rooted, in its turn, in the intrinsic constitution of an adventure, as that which is opened in its ground to the nonground of birth. By configuring my possibilities and the world for the first time, birth opens my present to a past that is older than any past that can be taken over, to a pluperfect that has never been present; by this very fact, it also opens me to possibilities that I do not project and to which I cannot respond but that are assigned and addressed to me by this event. These possibilities are rooted in a prepersonal history, a history strictly unable to be taken over: the *advenant*'s *prehistory*. This history, which precedes me, and is first the history of others, is bestowed on me by the event of birth, as the *source of possibility in general* for the human adventure. In being born, I am anticipated and preceded by possibilities that transcend any projection of mine and that are therefore assigned to me in excess of any understanding. Incomprehension is first and basic in virtue of the precedence of evential possibility over any projection of understanding. Opening on a prehistory I do not at first understand but from which I must understand myself, birth is that gift that surpasses any power of appropriation and that forever makes the human adventure an enigma. Because he can only come into the world by being born, an *advenant* is handed over to the heteronomy of this gift, he can grasp the meaning of his history only by connecting it to a history that is not yet his and whose meaning precedes all understanding and thus overhangs him from the outset. In this respect, to be born is to have *a* history before having *one's own* history: a prepersonal history, literally unable to be taken over, introducing into the human adventure an excessive meaning that is incommensurable with my projections and thus radically inexhaustible. Starting from such a sense, which runs through my adventure and of which I am not myself the origin, a destiny is laid out for me. However, this destiny, which fundamentally signifies the delay of my own adventure with respect to every possibility and every meaning, is in no way a fate. For, if I cannot take over this past, if this prepersonal past, coming before all memory and forgetting, preceding birth and opening to it, is a pluperfect I always "come after," it is also what makes the possible always "go before" me and thus well up from the future. The nonground of birth, by its very opening, within or "behind" an adventure, of possibilities that precede the adventure and of which it is not the measure, also thereby opens a future "ahead" of every projection, a future from which I am assigned every *eventuality*: possibility of which I am not the measure, which overhangs my adventure and even my death, since it can be "shared" with those who come after me and taken up by them. The eventuality of this possibility can come to me from an ab-solute future [*à-venir*] without relation to my present, only because that future is in some way "already included"—in a sense that only an evential analysis of time can make clear—in that past that is also ab-solute and older than any past that can be taken over, experienced, or recalled: the past of my birth. Thus, the possible can rise up from the future, with its evential meaning (as *eventuality*),[17] only because an event already happened immemorially, the event of my birth, which lets this possibility happen with its excess of a meaning that is irreducible to my projections and to any "understanding [*Verstehen*]" conceived as the finite projection of a potentiality-for-Being.[18]

But isn't there an untenable paradox here, in that understanding has an original delay with respect to the meaning that is assigned to an *advenant* from the nonground of birth, and yet meaning happens *only* by means of understanding? We must grasp anew here the extent to which this paradox is neither absurd nor gratuitous but is rather rooted in the "thing itself."

Is it not manifest nonsense to propose the possibility of an understanding that is originally exceeded by its very meaning, and therefore the possibility of an incomprehension that is first by right, preceding and rendering possible all subsequent understanding? And is it not the same for the assertion that possibilities befall an *advenant* before any of his own projections, and therefore before any possibility of him *understanding* them? Granted, such possibilities cannot simply appear to an *advenant*, in excess of any "potentiality-for-Being"—and thereby address a *meaning* to him—unless he understands them as such. However, although this is a necessary condition, it does not follow that it is a sufficient one. That understanding is required for something like meaning to be able to happen does not exclude—in fact, on the contrary, it implies—that this understanding itself, with the structural delay that belongs to it, is more profoundly determined by the event of birth. The understanding thanks to which meaning happens for an *advenant can happen in its turn only because there has first been birth*, that is, because it is originally open to the nonground of a meaning that precedes and exceeds it from the outset. The condition for the manifestation of possibility and meaning receives its meaning and possibility from this event. If it is a condition of appearing as such, it appears to be more originally conditioned in its turn by the appearing of this condition. The nonground of birth is thus again that by which every condition topples over and inverts into uncondition. All understanding is open to the excess of an inexhaustible meaning by the original disparity in birth of originary and original. Although original, understanding is not itself the origin of meaning, which it can therefore appropriate only according to an original delay with respect to its origin. It is exceeded by that which it conditions only insofar as it is conditioned in return. The human adventure is thus entirely constructed on this inborn fissure [*faille native*], on this nonground that it can neither grasp nor make possible but which rather determines the excess of possibility and of meaning in general over all appropriation by understanding.

But what are these prepersonal possibilities, which precede me in a history that is older than my histories and to which I am connected by the event of birth itself? They are first of all the possibilities of others: not only my parents but also others *in general*. In the event of birth, another is already announced. To this extent, birth puts me originally in the presence of an otherness that is assuredly still "anonymous," since it can be understood as such only in its "relation" to my selfhood. I am not born alone; any isolation or solitude are instead derivative phenomena with respect to the presence of this otherness, which is anonymous but nevertheless already inscribed in the event of birth. But what exactly is the meaning of this otherness? If birth is the event in which the world is given, others can certainly not be its source, since they are announced as such only *arising from* such an event. It is after the event of the world's advent, and *on the horizon* of the world, that others can appear for an *advenant*, with the meaning that they have for him: in particular, with the meaning of "parent." Therefore, it is not others who open a world for me, but it is rather starting from the *impersonal* event of birth that others can in their turn enter my horizon—as parents, for example. Far from being subordinated to a prior otherness, an event is its own origin, since it is from it alone that what "precedes" it receives meaning. In addition to this purely phenomenological observation, there is also the following consideration: far from others being able to be the origin of this gift of a world—which would amount to elevating them to the rank of a kind of divinity who, strictly speaking, would *create* me, as the biblical God created the angels, instead of merely fathering or begetting me—they are themselves born. Having been endowed with a world, they can merely "pass it on" to me, so that I share in this endowment. Their adventure too is arrayed starting entirely from this *impersonal* event. Even though it is in fact another who *brings me into the world, she does not open the world as such to me.* Birth alone, in its impersonality as an event, is "capable" of such prodigies.

The linguistic dissymmetry evident in the act of naming is thus less an indication of others' primacy over me than of an irreducible heteronomy of the Self with respect to this event as such. Even if others originally announce themselves through the event of birth, they depend no less, in their manifestation, on this event. They can themselves precede me only because, first and fundamentally, this *event* precedes me, by exceeding my own powers. Thus, to be "named" is to be anticipated by the verbal initiative of another, "called" by a word that overhangs me and that I can never completely appropriate, since my name, symbol of my self-ownership, of my "identity," is at the same time symbol of this initial dispossession. But this speaking initiative of another is possible in its turn only beginning from the event's radical anticipation—an impersonal anticipation that the inaugural dissymmetry of naming, among other manifestations, merely reflects.

It follows that birth only ever takes place as an innerworldly fact for others. For the one who is born himself, the *advenant*, it is an event that, strictly speaking, never happened as a fact; it is immemorial in a positive sense—which does not mean a lack or privation of memory, a secondary and derivative forgetting, but rather defines the most primordial mode of givenness of this event. A radically nonactual event, it is also that by which the difference between facts and events is established. Transcending par excellence any actualization as fact, never being able to be experienced factually by an *advenant*, birth is also not datable for him, and even less by him. It is datable only for others, and my "date of birth" translates in its own way this primary dispossession of my adventure, according to which the fact of my coming into the world constitutively eludes me. Though it is radically unable to be experienced as a fact, we will see that birth is nevertheless constantly undergone as an event, according to a non-empirical undergoing, by means of a privileged feeling, despair, that makes its meaning appear.

Now, if birth is what fundamentally determines the meaning of all other events and in so doing also determines the meaning of the one who provides for them or takes over their reception [*accueil*], the *advenant*; if every subsequent event gives an *advenant* the possibility of being born again, by submitting himself to a transformation, and appropriating the possibilities which thus befall him, then the question arises of how we should conceive such a "rebirth." Evidently, it is not a matter of a "second birth" but rather of this capacity to undergo an event, at the risk of a radical transformation of my possibilities and of myself, which capacity is the original phenomenon of selfhood. What, then, is the eviential meaning of such a selfhood? To approach this question, it is first necessary to answer this other one: if an event, in general, is what reconfigures *all* my possibilities articulated in a world and not simply one or another factical possibility; if, from the instant when an event arises, it is *the totality of the possible* that appears in a new light, then is there not at least *one* possibility that holds itself outside any possible making possible by the event: the possibility that I am myself, inasmuch as I am *capable* of undergoing events? If this is the case, it would be legitimate to lead selfhood back to ontological structures that precede an event and, thus, to submit the event to a prior instance. But such is not the case, and it is this that must be shown. To this end, it will be helpful to dwell a little longer on what has been called to this point "possibility." For, as soon as the event of birth leads us to reconsider concepts as fundamental as world and selfhood, we cannot leave the concept of possibility untouched. We have already seen that birth, in opening to an *advenant* possibilities that precede his projections and of which he is not the origin, possibilities rooted in a prepersonal history that overhangs him immemorially, thereby also opens a possibility that exceeds any projection and that comes to him from the future: eventuality. I use this term for the properly evential sense of possibility, such as we are led to by a hermeneutic of birth. What is such a "possibility" if, on the one hand, birth alone originarily makes it possible, and, on the other hand, it is only on this condition that it can be what arises originally with every subsequent event, what every subsequent event reconfigures by its very arising?

§14 Eventuality

Events have been characterized as what reconfigures the possibilities of an *advenant* articulated in a world, in and by its own arising. But how should "possibility" be understood here? How should the "relation" between events and possibilities be characterized? More precisely, what should be understood by the verb "reconfigure"?

When innerworldly facts occur, they too have a "relation" to the possible: facts actualize a prior possibility, one that is already given on the horizon of a world; they realize this possibility as such. The possibility of falling was there, in the fruit: the "reality" of such a possibility signifies nothing other, in this instance, than its propensity to be realized. The more the fruit ripened, the greater, the more real, was the possibility that it would fall from its branch. *For an innerworldly fact, in general, "possibility" therefore signifies "propensity to be realized."* The reality of a possibility grows in proportion to its actualizability. Actualization is, as such, the becoming-fact of a fact. The closer an innerworldly fact is to its actualization, the greater is its possibility; that is, the more real is its propensity to be brought about. The "reality" of the possible and its possibility are here one and the same thing. It follows that *for an innerworldly fact, the possibility of the possible is its actualizability.*

Is it the same with the possibilities that befall us, in general, in our human adventure? Does the possibility of the possible for the *advenant* consist in its actualizability? If such were the case, it would mean that possibilities were in me in the way they are in an apple. They would preexist their realization, as possibilities determined and given in advance; their reality would increase in proportion to their actualizability. After all, such an interpretation is not entirely untenable. Can one not maintain that, by being born, each *advenant* possesses a horizon of determinate possibilities—biological, social, historical—and that he simply actualizes them throughout his adventure? In such a conception, there would be no "creation" of possibilities but simply actualization by the *advenant* of preexistent possibilities. Alternatively, one could put a different interpretation on the assertion that the possibility of the possible for an *advenant* consists in its actualizability. Instead of holding, as this first thesis does, that possibilities are determined from the outset, thus reducing to nothing freedom conceived as freedom of indifference, one could adopt an opposite premise and propose an original horizon of virgin possibilities that are in themselves empty and indeterminate: the adventure of an *advenant* would then consist in a progressive *determining* of the possible, or rather, of *possibilities*, which in being realized would be mutually constrained and determine one another by gaining actuality: *ad-vening to oneself* would be actualizing the possible by constraining the amplitude of the initial possibilities, conferring determinacy on these empty possibilities by *determining* them in their compossibility or incompossibility.

However, whether one begins according to the first thesis, with determinate possibilities, or according to the second thesis, with absolutely empty possibilities, which is to say, whether one grants, in the first case, the *advenant* a practically null freedom of indeterminacy or, in the second case, an absolute and quasi-demiurgic freedom, a primary ontological *fiat* over possibilities that are entirely undetermined, in each thesis the same question is left in suspense: *Does the possibility of the possible for an existent consist in its actualizability?* This question becomes even more crucial when a closer examination shows that these two apparently contradictory conceptions are in fact equivalent. For it is almost impossible to see how, in the second conception, the modal status of the possible can be changed: how could a possibility that is at first entirely undetermined, in the course of a human adventure become determined, a "logical possibility," to use Leibniz's term, become a "compossible"? Out of a concern for coherency, one is thus forced to admit, as Leibniz himself states, that in the beginning *there are only compossibles, already determined* possibilities, which are all contained in the complete concept of each individual and thereby to extend the determinacy of the possible more and more, to the primitive concept of the world, such as it is presented in the divine understanding to a creative will. Once possibility is envisaged on the horizon of its actualization as fact, it is necessary to endorse determinism, since it relies on precisely this idea of possible causal explanation and submits freedom itself to the condition of such an explanation. However, determinism accounts for freedom only as long as it conceives every possibility starting from its actualizability; if one could escape this horizon, the problem of freedom itself would be posed anew. Granted, in the preceding example, the horizon of virgin possibilities that was presupposed can only be an illusion, as much as is the indeterminacy of the choice that accompanies it. Thus, the second thesis brings us back to the first one. But do not both of them show their inadequacy for understanding possibility as it is offered to an *advenant*? Is not a definition of possibility as actualizability valid only for *innerworldly facts*? If the human adventure cannot be characterized as a succession of facts and can only be interpreted with the event, in its evential sense, as its guiding concept, is it not the very characterization of "possibility" that should be rethought? And, if so, how should it be conceived?

Of course, there would be another way to maintain that possibility, for an *advenant*, originally has the sense of what is actualizable for or by him: rather than beginning from determinate possibilities or empty possibilities that would be in him as they are in an apple, these possibilities could be understood right away from the projection that makes them possible. Does not an *advenant* constitutively have the possibility of projecting himself toward possibilities in order to make them his, and thereby realize them? A projection carries me toward the possible, and thus *makes it possible*, only if it is a projection of *realizing* this possibility. But such a "realization" is itself *rendered possible* by the original making-possible of the projection. The possibility of the possible—and therefore also its "reality"—would then mean its *making-possible* by a primordial projection. Surely we are now approaching the first sense of possibility, as it is arrayed for an *advenant*? Perhaps, but on condition of being attentive to the very movement of this making-possible. For a projection can give form to the possible—and thus "make it possible"—only by shaping itself on the possibilities already offered to me in a particular horizon; an *advenant* can give himself ends in the world only by understanding himself in the light of the possibilities articulated therein. A projection in which I launch myself toward a possibility, that I freely put forward, and for whose possible realization I aim, still unfolds entirely on the horizon of the world: *it cannot open the world as such.* This is why making-possible by an event is more original than making-possible by a projection. The former alone *opens a world* through (re)configuring its possibilities. Thus, apart from understanding possibility as actualizability and as making-possible by a projection, a third sense of possibility is apparent, which we must now attempt to elucidate.

What happens when "something" happens that makes history in my adventure? The very possibilities that had previously been articulated for me in a world and from which, or in conformity with which, I had been able to understand *myself* now appear in a new light: one that has arisen only with the event, insofar as it is *world-establishing*. Even if an illness strikes me down, even if bereavement desolates me, I will still retain my "vocation" as a painter or writer, for instance; I will still retain my liking for traveling or for women. But if this was precisely a genuine *event*, I will no longer be a painter or writer *in the same way*; "something" will have changed forever: I will no longer travel in the same way, and the way I look at the countries through which I pass will also be different. The drawn and dry phrases with which Flaubert begins the penultimate chapter of *Sentimental Education* are well known: "He travelled the world. He tasted the melancholy of packet ships, the chill of waking under canvas, the boredom of landscapes and monuments, the bitterness of broken friendship. He returned home. He went into society, and he had affairs with other women. They were insipid beside the endless memory of his first love. And the vehemence of desire, the keen edge of sensation itself, had left him."[19] A counterpoint to the event that opens Flaubert's narrative, the encounter with Mme Arnoux, this text reveals its character as an *event*. It is not only particular possibilities that are transfigured by this encounter and offered to Frédéric in another light, but all his possibilities that tremble and take on a new meaning for him. It matters little here that his character is weak, cowardly, and insignificant; it matters little which psychological traits could explain his attitude, his sudden attraction to travel and desire for flight, his frustrated ambitions and disillusionment. What matters for an evential hermeneutic is nothing of the psychological, nothing that bears on the "personality" or "life" of the character, but the meaning-character of the event itself, inasmuch as it reconfigures an *advenant*'s intrinsic possibilities *as a totality*, and not only certain possibilities among them. Now, what precisely does this "reconfiguration" mean? In fact, to state that an event "reconfigures" an *advenant*'s possibilities is, in all rigor, to maintain that the event, by its very arising, *makes possible* these possibilities. What else could such a thorough modifying of possibilities be, making them appear in a new light, if not *making them possible* anew, or making them possible differently, given that "possibilities" actually have no other "reality" than their possibility? But, once again, in what sense should such a "possibility" be understood if it is originally opened by an event, and by it alone? In what sense is "possibility" to be understood if an event brings new possibilities to pass, rather than being limited to actualizing prior possibilities as a mere fact does? When an event reconfigures an *advenant*'s most intimate possibilities, it does not limit itself to rearranging or redistributing them. It *opens* new ones and, correlatively, closes old ones; that is, in each case, it *makes them possible*. The possibility of rendering possible, the making-possible, is a characteristic of events in their eventuality. *Hence, the possibility of the possible is, literally, its eventuality.* The word "eventuality" here is not being used in its current sense of a contingent possibility, which might occur *or not*. Eventuality instead defines the possible, in that it arises from an event prior to any projection. Such possibilities are impersonal and anonymous, or rather prepersonal, since they give me the possibility of advening to myself by advening myself precisely as other. It follows that an *advenant* can receive possibilities toward which he can launch himself anticipatively *only from* events, to which he is exposed from the outset, as to *the very opening of possibility in general.*

We have ended up with a paradox: on the one hand, there can be no possibilities at all for an *advenant* without projections; on the other hand, there can be no projections without possibilities. How can this strange entwining be conceived? One could try holding, with Heidegger, that possibilities and projections are co-originary, to the extent that they are both rooted in Being itself as *existing*: possibility would belong to facticity, to an inheritance from which projection could not set itself free but that exists only because Dasein first of all ek-sists, projects itself toward the possibility that it itself is on the background of impossibility. However, would not making all possibility depend on Being itself as existing amount to reducing the irreducible delay that structures every projection, in that projections arise against the nonground of birth, and to abolishing the original being-out-of-phase that constitutes every projection in itself as a differentiated response to the surplus of events?

Thus, more original than the possibility configured by a projection toward which I launch myself, and at which I aim by putting it forward, is eventuality, which gives such a possibility its meaning by giving it a future-loading. For this exceeding possibility, which bursts forth with an event and is opened to me by it, comes to me from an ab-solute future, literally without relation to my present[20] and therefore also without relation to the possibilities that a projection predetermines. Eventuality in its pure sense is that possibility which transcends every projection and *is given to me only peradventure.* In fact, possibilities only really befall me if they open to the impossible, to what I was neither seeking nor projecting but which, coming about peradventure, can alone give my projections the meaning that is theirs. Any real projection is one that, conditioned in its turn by the future's excess, lets the future come to be in its difference from and otherness to my present. What would be the meaning for me of authoring a book, of an encounter, of a journey, if the projection that carried me into these did not also open in me a fissure that allowed the unprojected to grow, if the possibility I projected was not transformed— thereby transforming *me*—by encountering this *other* possibility, this *eventual* possibility, which was not already configured by my projection? What would it mean for me to decide to write a book, unless in writing it I discovered my own thought in a way that no anticipation or approximation could have revealed it? This eventuality of the possible is what rebounds on me and is delivered from a future that exceeds my present, conferring "gravity" on the projection and unsubstitutability on the one who projects. For, as we shall see, selfhood, in its evential sense, always means an *advenant*'s capacity to appropriate eventual possibilities, articulated in a world, that surface from an event, and to understand oneself from them. Now, such a "capacity" is inseparable from the risk that in such an undergoing one might be *altered* through and through. Selfhood and otherness to oneself are seen here as intimately linked—and their very entwining is time.

So, by contrast with possibilities that I project, which emerge spontaneously on the background of my presentified past and remain a configuration of my present, eventuality is that possibility which does not come from me but rather comes on me, which I do not attain but which literally lands on me and submerges me; without such an eventual possibility, every projection would be in vain, for it would have no hold on the future in its absolute difference from my present: a projection clutching at dead possibilities, dead even before they had been possible, since they would be incapable of taking hold of the future and thereby making me happen to myself by calling me to more than what I know of my capability. In fact, it is wrong to say that "no one is bound to the impossible [*à l'impossible nul n'est tenu*],"[21] for we are genuinely *bound only* to the impossible! The eventuality of the possible, opened by and from an event, is what truly *binds* me, by calling me to more than my capability and even to the impossible. It is to the impossible that our projections are dedicated: not to the *absolutely* impossible, but to what is properly and strictly impossible with respect to any actualization or anticipation, that is, with respect to the two senses of the possible singled out previously. This possible that binds us and to which we are bound is what I might call a "task." However, such a designation could still mislead us. It is a meaningful designation, for example, in the domain of decisions, where even though we decide about the possible, about the undecided, we do not decide on *what becomes* of this very decision. As we will see, deciding on what is undecided is at the same time to commit ourselves to the undecidable, to open ourselves to an *inexhaustible* possibility that transcends all decision. By contrast, the designation says nothing to us about paths that lead to possibilities, without our knowing, in the search that guides an encounter, or in the desire that works obscurely in the quest for a work of art. Would we say that the eventual possibilities given to me when I write a poem or when I paint a picture are a "task" for me? Here, the connotation of "obligation" obscures the *gratuity* of the possible, inasmuch as it is given to me *without reason*, in excess of any projection: eventuality of which I am not the measure.

However, would it not be a gratuitous paradox if the purest sense of the possible, its true sense, were the impossible? Not if we examine more carefully this intertwining between events and the possible, in which, by virtue of the load of possibilities it holds in reserve, an event not only exceeds its actualization as a fact, but is also what makes a possibility possible, thus nullifying the idea of an autarchic freedom or a primary ontological *fiat*. For it is not as if there were *first of all* a totality of projections by which an *advenant* would open up the possible by forging himself a destiny to order, and then, *in a second moment*, factical possibilities arising from events, which would condition his situation in the world, like earth in which his projections would blossom. There is no *formal* potentiality-for-Being—determinable, for example, as anticipation of death[22]—that would precede the situation in which I have to decide myself. On the contrary, any possibility that is assigned to me is already opened, and thereby determined, by events and by the world-configuration they push forth.

This is why the eventuality of the possible is in no way opposed to its actuality, since events—with the exception of birth and death, as we will see shortly—*also* take place as facts. Indeed, far from the eventuality of the possible being opposed to its actuality or its actualization, it is inseparable from these. For events are not only what befall me in excess of their actualization by making possible both possibilities and world. They are *also* facts, and it is only as such that they can bring to a human adventure that excess of possibilities by virtue of which they are irreducible to their innerworldly actualization. As my possibilities are progressively determined and take on actuality for me, as events progressively "are realized" and give my history its unique configuration, *so thereby does that possibility, which I myself unsubstitutably am, receive its possibility*. I am summoned by a possibility that opens and stretches to infinity in happening to me from a future that is strictly unable to be anticipated. The more that my history takes on form and shape, the more is specified—or, better, the more is *made possible*—my possibility in what renders it unique. An event is what, by opening and *determining* my possibilities, by conferring their possibility (their eventuality) on them, abolishes its own "conditions of possibility": it *bursts forth before being possible*, in the sense of an empty "possibility," but makes possible my essential possibilities, by giving them possibility as well as actuality. This making possible of the (eventual) possible does not contradict its actualization and does not simply apply to the possibility that I myself am; it also applies to the possibility that I am not. As I advance in producing a text, as initially indeterminate possibilities are progressively "realized" by acquiring actuality, as I progressively learn what it is that I want to say by discovering what I do say, so *grows* the *singular possibility* that this text is, and thus it increases in *possibility*. The event of writing a book, in its suspended occurring, by realizing possibilities that are indeterminate at the outset, makes possible the unique possibility that this book itself is. Such a possibility is *at work* in every work, for example in a poetic one; Claudel encapsulates its meaning most closely when he writes: "The point of poetry is not, as Baudelaire says, 'to dive to the depths of the Infinite to find something new,' but to [go to] the depths of the definite to find the inexhaustible there."[23]

This is what is going on for an *advenant* in the event of a decision, where I am in play *myself* as an unsubstitutable possibility: the more I realize my previously indeterminate possibilities, the more I decide about myself, and the more the eventuality of an exceeding possibility opens up beyond this decision (of realizing some particular possibility), the exceeding possibility that I myself am for myself, which is only given to me *by excess* and is therefore irreducible to any of my projections. This possibility comes upon me on the margin of its actualization, but it can come upon me in this way only because of its actualization, to the extent that an event from which eventual possibilities are assigned to me (in this case, a decision) *also* occurs as a fact in the world. Such an eventuality, which comes upon me in excess of its actualization, is at the same time, with respect to already realized possibilities, as with respect to any projected possibility, an *impossibility*. The very actualization of my possibilities, a decision as *fact*, releases the impossible for me, the unprojectable that dwelled in them (the decision as event) and that is one with them, since I advene to myself as *one single possibility*, an adventurous possibility that occurs only *per impossibile*, thereby conferring meaning on a human adventure. By thus reconfiguring my intrinsic possibilities (my world), every event—here, a decision—also opens to me *ipso facto* a possibility that I did not project and that, with respect to my actual or actualized possibilities (factual possibility), as well as my projected possibilities (projectual possibility), is strictly impossible. It is only by releasing this exceeding possibility, the *eventual*, that an event allows me to advene to myself, precisely by advening as *other*, according to the fissure that the event carves out forever in my own adventure.

By determining factical possibility—a decision as a simple fact issuing from a deliberation and, consequently, inserted in a prior context that is articulated according to the double chain of its motives and drives—a decision releases *thereby* the eventuality of an *other* possibility, which comes to me from the future. This other possibility is in itself undecidable and cannot be anticipated, but it is what alone confers on my decision the weight that belongs to it—by making it *an event*. This is what is going on with any genuine decision, which is only possible by renouncing all mastery and control of the possibility that it makes happen, and by allowing itself to be anticipated and oriented by an exceeding possibility of which it cannot itself be the measure. I can only really decide on the undecided if I set myself on the undecidable, on what can come and shatter my decision, on the excess of another possibility, on which my decision does not bear but that instead bears on my decision. Letting this possibility hatch, instead of simply enclosing it and bringing it to a halt, letting it decide me as much as I decide it: it is in this chiasm, which never closes over, that the possibility of every genuine decision dwells. In each case, my projection, a probe launched into the shadows of the future, "makes possible" a possibility only if it is itself already made possible by the latter, that is, if it responds to eventuality in its evential occurring, which always precedes me and is given only in excess.

Consequently, it is insofar as the possibility that I myself am is "realized" by gaining in determination, that what is impossible with respect to all realization, as with respect to all projection (since any projection is necessarily projected in view of a realization)—the eventual, the exceeding possibility that comes to me, without coming from me, out of an absolute future without relation to my present—gains in *possibility*, and I am called to more than my potentiality and, inversely, discover at each instant that I have potentiality beyond what I believed. All our projections are anchored to the impossible, as that which gives them their future-loading. A book is for a writer, a painting is for a painter, inaccessible by any projection; it can be reached only by letting this possibility reach them: an eventual possibility that their work harbors. Thus, every painter stands before his canvas, at the moment of daubing it with color, as one who has never painted in his life, in the state that Cézanne calls in its entirety "virginity of the world": "At that moment, I am as one with my painting. We are an iridescent chaos. I come before my motif and I lose myself. . . . We germinate. When night falls again, it seems to me that I shall never paint, that I have never painted."[24] The only way to reach this possibility that is inaccessible to our projections and inalienable is therefore to let it reach us. Rather than realizing prior possibility configured in a projection, it means letting the eventuality of the possibility happen by putting oneself at risk. It is the same for every genuine decision, which always makes a way for the impossible; that is, it takes us along paths that only the fact of deciding, just as, above, the fact of painting or writing, can reveal to us.

At issue here is the meaning of eventual possibility, insofar as this is strictly given to us only as the other side of our impossibility. Or, rather, insofar as possibility and impossibility are related to each other as the two sides of a single phenomenon, the chiasm to which every adventure is anchored in that it happens only *per impossibile*. The very possibility of the possible, and thus also its only "reality"—since the former does not contradict the latter—transcends any factical actualization just as it transcends any projectual possibility. Thus, an adventure can only be open to the eventuality that arises with an event because it advenes to itself, basically, *per impossibile*, and this is why the "im-possible," in its relation with the *advenant*, is first of all the most proper name for possibility.

§15 Selfhood and Responsibility

What is it that makes the *singularity* of this unique possibility that I myself am for myself, a singularity that is laid out starting from events, and that hangs over me as an *inexhaustible* possibility (taken away from me in death but in no way deriving from it) by opening my adventure to the infinity of a meaning that evades any possible totalization? How are we to understand that, although our adventure is laid out starting from the impersonal or prepersonal dimension carved out in it by birth, it is, nevertheless, in each case, my singular adventure? Do we not risk this problem becoming insoluble because of the way we have seemingly complicated its terms? Is it philosophically tenable to hold that an *advenant*'s adventure is not singular from the outset but that events singularize it despite themselves being impersonal? Perhaps—on the condition of attempting to understand this adventure better.

It is only from his history that an *advenant* can let himself declare *who* he is. Therefore, the question of his selfhood is inseparable from this other question: what are the conditions for an event in general to be able to reach me, transform me, and upend me, by reconfiguring my intrinsic possibilities? For "I" advene to myself as such only insofar as something happens to me, and something happens to me only insofar as I become myself, in undergoing an event.[25] "*Advenant*" is the name I give to the human being insofar as he or she is thoroughly implicated in what happens to him or her, such that, to understand *himself*, he must have a *history*. However, "history" here is not merely a succession of "events" whose fabric and pattern constitutes my "biography," such that my selfhood would be reduced to a narration of "events" that happened to me: to testify to *who* I am, I would need to give an account of myself. Such an understanding of "history," as a succession of innerworldly facts that simply happen to an *advenant*, remains purely *evental*. The *evential* concept of selfhood is based on a completely different concept of history: "I" am my history eventially understood starting from the events which *make history* for me, which open a history for me, along with the dimension of its *meaning*. History here is no longer the formal and empty frame within which a series of "events," conceived as innerworldly facts, can take place, but rather what bursts forth in each case from events: it is the "taking-place" of events that *gives place* to history by giving it *meaning*, and not history that is reduced to a causal chain of facts, conceived according to their *succession*, which is itself innerworldly.

Therefore, selfhood signifies an *advenant*'s capacity to be open to events, insofar as these events happen to him unsubstitutably, the capacity to be implicated himself in what happens to him, or the capacity to understand *himself* from a history and the possibilities it articulates. To what extent are these formulations equivalent, or do they at least follow from one another? To answer this question, we must consider these various definitions more closely.

Considering things more analytically, it is possible to identify three fundamental moments for elucidating the phenomenon of selfhood. First, openness to events in general: the *advenant*'s *passibility*. Second, the possibility of the *advenant* being himself implicated in what happens to him, which in turn depends on, and is inseparable from, the passibility of his being impersonally exposed to events. This implication is, in fact, inherent in the addressed character of events, which is evident in the passibility with which I am exposed to them, since I am *open* to events as such only if I can undergo them *myself* unsubstutitably. Third, it is only to the extent that an *advenant* is open to an event, and is himself implicated in what happens to him, that he also can advene singularly, incomparable with any other, from the impersonal possibilities that articulate his history in its incomparability: that he can *appropriate* these possibilities and thus acquire a *singularity*.

These three fundamental and inseparable moments—(1) passibility, (2) implication, and (3) singularity—co-determine selfhood and its evential meaning. In fact, to the extent that an *advenant* is open to events, he is able to be implicated himself in what is assigned to him in an impersonal mode and, because he is thus implicated in what happens to him, he is able to advene singularly starting from impersonal possibilities, arising from events, which punctuate his adventure. An evential analysis of selfhood must begin with a description of these three foundational determinants.

An *advenant* is open to events simply by the "fact" of birth. As we have seen, this possibility is prepersonal; it is an opening to events as impersonal. For even though events are always addressed, in their proper phenomenological tenor they conserve an essential anonymity. Events are "singular," unique, "unrepeatable," and, nevertheless, even in their extreme individuation, remain neutral, as Gilles Deleuze writes: "It is the 'they' of impersonal and pre-individual singularities, the 'they' of the pure event wherein *it* dies in the same way that *it* rains."[26] But this unreserved exposure to what can touch me and strike me, prior to the traditional division between a subject's activity and passivity, because selfhood is only possible through it—this *possibility* may be arrayed differently depending on whether or not an *advenant* is capable of being *himself*, that is, whether or not he can appropriate the event by integrating it in a new projection of the world and, by persisting in his own openness, face what happens to him. This is why, in despair, when he appears incapable of facing events and meets what happens to him as though it were happening to another, when the world no longer becomes world but collapses,[27] his possibility itself appears as modified. Selfhood's bankruptcy leaves an *advenant* radically incapable of relating to events in the first person, and entirely handed over to the nudity of a pure exposure to what strikes him and upends him, before any possibility for him of undergoing this unsubstitutably, nor therefore of responding to it.

Thus, this passibility to an event, from which I can never escape, is arrayed differently, depending on whether or not I can relate myself to it in the first person and be implicated in it. The second moment of selfhood is implication, by which I seize an event as being addressed and assigned to me *as to no other*. Even though this implication may well be the matrix of any individuation for an *advenant*, it refers to no subjective instance that is already individuated—no "me" or "I," which would ground its evident givenness to itself. On the other hand, it is only in virtue of such an implication that an *advenant* can appropriate events and illuminate himself in their light, so as to pierce the shadows of his own "identity"—that he can understand himself in his *singularity*, starting from the possibilities configured by events.

Hence, the three moments analyzed here come together in the unitary phenomenon of selfhood, in its properly evential characterization: *the possibility for an* advenant *to be open to events, thereby responding to what happens to him, and appropriating the possibilities that events assign to him* [lui destinent], *so as to be able to advene himself singularly across a destiny.* I will call this capacity of responding to events in their impersonal occurring *responsibility*, in a sense that should not be confused with ethical or juridical imputability. Here, "responsibility" signifies the possibility of an *advenant* to be open to events and to relate himself to this openness by answering for his history. This capacity to relate oneself *first hand* to one's openness and to appropriate what happens to one by redeploying the world that an event has configured according to a new unitary projection is another name for selfhood in its eventual sense. Responsibility is the possibility for an *advenant* to be responsible for his passibility, that is, for what he is radically incapable of taking over—for the primary and measureless exposure of himself to the event of his own adventure. *Selfhood, as the possibility of answering for my passibility, is responsibility.* Understood in this sense, responsibility signifies anything but imputability, which arises only when I am the cause of an act, or its ethical-juridical agent. Yet I am never the cause of an event because, even when it can be determined that I am the one by whom it happens, as in the case of a decision, for instance, I am *only* ever the cause of *the fact* and never of the event—the event setting itself free in principle from any cause by its an-archic arising. Never being its cause, I am therefore responsible for it in a completely different sense from moral imputability.

For example, no tribunal, nor moral conscience, nor juridical or ethical action can ever impute an illness to me. If I can be declared "responsible" for it, it is in a more original sense of responsibility, which in turn makes any imputability possible. I am responsible in the sense that I must endure my ordeal myself by appropriating to myself the eventualities that are assigned to me through this event. To have the capacity to relate himself first hand (possibility) to a powerlessness that runs through his adventure (passibility) is, in fact, the condition for the *advenant* being able to happen to himself (be singularized) from what happens to him. *To be able to hold open the opening of his passibility by holding himself there, to have the capacity to persist in this openness, through which an advenant is exposed to more than he is capable of—this is what I call "responsibility."* I can answer *for* myself and be "responsible" only if I can first answer *to* an event in its impersonal occurring, only if I can face what happens to me. It is solely on this condition that I can also be responsible *for* an event—that in itself cannot be taken over—that is, I can hold myself free *for* it, open and available, by submitting myself to a transformation. Selfhood is constituted wholly in the original delay with which it answers to an event's solicitation, by answering for what cannot be taken over.

Thus, events, as what befalls me and gives me a history, summon me to a kind of responsibility that is different from responsibility for what I will. To be oneself is to persist in this openness of measureless exposure to events, to set oneself free for them, to be *available*. Responsibility is strictly this empty space of pure availability to what happens to us. "Availability" here does not simply mean "passivity," but neither is it of the order of some sort of "activity": to be available is to be open in such a way that I can be responsible for what happens to me by unsubstitutably undergoing it. Such a "being-oneself" or "selfhood" is in some way impersonal, with respect to any egoity and any individuality, since they are made possible by it. Rilke says that the pinnacle of selfhood is "anonymous,"[28] and adds in another letter: "Nothing has ever reached further, as an extreme state, than availability."[29] Similarly, Paul Cézanne describes the highest selfhood as a withdrawal and a "being quiet": "He [the painter] must silence all prejudice within himself. He must forget, forget, be quiet, be a perfect echo."[30] Such a total availability to events is how we allow them to reach us, upend us, and transform us. Persisting in the openness of this availability allows us to appropriate the possibilities that are assigned to us and, consequently, to be responsible for them. This availability is synonymous with selfhood in its eventral sense.

The meaning of "responsibility" has now been made more precise. Returning to our earlier example, I am of course not responsible for an illness in the sense of it being imputable to me. Nevertheless, in another sense, the event of this physical ailment does depend on me, in that I must be able to face this event and appropriate to myself the possibilities that it assigns me. Such an appropriation presupposes an *advenant*'s self-ownership, that is, the possibility of answering for this event and of advening singularly through undergoing it. In this other sense, I am indeed responsible for this event. Moreover, it is only insofar as I am thus "responsible" for the illness, according to this eventral concept of responsibility, that I am also responsible in the everyday sense for my attitude toward it—for myself as ill—in the sense that this attitude is imputable to me. The eventral concept of responsibility (I am responsible for my acts, as *facts* of which I am the *agent*) is therefore founded in its eventral concept.

But is not any responsibility inseparable from some culpability? And does this not imply that one can name a culprit, assign an act to an agent, and determine its cause by finding an author for it? Not at all. In fact, I am strictly innocent of my passibility, just as I am—and precisely to the extent that I am—of my own birth. The possibility of relating myself first hand to my passibility (responsibility) is therefore entirely distinct from any culpability in the ethical or juridical sense. Not only am I never culpable for an event as such, since I am never its cause, but on the contrary, culpability can be apparent and unfold in an infraethical form in situations where responsibility in the eventral sense falters and collapses. Thus, it is precisely the lack of selfhood that makes an *advenant* who is submitted to particular traumas perceive himself as both culpable and victim—and more culpable the more he is victim. This will be demonstrated in the next section by an analysis of terror.

Only responsibility understood in its evential sense makes possible the third moment of the complex phenomenon of selfhood: singularity. Indeed, only insofar as an *advenant* is open to events—that is, at the same time himself implicated in what happens to him and able to be responsible for it—is he also able to advene to himself singularly, to determine *who* he is in light of his history. Selfhood is the ground for an *advenant*'s singularity, as it is historically arrayed from the events that befall him and the possibilities they articulate. But how are we to understand this singularity? How are we to determine its source? Such a singularity does not come from the resolute anticipation of a signal possibility: that of my death (Heidegger). Rather, it comes from events themselves inasmuch as they singularize me, that is, in their ceaselessly configuring my possibilities differently, by conferring a particular unity of meaning on my history. How are possibilities unified in *a* destiny, conferring singularity on an *advenant*? The answer to this question requires that we broach the problem of history.[31] However, what is already evident is that an *advenant*'s singularity is in each case determined starting from the concrete possibilities that befall him and that confer on his destiny its unique configuration; these possibilities can be upended in their turn by new events, so that an *advenant* can no longer understand himself in the same way at different periods of his history. Hence, this singularity is able to change, as my history is modified and my possibilities are seen to be configured differently. For *an event is that which has changed me.* But how are we to understand the relation that is established here between selfhood understood as responsibility and the singularity, in each instance shaped, that arises from my history as what singularizes me? To be able to happen to myself in my singularity through the events that happen to me, I must already be capable of holding myself open to events and of advening from this openness; I must therefore already be *myself* in the sense of selfhood or responsibility. Therefore, selfhood, eventially understood, does not mean my singularity as it is shaped in each instance and in relation to which I can be said to have changed; rather, it means what founds the possibility of my singularity. Two paradoxes follow from this. First, selfhood, the capacity to be implicated myself in what happens to me and hence be responsible for it, is what founds the possibility of my individuation, is not already individual but rather preindividual, the matrix for any individuality. Second, selfhood understood in this sense founds my singularity, which differs in each instance at different periods of my history; it contains in itself the possibility of any change: hence it is prior to the opposition of identity and change that sets the horizon for traditional conceptions of the Self.

In having to answer unsubstitutably for what happens to him, and in himself being unsubstitutable in this response in which selfhood is rooted, an *advenant* is *one and the same* across his whole history. This unity signifies *unsubstitutability in responsibility*. An *advenant* has a unity insofar as the task of responding to the injunction of events falls on him *as himself*. He does not have unity as singular, as being determined as such and such. On the contrary, his singularity is ceaselessly arrayed differently across his history as it moves through its stages, the constellations of meaning established by events. Far from promoting a gathering of his histories, singularity, always plural, always multiple, instead marks their irreducible dispersion. It is only as himself, as open to events and having to be responsible for them, that an *advenant* is a unity, and not as an individual in the riches of his concrete features. It follows that his selfhood is not individuated from the outset but instead precedes any concrete individuation. The possibility of an *advenant*'s singularity lies in his selfhood, which implies that the latter is not already singularized itself. The ground of an *advenant*'s self-ownership and of any appropriation of events by him is not first something that he has as his own, but it is rather his capacity to come into his own by being transformed. If selfhood makes an *advenant*'s individuation possible in this way—an individuation that should be thought of here in its transitive and verbal sense, as the event of my always being on the way to happening to myself—it is therefore preindividual and the principle of any individuation. It signifies the freedom of being free for events, as an *advenant*'s capacity to persist in his own openness, to face what happens to him, his possibility of appropriating what happens—a possibility that is rooted in the measureless possibility of his own adventure.

From this follows the second paradox we identified above. Selfhood, as possibility of my passibility, responsibility, is the capacity of holding myself open to what happens to me, so as to appropriate it as such. Now, by upending the world through and through, events impose on me the necessity of understanding myself otherwise, through undergoing them. Consequently, selfhood signifies nothing other than the capacity for change, the power to refashion myself, to happen to myself differently, starting from the events that punctuate my adventure. Far from defining itself primordially by the "constancy" and "stability" of an inalienable Self, far from radically opposing itself to any change with respect to itself, selfhood is originally *a potentiality to transform ourselves by contact with what happens to us.* Openness to events signifies nothing other than precisely this capacity to refashion not only my projections, my relation to my possibilities and to the world, but also my singularity itself, as it is historically arrayed starting from events and the possibilities they configure.

Thus, it is not responsibility in the evential sense that presupposes an *advenant*'s self-identity but, inversely, his singularity that is wholly founded in his capacity to be responsible for what happens to him (by being transformed).

Such a primary and underivable responsibility still differs from that of Dasein with respect to Being as "*his*" (determined by mineness, by *Jemeinigkeit*). For Heidegger still subordinates responsibility to selfhood determined existentially as anticipatory resolution. Indeed, only a Dasein that is resolved in advance can "hear" the call of conscience that he silently addresses to himself from the isolation of his thrownness, and hence *be responsible for his Being*, be responsible for Being as his, by bearing witness to an authentic potentiality-for-Being. To be responsible for Being as one's own is thus nothing other than existing resolutely in the projection of an autonomous potentiality-for-Being—since only resolute Dasein can reach that "self-subsistence of existence"[32] of which Heidegger speaks. At the same time, it is thereby to raise oneself by one's self-constancy (*Selbstständigkeit*) above the contingencies and circumstances that belong to the facticity of a destiny, so as to take them over as such. To be responsible for Being is moreover to be responsible for oneself, since Dasein is always mine (*je meines*), enclosed, as Levinas says, in the "immanence of *Jemeinigkeit*," such that this "responsibility" is only Dasein's way to be resolute, to exist the "self" as *subject*. It is quite different with evential responsibility. As subjectivity is originally a response to an event—that is, to what exceeds it through and through by opening it to more than itself, to the otherness of an anonymous gift, the gift of the world, which is originally declared in the event of birth—an *advenant* is always responsible for more than himself, insofar as he is always already exposed to other than himself. To be responsible for birth in this way, and thereby for every event, is therefore to be unable to reduce the event of being (birth) to the event of Being (understanding), to be unable to gauge the meaning of one's adventure by Dasein's ontological transcendence. If the exemplary being is responsible for Being by existing resolutely (his death) and thus reaching full autonomy, an *advenant*, by contrast, is responsible by being washed over and enveloped by an event that opens his adventure to an essential heteronomy, being unable to circumscribe this in a resolute projection nor to take it over in the first person. This is why one should not say, as Heidegger does, that Dasein is responsible for Being because he is responsible first of all for himself, because he is resolute, but rather, that Dasein can be responsible for himself (for his possibilities freely anticipated in a finite projection) only because he is more originally responsible for what happens to him, only because he is open in himself to more than himself.

On the basis of this evential phenomenon of responsibility, it becomes possible to show the *derived* character of Heidegger's characterization of existential selfhood. Selfhood understood as responsibility articulates three fundamental characteristics of an *advenant*, which have been brought to light by our earlier analyses: (1) passibility, in that it appears to be irreducible to any facticity and prior to it by right; (2) eventuality, which is the excess that all possibility has over an *advenant*'s projections, in that it is assigned to him from events; and (3) understanding, which is originally delayed behind the meaning of what is to be understood and makes it possible to appropriate the eventualities that allow an *advenant*'s advent to himself in his singularity. Synthetically, responsibility therefore signifies the original exposure to events, in that they make possibilities possible prior to any projection, originally precede all projections and all understanding, and thus are alone what allows an *advenant* to reach himself and the singularity of his destiny. Defined in this way, starting from eventials, responsibility anticipates and founds the existential structures of pro-jection (*Ent-wurf*) and thrown-ness (*Ge-worfenheit*), in which Dasein's selfhood is rooted. It is prior to the exemplary being's existentiality just as much as to its facticity, and in fact it makes them possible, since all facticity presupposes a passibility with respect to the very event of birth, and any pro-jection presupposes a "being-anticipated" by eventual possibilities. Responsibility also precedes any *Eigentlichkeit* and any (self-)authenticity of Dasein, which involves the fundamental mineness of Being. This is because responsibility with respect to Being as in each case mine (*je meines*), as what I make possible in each case in a free projection, as *potentiality-for-Being*, the being in care of its Being—attested in resolution—presupposes an openness to events in their transcendental neutrality, a responsibility as yet impersonal, where the one who is responsible is not already "himself," singular, *subject*, but can only become this through this very response, where, given over to more than he can take over and exceeded by a possibility that overhangs him, he has to be responsible for what happens to him before existing authentically (*eigentlich*) or being ever able to resolve himself to it.

How do things stand at this stage with the second paradox we raised earlier? Is it not actually contradictory to define selfhood as a capacity for refashioning through unsubstitutably undergoing events? Is not the attempt to distinguish selfhood from any idea of constancy, or even "self-constancy," from Dasein's self-subsistence (*Selbstständigkeit*) destined for failure? Is it not necessary that "something" remain constant if I am to affirm that it is myself in each case who is "transformed" through undergoing an event? In fact, this objection can only have genuine weight to call our analyses into question if it is demonstrated that such a "constancy" is necessarily presupposed by the concept of selfhood in general. We will have to show, to the contrary, by progressively shedding light on the evential meaning of time, that such a "constancy" has to be supposed (as standing in opposition to any "change" or "alteration") *only where one is still governed, in an implicit way, by a "metaphysical" (intratemporal) concept of "time"* [33]—where "remaining the same" *is still opposed* to "becoming other," or where this opposition is itself expressed in the opposition of two temporalities (e.g., in *Being and Time*, as it is already, in another way, in *On the Phenomenology of the Consciousness of Internal Time*):[34] original and authentic temporality, from which any change, *genesis*, or "becoming other" is excluded in advance, under the constraints of ontological formality (*Formalität*)[35] and inauthentic temporality, as a succession of nows. But can this opposition between two temporalities be maintained, and at what price? Does it not still bring a "metaphysical" imprint into Heidegger's existential conceptuality?

From an evential point of view, on the other hand, selfhood is prior to the alternative of constancy and instability, which reproduces, on the existential level, the traditional opposition of identity and change. Prior to these divisions, selfhood is neither constant nor inconstant; it is the very capacity for an *advenant* to refashion himself, to happen to himself by differing from himself. This is why selfhood is only fully manifested where an *advenant* is called upon to *integrate* an event by transforming his projections and understanding himself differently, or to allow himself to be "disintegrated" by it, sinking into despair. We will see that such a "trans-formation" of oneself and one's projections is not the mere "transit" from one "state" of an *advenant* to another, which transit would be conceivable in light of linear temporality. Rather, it is the primary-surge [*prime-saut*][36] (*Ur-sprung*) of an origin, which is pure bursting forth of itself in itself, as absolute difference and fissure, in the verticality of a present-source that ab-solves itself from any relation to a prior past.

Meanwhile, the strongest objection that will be raised by these analyses will doubtless be the following: is not conceiving selfhood as the condition of possibility for any singularity—and, thus, for any change—to fall back inevitably into a variety of formalism, from which these analyses were supposed to free us? In fact, selfhood cannot be thought here as a *formal* condition preceding events, as a reception [*accueil*] condition to which they would have to be submitted before they could occur as such. I have already shown in what way such an interpretation, which relegates an *advenant* to the rank of a "subject," understood as what always lies "behind" or "under" what happens, is excluded in principle by the phenomenological modalities according to which events *show themselves*. If selfhood is therefore the "condition" for any singularity and for any change, it is more originally conditioned in turn by the event in which it originates, it is precisely an *uncondition*, in the sense with which I have used this word earlier. This is why selfhood, even if it is original, in the sense in which it is a founding characteristic of an *advenant*, is not originary, for it is rooted in event as origin and the origin-event of the origin, in birth as proto-event. Selfhood can be this capacity of an *advenant* to hold himself open beyond measure to events only because events, in and through their arising, have more originally opened the playing field where such a holding-open is possible. In addition, this is why selfhood, as originating in events' neutrality and in the prepersonal dimension of the human adventure, such as it happens from birth, is able to be lost, to succumb to the excess of events that cannot be assimilated by an *advenant*, that are impossible for him to integrate, that disintegrate any genuine possibility of reception [*accueil*]. This is what the analyses of despair and terror will show shortly. Consequently, selfhood is neither first in itself nor inalienable. Rather, it is a possibility, a "capacity," in a paradoxical sense, since it is just as much a capacity for nothing, for simply holding oneself open, persisting in openness, and—only to this extent—a capacity for laying out anew, in a new world-projection, the possibilities an event makes possible. Thus, selfhood is a capacity that can, in its turn, be alienated or lost.

§16 Despair and Terror

(a) Passibility to Events, and Feeling

There is no such thing as a neutral event. Everything that happens to us is already laden with joy or sadness for us, already tinged with anxiety, fear, or hope. I call all these states "feelings [*sentiments*]": a feeling, in general, is the way in which an *advenant feels himself in facing what happens to him*. There is never a pure passibility to an event without its already being modalized, affectively colored by feelings. The reflexive character of feelings, as feeling oneself to be . . . (in some affective state or other), belongs to the very mode of their phenomenality. Of course, feelings can be more or less "reflexive," in the everyday sense of the word, with an *advenant* being more or less "turned toward himself" and absorbed in himself. Someone who is carefree, for example, shows a particular absence of care and worry (in both senses of the Latin: *cura*) for himself. This is true *a fortiori* for feelings like joy, which, as Schelling remarks, has this trait in common with gracefulness: it is only possible if one is unaware of it. "What goes on there is akin to certain human qualities that exist only if they are *ignorant* of themselves. Thus innocence no longer is when it knows that it is innocent, just as grace that seeks to be gracious is no longer grace, and nothing in the world is more odious than a feigned naivety."[37] Where it is greatest, and literally exults, joy overflows, pours out, and radiates; it does not turn back on itself and is *oblivious* to itself in a strong and positive sense, which does not mark any deficiency or weakness with respect to a prior self-consciousness but on the contrary a surplus, an excess: joy radiates outside itself, communicates and diffuses itself. A joy that did not communicate itself would be a weak joy; even great interior joys, which are deep and solitary, are inseparable from an expansive feeling and a desire to share them with another. However, even in constantly excentric joy, open to others and radiating toward them, an essential "reflexivity" is also present, in that joy is a feeling, a way of feeling oneself to be facing what happens to us. Such a "feeling [*ressentir*]" is not necessarily turned toward oneself nor self-absorbed; rather, it demonstrates the following phenomenological characteristic: the "Self" is present in it as such, before any "reflection" by the *advenant* on himself. What does such an assertion signify phenomenologically? How does an *advenant* relate to himself in feelings? How should we specify this "Self," which appears to be implicated, prior to any reflection, in any affective "state"?

Feeling modalizes our openness to events in general, or passibility. Through passibility, feeling also determines our very openness to the world that is made possible by events. It is from the world and the possibilities it articulates that an *advenant* can understand himself in his singularity, as one to whom such possibilities befall, insofar as he grasps them anew in a unitary project. Hence, the self-reference of feeling in no way signifies a thematic return on oneself, a "reflection" accomplished by a "subject"; it simply indicates that in any feeling, what is at stake is *selfhood as responsibility*. This is the case *a fortiori*, of course, for certain feelings where this "reflexivity" seems to be exacerbated, as happens in moroseness, boredom, nostalgia, melancholy, or sadness: each of these feelings is imbued with a withdrawal and turning back on the self that are the inverse of joy. This is even more evident in the case of sadness, which is opposed to joy's expansiveness and is a dejection that robs us of our strength, extinguishes our desires, closes us in on ourselves, and deprives us of any full relation with others.

Who has not undergone great sadness, which passes right through our very depths, leaving us discouraged, abandoned, perhaps even devastated? But the characteristic feature of sadness lies in its alternation between dejection and revulsion, which is precisely what makes it still *ours*, so that we are ourselves at stake in undergoing it and are not completely dispossessed and alienated by it from our own feeling. In one of his *Letters to a Young Poet*, Rilke speaks of such profound sadness, which passes through us like a great squall and does not leave us untouched:

> You have had many and great sadnesses, which passed. And you say that even this passing was hard for you and put you out of sorts. But, please, consider whether the great sadnesses have not rather gone right through the center of yourself. Whether much in you has not altered, whether you have not somewhere, at some point of your being, undergone a change while you were sad? Only those sadnesses are dangerous and bad which one carries about among people in order to drown them out.[38]

We will see shortly the name for this anonymity that dispossesses me of my own sadness. But sadness, as long as it remains *mine*, at the same time dejection and revulsion, suffering and struggle, even if it puts one out of sorts, even if it devastates, is not "bad," writes Rilke. He adds: "Almost all our sadnesses are moments of tension that we find paralyzing because we no longer hear our surprised feelings living."[39] This tension and struggle are consubstantial with sadness. In the vast solitude that it imposes, it is still *ours*, and it is thus that we endure it and have to endure it, this "flesh of our destiny": "This is why it is so important to be alone and contemplative when one is sad."[40] Now, solitude and contemplation are attitudes of an *advenant*. They are not a contingent isolation, the factical loss of others, but a way of advening that is possible even in the middle of a crowd—and surely there is nowhere else that the solitude of a sad heart is greater or more poignant. This is why Rilke still writes that contemplation and solitude, which are the first and best expression of sadness, are also its primary, and perhaps only, remedy.

A critical moment of the human adventure, where dejection and revulsion, suffering and struggle, alternate and confront one another, sadness as a feeling thus remains a way in which events "touch" and "affect" us by being addressed to us, uniquely, according to our unique destiny. This is why sadness, even if it is extreme, is still a benefit from the moment in which we make it our own and are present to it ourselves because, through it, it is to events themselves, to all our history, and to ourselves that we are present. Christian theology speaks in this way of the "gift of tears"— tears that are themselves a benefit, not only in prayer, but already in themselves. For the opposite of feeling as a way of appropriating events, even sad ones, as our own, is the *apathy* of certain psychoses: melancholic stupor, for example, or in a different way, the impersonality of despair.

(b) Despair as a Fundamental Feeling

While sadness is still a way of relating myself to what happens to me by suffering its ordeal, despair is characterized by a type of doleful apathy. In this state, unable to appropriate to myself what happens to me and to integrate events into a new projection of the world, "I" actually become *nobody*: my whole adventure sinks into a bottomless anonymity. Despair is not only the collapse of my possibilities—"the impossibility of something possible [*die Unmöglichkeit des Möglichen*]" [41]—but also the incapacity to welcome the events that befall me and that are literally unbearable. Consequently, it is also the impossibility of advening through these events. Here, an *advenant* falls short of himself and of all projection; overwhelmed by events, he cannot recover his grasp as *himself*. Everything sinks in a kind of anonymous vigil, where "I" am there without being there, in an impersonal stupor where suffering, at its peak, becomes almost painless. All possibilities are absorbed and overwhelmed in a bottomless passibility, from which any "passion" or *pathos* is excluded and in which the only way of being moved [*le pathétique*] is this doleful apathy. Nothing more is possible, the world no longer becomes world, there are no more events. Dispossessed of all possibility, delivered over to the endless and bottomless passibility of his own adventure, to the impersonality that pervades this adventure through and through from the moment of birth, an *advenant* no longer advenes to himself, but subsides without respite in this doleful stupor. The incapacity to integrate events into new projections of the world, the downfall within selfhood itself, go together with a radical disinterest in the world (which dis-interest should be understood in its strong sense, as a dis-implication of an *advenant* in what happens to him) and an absolute *detachment* with respect to that world. When one is sad, at least one clings to sadness and has in that something of one's own, something to struggle against, something to abandon oneself to. In moments of real despair, one only has a vigil that sets in without anyone—and that signifies literally the incapacity to be sad. There is suffering, but there is no longer anyone to suffer, *our* suffering is taken from us, as well as all possibility of abandoning ourselves or of struggling. *One* observes one's suffering by no longer being present oneself to it; all will, all force, abandons us.

Thus, in the great calm that sets in at moments of real despair, an impersonal lucidity is revealed, in which things take on a life of their own, and the world, now stripped of all meaning, is transformed into pure *spectacle*, unfolding before us and taking on a form that is even more gripping because it has been deserted by selfhood. Things deprived of a world (since the world as such has collapsed under the impact of an event that is strictly unbearable and resists any appropriation) invade and choke our adventure, populating despair's anonymous hyperlucidity and its impersonal vigil, but they no longer reach us, or they only reach the emptiness of our deserted "Self." Hence the particular intimacy—which must not be interpreted too hastily—that is established with impersonal death, as an essentially "inauthentic" and radically anonymous event where *one* dies without the possibility of taking over one's death or even being resolved to it. Despair's anonymous hyperlucidity observes the world's shipwreck as if *one* no longer was: simply, someone has died, this has already taken place long ago, it has always been so, we have not seen this death come, and all this has not even taken place. This is how it is with despair, as Kierkegaard describes it: a continuing death, a death that cannot die and that is nevertheless already dead, that cannot itself take on death nor take it over, since the very decision of suicide always presumes selfhood and a projection of the world, which are precisely what collapses in great despair. A few sentences of *A Sentimental Education* capture this well: "It would only take a single movement! The weight of his head pulled him forward, and he imagined his corpse floating on the water. Frédéric leant over. *The parapet was rather wide, and it was weariness that deterred him from throwing himself off.*"[42]

Despair thus makes evident our primary relation to death: in it, we experience ourselves as *already dead*, as Kafka very rightly puts it: "Anyone who cannot come to terms with his life while he is alive needs one hand to ward off a little his despair over his fate . . . for he sees different (and more) things than do the other; after all, dead as he is in his own lifetime, he is the real survivor."[43] Thus, we experience ourselves as having fallen short of any selfhood or projection and therefore as unable to "take over" death, incapable of suicide. But despair also makes evident an original relation to events in general, in their impersonal character, since here it is our human adventure that completely sinks into a bottomless impersonality. Thus, it can be seen that despair is the counterphenomenon of selfhood. As a *"negative"*—in the photographic sense—it is what best reveals selfhood's meaning: the collapse of my possibilities and their reabsorption into the bottomless passibility of my adventure is the negative image of selfhood, as capacity to face events and to appropriate the possibilities they assign me by redeploying them in new projections—as *insistence* in the face of events: an insistence that only really appears *as such* where it collapses, where *I* can precisely no longer "face up to," in the original and underivable phenomenon of despair.

Our one and only "adventure" consists precisely in this insistence in the face of what happens to us—an insistence by which we are ourselves, doubly held by the necessity and the impossibility of continuing, in that chiasm to which an *advenant* is shackled without remission to the extent that his adventure is possible only *per impossibile*. This insistence, which is solely possible at the risk of our own impossibility and to which we are delivered by the very event of birth, is only really revealed in despair, in the collapse of a "Self" lacking selfhood, in the impersonal mode of that universal vigil without anybody, where the world no longer becomes world, in the relation to that other anonymity profounder than death so well expressed, after all, by Beckett's ironic phrase—but is there a more eminent expression of despair than irony?—that says everything that needs to be said about our adventure, a transcendental expression, prior to any empirical specification, prior to any success or failure, happiness or sadness in "life": "The end is in the beginning and yet you go on."[44] An expression that is not neutral by accident, since it is spoken from that bottomless and endless impersonality of despair and stands out in relief only by bringing to light this fundamental anonymity, which pervades and dwells in any adventure into which one is born [*aventure native*].

Fundamental feeling of the loss of all feeling, bottomless feeling of the bottomlessness of all feeling, despair is hence not extreme sadness. In it, an *advenant* falls short of any selfhood, and therefore also of any sadness and of any feeling in general. And since there is selfhood only in a relation to a world, as the totality of possibilities articulated among themselves and taken up in a projection by an *advenant*, annihilation of any selfhood is inseparable from a collapse of the world. In despair, I am unable to relate myself first hand to events by appropriating the possibilities they open up, and I also fall short of any capacity to have a *world* in the evential sense. Or, rather, this spectral "world," a mere homonym of the former, where *I*, properly speaking, no longer am, or only am in a weak sense, is no more than the whole of my possibilities robbed of their possibility [*possibles dé-possibilisés*]. "*Ich bin nichts mehr, ich lebe nicht mehr gerne* [I'm nothing now, and listless I live on],"[45] writes Hölderlin. Despair is evident in this annihilation of oneself and of the world, which renders life literally unliveable and where one feels already dead.[46] Such a *collapse of the world* is necessarily accompanied by the collapse of all relations with others, on which selfhood itself depends in principle,[47] the impossibility of calling for help, prostration, and mutism. The literally unbearable impersonality of the event entails a sudden and simultaneous anonymity of others, the dissolution of beloved faces, sinking in their turn into complete neutrality. Falling short myself of any capacity to act for another, I no longer hope for intervention or rescue from others, I can no longer hope for *anything*. It is precisely to the extent that I am no longer myself, in facing an impersonal event that nevertheless befalls *me*, who has to carry its burden, in this failure of selfhood, that I am by the same blow stripped of my relation to others, with beloved faces confused, blurred, and lost in the midst of things, in this deserted and depopulated world where a moment never ends and the present is perpetual.

And so, it is only when an *advenant* falls short of himself, when he reaches "the depths" of despair, that he also reaches the depths of distress, isolation, and *solitude*. This abandon and distress, as the *loss of others*, should no longer even be called solitude, since solitude is still a way of being oneself, precisely as "isolated," while the distress that accompanies despair is at the same time the loss both of others and of oneself: *"solitude" more solitary than any solitude* where at least selfhood persists and is preserved, even in its isolation.[48]

Thus, beyond any psychology or anthropology, the phenomenon of despair bears witness to a fundamental anonymity of the human adventure, which lets us bring to light, negatively, the evential meaning of selfhood. The latter is always a deferred response to events, such that I respond to what happens to me without ever being its origin. Rather, it is events, as origin, that alone allow me to respond, by *taking up and making possible* the possibilities they open and thus appropriating them as such. This response is itself constituted entirely by the disparity between passibility, as primary and fundamental openness to events, and the capacity to *hold myself open*, to insist in this openness: *availability* to events. Thus selfhood, which is the condition for something happening to me *first hand*, is still more originally an *uncondition*, since it is rooted in that more original passibility of my own adventure, which has the event of birth as origin and from which, alone, selfhood is modulated as possibility of *response*, responsibility, according to an *original* delay.

Hence, we can also see the relation of despair, the fundamental feeling, to birth, the nonground of an adventure. In despair, where the world no longer becomes world for me, where the possibilities opened by events can no longer be gathered into a projection, what comes to light "behind" the things that haunt a deserted world is nothing other than a birth that cannot be appropriated, as Beckett writes again: "I gave up before birth, it is not possible otherwise, but birth there had to be, it was he, I was inside, that's how I see it, it was he who wailed, he who saw the light, I didn't wail, I didn't see the light, it's impossible I should have a voice, impossible I should have thoughts, and I speak and think, I do the impossible, it is not possible otherwise."[49] In this litany of impossible appropriation, in the very impossibility of recognizing the one to whom this immemorial event has occurred, the one who has to endure its burden without ever being able to take it over himself in the first person, birth, the nonground of the world, the nonworld of a nonground that resists all projection, is what suddenly flickers, in the collapsed world of despair, in this world that is reduced to *nothing*—"nothing" that is no longer a modality of Being as no-thing, non-being, ontological difference, presence (*Anwesenheit, Anwesen*) of the present (*Anwesendes*), consequently irreducible to thought of Being as presence. This nonground of the event of birth, absolutely immemorial, in front of which we are nothing, which is absolutely unable to be appropriated, impossible for a subject to gather into presence, is what despair gives us to undergo. This despair is not a privation of hope, which would thus be conceived as original, but rather the very "ground" of an adventure, where one "hits rock bottom," irreducible to any facticity just as much as to any potentiality-for-Being: "I'm dead," writes Beckett, "and getting born, without having ended, helpless to begin, that's my life."[50] This is not a mere witticism, a paradoxical inversion, but rather birth's nonground, undergone in despair as first death, primary death, from which I am always already separated, for which I always already mourn: for this *inscription* in a prehistory that transcends any taking up or taking over is precisely what makes my adventure impossible for a subject to gather into presence.[51] Adventure as the continual being-mourning—mourning for Being as such. Through birth, as despair makes us suddenly "sensitive" to it, what wavers is the very hope of gathering any event into presence, according to a re-presentation; what we mourn is Being as presence: "It may be thought there was [something once], so long as it's known there was not, never anything, but giving up [*abandon*]."[52] We must give all their speculative weight to these phrases of Beckett: despair manifests that birth is always already mourning for Being, rupture of presence, unfillable absence, abandon, impossibility of putting the pieces together again, original scattering of Being, nonpresence and noncoincidence to oneself, loss that is earlier than any empirical loss, mourning for any "Self" as permanence in re-presentation.

(c) Terror and Traumatism

The collapse of the world and of the Self, which is evident in despair, is not seen only there. Analogous phenomena can be found in particular forms of psychosis or particular neuroses, where events, in the form of *trauma*, play an essential role. The collapse of selfhood here correlates to *a profound alteration of an advenant's passibility*—that is, of his original "relation" to events as such. In considering the phenomenon of terror, we can attempt to bring to light this alteration of passibility by analyzing how the impossibility of any response to a traumatizing event entails a profound modification of our relation to this event, which suddenly frees itself from the limits of this singular experience and invades our whole adventure through its incessant repetition in memory or dreams and, impossible to assimilate, becomes a genuine internal "foreign body," as Freud put it so well.[53]

Traumatism is an event that we cannot make our own. Though we are utterly exposed to it, this is as a *subject* incapable of facing it, *subjected* to the excess of what has struck us all the more painfully since it happens to us from outside,[54] takes us by surprise, avoids any grasp, and outwits any protection. Thus, the meaning of traumatism is originally revealed in the experience of terror. If selfhood is indeed the capacity-to-face what happens to us, so as to appropriate it as such, in terror by contrast *there is no longer any "facing"*: an *advenant* is delivered without reserve to the anonymous and faceless otherness of the terrifying, which overruns him entirely, chills him to the bones, transfixes him, and so on. In this respect, terror is profoundly different from fear. While the menacing always declares itself in a particular locality of the world, as Heidegger rightly emphasizes, and setting itself before us, makes us shrink back, the terrifying declares itself to us in a *proximity without distance* that abolishes any possibility of flight and leaves us paralyzed, numbed, and defenseless. This *absolute* proximity of the terrifying has nothing to do with the spatial distance that the menacing may have to us. While the menace of the menacing grows or decreases in proportion to its spatial proximity, the proximity of the terrifying is not able to increase or diminish: it is an *obsessive mode of enveloping*. The characteristic feature of this absolute and distanceless proximity is that it *annuls space* by annulling all distance, thereby thwarting any possibility of flight before that which, freed from any place and position in the world, *invades space as a whole.* The correlate of terror is *atmospheric.* It comes at us and is upon us suddenly, eliminating any escape. As Binswanger writes of Suzanne Urban, describing the initial scene of terror when the doctor discloses her husband's cancer,[55] terror becomes atmosphere for her. It is smell that best evokes this obsession, by scent's distanceless proximity, its unlocalizable and enveloping character: "As those close to her put it so well, she begins to 'smell danger everywhere.'"[56]

In its distanceless proximity, the terrifying envelops us from all directions; consequently, it leaves us inert and paralyzes any *reaction.* Not only does it eliminate any escape, but also, by inhibiting all fear, which is still a way of affronting and facing the menacing, even if by flight, it thwarts courage from coming to light. While fear calls for courage, terror leaves us stupefied. This immobility is as much "physical" as "psychic." The impossibility of any reaction is, first and fundamentally, the impossibility of *responding* to what comes to pass, that is, of being *ourselves* in face of what happens to us. Binswanger writes further of Suzanne Urban that, in the grip of terror, she can be described as "an irresponsible Self, incapable of responding"[57]—that is, no longer really a "Self" at all. In this respect, terror is irreducible to fear, it is not merely a variety of fear, a particularly acute fear, etc. The particular inertia by which terror shows itself equates more to a "blockage" of all feeling, by which an *advenant* would relate to himself and find himself affectively disposed in some way or other with respect to what upsets him. For the terrifying is not of the order of the upsetting but rather of the traumatizing, that is, of what evades any proper and *first-hand* experience. It strikes us in a very different way from what we can make our own and appropriate in the mode of *experience.* Indeed, we can only be upset by what we can also make our own by making it the source of a self-transformation. A traumatic event, by contrast, in breaking into a human adventure and resisting an *advenant*'s assimilation, is rather that which thwarts any transformation from self to self, any experience, freezing an *advenant*'s very adventure and preventing him from advening.

Terror differs from fear not only in that, as an experience of shock, it dispossesses us of any possibility of responding to it in the first person. By contrast with fear, which always takes its meaning from an external menace, terror arises also from an "interior" menace, from a menace such that selfhood itself is what is at stake. What terrifies me and deprives me of my powers is always a terrifying event or object, but it is also, always and at the same time, what that event reveals to me about myself. This is why the obscure presence of the terrifying is marked only in situations that reveal me to myself. For example, in war, on a battlefield, where the din of bombs, the moans and cries of the wounded, conceal the ground under my feet and expose me to the abyss of my own death. Or when an accident happens to me or to another, revealing to me my impotence under destiny's blows. Terror is inseparable from this revelatory power: the *intimacy* of the terrifying stands out in these terrifying situations, where, for me, it is always a matter of my own death. This is particularly evident for the traumatisms that psychiatry groups together under the label of "fright neuroses [*Schreckneurosen*]."[58] The revelation at stake here is certainly not a theoretical consciousness of death *in general*: of course, I am already familiar with death as a universal phenomenon; what is revealed to me is death as *my death*, that event which is all about me in my unsubstitutable selfhood. Consequently, if there is a "revelation," it is one in which I am implicated myself, entirely, in which I am upended (or, rather, traumatized), the revelation in question being nothing other than this precise upending itself. Not simply knowledge, where an *advenant* could remain "exterior" to what he knew, but unsubstitutable ordeal, an experience that I must pass through myself, at the risk of myself, where what is at stake is me in my selfhood. This is the source of the difference between fear and terror. Of course, any fear is fear for myself; any danger that hangs over me thereby brings me back to who I am. In extreme or mortal danger, it is indeed my death that is put at stake by the menace and thus calls forth a boost of courage. Hence, not all mortal danger induces terror, only that one where the intimacy of the terrifying dispossesses me of my possibilities, paralyzes my defenses by preventing any reaction, makes the ground drop away from under me, and thus exposes me to myself, under the overhang of death, entirely delivered over to its anonymous "power." It reveals to me that I am *nothing*. Thus, terror and fear have completely different relations to death. An *advenant* who is menaced by danger relates to death as a possibility that is still his own, a possibility *that is merely possible*, freely anticipated and able to be anticipated and, thus, still "represented" and "dominated"—an avoidable possibility, at least "for the moment." The intimacy with death that is revealed in terror, by contrast, is such that my selfhood collapses, unable to respond to what happens to me; I am entirely delivered over to the anonymous empire of death, to the impersonal "one dies," which is its most proper sense.[59] Here, death is no longer something that I can avoid, but is what surrounds and envelops me, taking all power away from me, not only over it, but first of all over myself.

Thus, it is precisely to the extent that, in terror, I can no longer respond to what happens to me, am unable to react, and am subjected to an event I can no longer make my own, to an event as traumatism, that I am also, and by this very fact, reduced to the status of pure *subject*. This subjection to events is evident in the complex phenomenon of *fascination*. For there is no terror without fascination, without that captivation by the terrifying, which belongs to terror as such. But what does "fascination" mean here? It is, as we will see, an attitude that is in some way double, whose two "faces" are nevertheless like the obverse and reverse of a single phenomenon: on the one hand, the impossibility of understanding and "recognizing" oneself in what happens to us, an impossibility that belongs necessarily to all traumatism; on the other hand, a seizure by the event, which can no longer appear except with its "objective" face, as pure chance or fate utterly deprived of sense, holding us more in its grasp the less we can recognize ourselves in it. Here, events are no longer that from which I can understand myself in my singularity. Rather, precisely to the extent that I am no longer capable of appropriating their meaning, they are that which reflects my image to me as a hallucinated double, and that of which the occurrence stupefies me, grips me, and leaves me thunderstruck. Thus, *the less* I am able to understand myself from what happens to me—because of traumatism's excess beyond any possible appropriation—*the more* it holds me in its grasp, in the mode of fascination. The *advenant*'s lack of implication in what "comes to pass," his lack of selfhood, are here contemporaneous with an extreme subjection to the traumatizing event. This fundamental aspect has been well brought to light by clinical psychiatry with respect to particular neuroses that arise from trauma: "All traumatic encounter is *over-invested* to the point, sometimes, of completely concealing any subjective implication."[60] In this case, an *advenant* is nothing more than a mere *victim*, entirely submitted to what happens to him, unable to integrate events into a history, and thus advene freely from them. "Invoking chance, under its objective aspect, reinforces the feeling of arbitrariness."[61] This is made evident by complaints that are limited to rehearsing this single event in all its modes, so as to seek its causes ("Why has this happened?") and diminish its absurdity. Such an attempt is all the more in vain as the event's *meaning* is unfindable, in that the event is itself impossible for an *advenant* to assimilate or integrate. By a kind of compensation, this arbitrariness gives way to interpretations in which traumatism's radical non-sense is transformed into a kind of intentional aim, where the victims of an attack, for example, "feel that they are deliberately aimed at, and express a feeling of guilt for having been present on the site of an attack."[62] Here, "survivor's guilt" is the only way in which an *advenant* can "respond" to what has just shattered any possibility of response, make his own what he can in no way appropriate, make himself responsible where all genuine responsibility has collapsed.

The lack of selfhood gives way to what clinicians call modalities of replacement, where the accent is no longer on oneself but on others, and an *advenant* effaces himself behind a group or cause, or, inversely, by identifying himself with a victim, lays the responsibility for his suffering on others.[63] Reactions of a shattered and cornered Self who finds in others a substitute for his own deficiency.

Thus, an *advenant*'s incapacity to advene to himself freely, his submission to an event that crushes him, entails a modification of his passibility: a traumatic event, constantly recalled and relived in the mode of intense memories or repetitive dreams, ceaselessly invades the present, entirely pervades it, and forbids in advance any other genuine event from coming to light. The patient is unrelentingly led to traumatism, and his protests mark both his desire to be freed of the trauma and the necessity of always coming back to it. By absorbing into itself in advance the possibility for any other event, traumatism reduces the patient's time to gloomy rehearsing of an achronous present stemming from the covering over of the genuine present by a past that cannot be overcome, which ceaselessly presents itself in it, interpolated and "transported" into this present, so to speak, by recurring relivings that restrain the present's amplitude, close off any future, and thus prevent time from temporalizing. This repetition of a traumatizing event, in the form of dreams, memories, hallucinations, or compulsive actions, freezes one's whole adventure and reduces temporality to a mere repetition of the identical, an indefinite stagnation of a perpetual present, closed to any futurition. A genuine "internal foreign body," traumatism imposes its law on me, comes to haunt my detemporalized present endlessly, and, emancipated from its roots in the past, omnipresent, seems to have its own life—a life that has stopped short: it imposes on me inflexible scenarios of dreams and "existence," altering my passibility to the point of taking away the possibility of any other event happening to me.[64] This past that is interpolated into the present and cannot be overcome makes any genuine *memory* impossible, as memory presumes a distance with respect to the past. Traumatic neurosis is thus often identifiable by "the inability to recall important elements of the trauma."[65]

And so, the defeat of selfhood makes evident once again, in negative, its properly evential meaning. This reveals the thematic and structural unity of the preceding analyses. By making selfhood succumb under the weight of an event that is impossible to appropriate, traumatism brings selfhood to light as *capacity for appropriation*. Being able to appropriate an event that happens to him first hand is, for an *advenant*, to be himself.

A fundamental conclusion follows from this: since selfhood as responsibility always refers to the way an *advenant* stands in relation to events, this selfhood is also implicated in those events where another is manifested. For example, in the phenomenon of an encounter or, by contrast, in bereavement. This is why the otherness of others codetermines selfhood in its evential sense. The latter is never defined in an autarchic way; it originally puts in play a "relation" to others, starting from events in which they *declare themselves.*

§17 Selfhood and Otherness: The Phenomena of Bereavement and Encounter

In being born, an *advenant* receives the world in such a way that he never finds himself *alone* in it. Therefore, an original dimension of the human adventure is a constitutive relation with others. Of course, this is not in the sense of a mere formal ontological constitution, as in Heidegger's *Mitsein*, but in the sense that others always become evident as such for an *advenant* starting from *events*. This is especially so in bereavement and encounter. As in any genuine event, *an advenant in his selfhood is at stake* in these phenomena. Such events do not simply happen to us "from outside," leaving us unchanged; they strike us in the most intimate of ways, at the heart of our possibilities articulated in a world, from which we understand ourselves. Thus, with the irruption of another into the world, with an encounter as *event*, the whole world is transfigured: one "world is collapsing" and another "is rebuilding itself," as Kafka puts it.[66] It is the same with another's death and the event of bereavement, where the retreat of another's world does not leave my world unchanged but irremediably carries it, and me, with it. Encounters and bereavement attest to the inextricable entwining of our worlds, one *to* another, one *in* another.

In interpreting these phenomena, I am not simply concerned with analyzing contingent situations that have been chosen at random from the human adventure, but rather with pursuing and deepening the questioning up to this point about *the evential meaning of selfhood.* To what extent can these phenomena, which at first glance concern others—or, strictly speaking, "me" in my "relation" to others—provide a response to the question: *who* am I myself?

(a) Bereavement and Separation

Bereavement is the absolute experience of separation: not a contingent and reversible separation, a remediable separation whose "milieu" would be physical space, but a separation that is in itself absolute, irreversible, and irremediable, that happens in time and is sealed by time: the absolute of separation is temporal, because temporality is the only "dimension" in which an *absolute* separation is possible. In bereavement, such a separation is given to us to *undergo*: the deceased has "left us," not to go "elsewhere," but because the time in which he was still present is henceforth "inaccessible" to us. Here, another's death has the sense of an event that happens to the survivors; it is a phenomenon that is shared by those who remain. But how can such a death, which the other alone undergoes, touch us in our unsubstitutable selfhood, at the heart of our possibilities articulated in a world?

Of course, another's death cannot be experienced as a fact. Indeed, dying means no longer being of this world, losing the world as such. While such a "loss," which happens to another, can be accompanied for us by bodily signs, it cannot itself be the object of an experience. For there is no proper experience except of what is our own, and we always remain strangers to another's death, irremediably exterior, powerless spectators of what conceals itself from any spectacle—since, in one sense, "nothing" takes place in another's death, and this *nothing* is death. The spectacle of a human cadaver sometimes arouses an indecent curiosity the size of which is in inverse proportion to its capacity to grasp anything; it remains entirely closed off from "what comes to pass." For what "comes to pass" is strictly "nothing," nothing that can be apprehended as a fact in the world, but this nothing of the event is precisely what is striking here and is more striking the less it is visible, the more it escapes being seen. Nothing is less spectacular than death, and this is why nothing accentuates more the indecency of curiosity, but this curiosity exposes instead our incapacity to endure what touches us in the depths of our heart without ever "appearing" as a *fact* in the world: *the event itself*. In what sense, then, is the event of death an event that is *undergone*—in a radically nonempirical manner—by those who remain?

To be able to conceive of bereavement as *absolute* separation, it is not enough for another to "disappear." The disappearance must bring a cataclysm with it that is not only the loss of the beloved whose absence I feel but just as much *the loss of myself:* loss that must be understood in the strong sense, as a real *death*. We not only die to the beloved [*mourons . . . à la personne aimée*],[67] but through this first death we die to ourselves; that is, we die to the only one we could have been unsubstitutably *for* the beloved, and for him or her alone. But how is such a phenomenon possible? How can bereavement, another's death as endured ordeal, death *to* another, be indissolubly death to oneself? How can we specify this "self" that staggers in experiencing bereavement, the one to whom I die in dying to another?

In the event of bereavement, as in any event, I am in play myself in my selfhood. If every event is an *advent* for me, and allows me to understand myself and to advene to myself as myself, then it is the same for the event of an encounter, where my world is opened to dimensions of another world—another's world—and, correlatively, in the event of bereavement, where this world closes over again, and so closes over my world as well, together with the constellation of possibilities that were only mine because they befell me from encountering another. In other words, since my singularity originates in an event, it also originates in those possibilities opened by that event. These possibilities are *entwined* with another's possibilities in a *common history*, which is just as incomparable as the other is himself incomparable, and for which his death constitutes the *dénouement*, in both senses of the word. What the event of loss radically separates us from is not only another as he presents himself in the world, but *this world itself*: only on this condition can another's death touch us at the heart of our ownmost possibilities, in our most intimate singularity.

Thus, bereavement is this *dying to . . .* another that is endured by those who remain, this "dying to the one who has died": the duplication in this expression should not be understood here as an "effect" that another's death produces in those who survive him, for death can produce such an "effect" only to the extent that we are capable of undergoing it in bereavement, to the extent that it has already occurred and been undergone. This duplication belongs instead to the phenomenon of bereavement in its most original sense. Proust puts this with a force that is probably unequalled: "Nothing, I told myself, but a veritable extinction of myself would be capable (but that is impossible) of consoling me for hers. It did not occur to me that the death of oneself is neither impossible nor extraordinary; it is effected without our knowledge, sometimes against our will, every day of our lives."[68] *The intrinsic and indissoluble link between death to another and death to myself is what constitutes the evential meaning of bereavement as such.* Of course, the whole question of understanding this double (or redoubled) death remains open. For Proust, it has the exclusively empirical sense of an inexorable oblivion, a loss of habits that connect me to the beloved; moreover, it depends on the thesis formulated explicitly in numerous passages of Proust's work, that "I" am only a succession of (plural) "I's," and that time is a rhapsodic sequence of discontinuous instants: "It was not Albertine alone who was a succession of moments, it was also myself."[69] This proliferation of Albertines and of "I's" originates in the power of forgetting and in its correlate, the power of habit, the capacity to acquire new habits, that is, strictly speaking, to *forget*. However, the empiricist character of what we might call Proust's "theses" takes nothing away from the profound truth of his analysis of bereavement, which rests, again, on the intimate correlation between *dying to* . . . another and *dying to* . . . myself, but the meaning of such "dying" still demands to be further elucidated.

Perhaps no one has described the suffering of separation with greater depth than Proust. However, notwithstanding his greatness as a writer, he failed to capture its eventual meaning: for, thinking as an empiricist, Proust believes that experience, by repetition alone, not only creates habits in us but also *teaches* us something about the future: "Time passes, and little by little everything that we have spoken in falsehood becomes true; I had learned this only too well with Gilberte; the indifference I had feigned while never ceasing to weep had eventually become a fact."[70] What happened with Gilberte is repeated with Albertine. Suffering, by becoming a habit, brings its own relief; time is the best anesthetic, the best analgesic. From his experience with Gilberte, the narrator of *Remembrance of Things Past* concludes that (feinted) anticipation of separation always leads to a real separation: this is a *fact of experience*. But is there such a thing as "facts of experience"? Is experience, in its properly human, eventual, dimension, the experience of *facts*? If events are always unique while facts recur, then the experience of a "fact" produces no "fact of experience," nothing one can hold on to or hold up before the wounding novelty of an event. While facts can be repeated, events are unique. The loss of Albertine is not the same as the loss of Gilberte. A loss is always unique and incomparable with any other, for it is the very possibilities the narrator has in common with Albertine that waver and collapse with his beloved's world. This is what emerges from the refinements, hesitations, and voluntary retractions that are scattered through the rest of the text: undergoing Albertine's death will prove to the narrator the contrary of what his conception of habit has led him to conclude about the progressive extinction of suffering: "All my life to come," he writes, "seemed to have been wrenched from my heart."[71] For with the revelation of this death, the narrator is now confronted with *a pure event as itself*, whose sharpness has been blunted and whose violence has been hidden by his theory of habit and the ruses of suffering.[72] What had been concealed was the *originality* of events, their utterly unpredictable and irremediable character, which tears up habit's framework and leaves experience naked, without resources, radically exposed. Suffering that is undergone always surpasses what can be anticipated or imagined, to the very extent that it is *undergone* and not imagined or anticipated. There is an excess of the "real" over the "possible"; this excess absolutely resists being reduced or diminished, but is revealed in critical situations of a human adventure. In face of suffering in its extreme violence, our explanations are always too short, and experience's ruses are too naïve: "But this explanation was still fragile, it had not yet had [will it ever have?] the time to thrust into my mind its beneficent roots, and my pain could not so quickly be assuaged."[73] Why? Because suffering lives in us, so to speak, with a life of its own, because it has a temporality on which we have no grasp by ruses of habit or by reasoning. On seeing familiar objects, formerly connected to the idea of Albertine—Proust, an empiricist, is also an association-ist[74]—"a sudden flux of pain would overwhelm me."[75] What is the most painful in the loss of a beloved is all the *incidentals* by which their memory bruises us in ways that have not yet been smoothed over by habit and that are always new and unforeseeable. Proust does not suspect that it is this *novelty itself* that is the most wounding, because he interprets the suffering of separation as though it arose only from breaking a habit, from loosening the ties that custom has weaved with its implacable tyranny. These explanations remain psychological and cannot reach the eventital meaning-character of bereavement.

However, Proust provisionally rises above this empiricist and associationist psychology, noting that the suffering connected to bereavement comes not from precise memories, lived experiences of consciousness that would in some way be "present," *Erlebnisse*, but from the *world itself of the beloved*. This is why when a beloved withdraws from our life, it is our life itself that withdraws, is emptied of itself and of everything, with the result that the emptiness left by the beloved is so vast that it is as if the whole sea had withdrawn, leaving relics of its presence in the backwash on the beach: "I was so incapable during those days of forming any picture of Albertine . . . just as my mother, in the moments of despair when she was incapable of ever picturing my grandmother . . . might have accused and did in fact accuse herself of not missing her mother, whose death had been a mortal blow to her but whose features eluded her memory."[76] The experience of loss and bereavement cannot be reduced to psychological lived experiences, since it is undergone in its greatest intensity precisely where memories are missing. In loss, one undergoes an event that is as such unexperienceable, that plunges its roots into our very adventure and makes it shudder. The narrator is thinking of this event when he speaks of this new and unknown suffering that is brought about by Albertine's death: "*The world is not created once and for all for each of us individually*,"[77] and, a little later: "So then my life was entirely altered."[78] Memories may well be the psychological cause of the suffering connected with separation, but they cannot be its evential *origin*, by which they touch us and strike us and without which we could not experience the pure and imageless pain of loss. For the *encompassing* character of separation, the *total* emptiness that it leaves in us, cannot be exhausted by any memory. This is expressed admirably, and fugitively, in a unique phrase that on its own captures the phenomenological meaning of the event of loss, with which *the whole world trembles*: "Albertine had seemed to me to be an obstacle interposed between me and all things, because she was for me their container, and it was from her alone, as from a vase, that I could receive them."[79] With Albertine's death, his world itself, the world the narrator shared with her, the container of all things, disappears. Not merely a portion of his possibilities, those projects that "attached to her alone," for, by modifying particular possibilities, as with any genuine event, separation always reconfigures possibility in its totality. With Albertine's death, it is the former world as a whole that is engulfed in a concluded and accomplished past, from which I am forever separated, that shudders and collapses. Thus, it is precisely in the loss of another that the very mode of her presence is made evident with the greatest intensity, a presence that plunges its roots into our own, a tangled and lush presence that pervades our world by opening it to an other world—incomparably[80]—as will be evident shortly in the phenomenon of encounter.

It is thus mistaken to affirm, as Heidegger does, that another's death teaches Dasein nothing about its own death.[81] What takes place is much rather the contrary: in undergoing bereavement, *dying to . . .* another is inseparable from death of and to . . . myself, a collapse of *my* possibilities that were only possible for me by "existing" for the sake of the other and thanks to her presence. Bereavement can be this event that occurs to survivors only because another's death reconfigures all my *own* possibilities, which implies that my own possibilities were never separable from those of the one whom I mourn. This is why lost love, where the other doesn't *actually* die but is "as though dead" for us, bears the same essential characteristics of bereavement as absolute separation. That this case can be understood in terms of bereavement, as evential, in no way indicates a "metaphorical" usage of the term. Rather, any "metaphor" or linguistic "metaphoricality" is founded on an evential sharing of meaning between these two phenomena. When we speak of lover's bereavement or "dead loves [*amours défuntes*]" (Baudelaire), we are not metaphorically transferring to a new "domain" a meaning drawn from the phenomenon of another's death: on the contrary, in both cases, it is a matter of an *absolute separation*, in which what is lost is that which made the other unique for us and made our history incomparable. What is lost are the possibilities that our history harbored, our compossibles, the possibilities that articulated our adventure and gave it its singular figure. Bereavement is this breakdown into unmatched possibilities.

Loss more profound than any empirical loss, bereavement is therefore a "loss" in a paradoxical sense: not the loss of what I have (since losing something I have, a possession, is only the opposite of acquiring it and is never losing oneself) but the loss of what in no way belongs to me, what is entirely free with respect to me but that I can never lose *as such* without losing myself along with it. If bereavement is not merely a worldly event, an "objective" fact, but is rather an unparalleled event that strikes me in the heart *like no other* and upends me most intimately, this is because this event is a matter of my selfhood: for my selfhood is not given apart from the "relation" to the other that is established by an encounter, nor apart from the world that this encounter makes possible. It is by such an event, under the gaze of another and for her, that I myself fully acquire unicity and singularity. And so, the suffering of bereavement lies especially in that, being stripped of a beloved, I no longer fully belong to myself, since the one in whose sight I was unique and irreplaceable no longer exists. That of me which dies with her death, or with absolute separation from her, is my singularity-for-another, in that this is what *happens to me* only starting from the event in which our common adventure is bound together: I can never be the same for everyone—not because of an ontological "bad faith" (Sartre), which always makes me play a part, put myself in a role—but on the contrary because I am never myself (singular) except *for-another*, in an absolute and absolutely singular relation of two absolute singulars, because singularity, understood eventially, is something that *happens to me* starting from my various encounters with others, according to the twists and turns of our histories.

The relation of love is exemplary here but not exclusive. More than others, perhaps, it is the encounter of two histories, where we are both in play in our selfhood. It is an encounter that can only be conceived if one thinks about the possibility of common possibilities, of compossibles: an inextricable crossing over, where our possibilities, without ever coinciding or merging in a kind of fused unity, entwine to form a single history, the history of our love—a unique and incomparable history, where it is no longer completely possible to distinguish what derives from the initiative of one or the other, and where, without ever "being only one," I and another happen one-for-the-other. *Eros* here does not exclude *philia*: on the contrary, the concept of love should be understood with the widest possible extension. In both cases, love always aims directly at another and not at her "qualities"—thus invalidating the Pascalian alternative[82]—and, by a kind of infused gnosis, it strikes the heart of her singularity "without qualities": this whole that can be neither conceptualized nor fully analyzed, the corporeal whole that she is for me, it strikes her in her incomparable and singular history.

This death to another as death to myself (bereavement), to this "self" of singularity that is such only starting from the *impersonal* event of an encounter, where another *is presented* for the first time, this *dénouement*, in the proper sense, of the eventualities whose entwining articulates our common adventure is profoundly compared by the author of *Remembrance of Things Past* to the suffering experienced by amputees in their "phantom limb." On a fine and sunny day, ideal for a ride, it occurs to Marcel that Albertine probably would have taken her bike for an outing in the Touraine: "But, as with people who have lost a limb, the slightest change in the weather revived the pain I felt in the limb that no longer existed."[83] The loss of a beloved is so much a loss of myself that it can be compared to a slash in *my* flesh; but while an amputee's pain remains localizable—precisely in the "phantom limb"—the pain of lost love is not. It is an omnipresent and ubiquitous pain, which is made most intense by trivial details—objects that belonged to her, turns of phrase she had the custom of using, etc.—which are in this world like vestiges of a former one: details in which the former world gleams with a sudden intensity, as though we were transported there anew. Here, as in the case of an amputee's wounds, it is a matter of a wound that will not "heal," if "healing" means restoring corporeal integrity: a unique and irremediable wound, which is produced in us by the loss of something unique, and of what was unique about me for her, or rather of what was unique about "the one" (the "who" of *singularity*) she loved, who only existed as such *for her*, in this "relation" of love that is absolutely singular and singularly absolute. Indeed, nothing can heal the loss of what can never be replaced. Thus multiple wounds can coexist in the same *advenant*, wounds corresponding to successive bereavements, to successive deaths to others and, consequently, to oneself.[84]

(b) Encounter

Even though there is a "first time" in every encounter, there is no first encounter. As long as an *advenant* advenes to himself and understands himself, his history appears to him as punctuated by multiple encounters. Some are already forgotten but populate his adventure immemorially.

There is no first morning for encounters, no virginal and dawnlike meeting by which others present themselves in our world for the first time, but rather this world always already harbors, in the play of its possibilities, those compossibles that befall me from an ongoing relation with another. To this phenomenological impossibility of conceiving a first meeting in the adventure into which we are born is added the extreme difficulty of conceiving the "first time" in any encounter, which is one of their decisive evential characteristics. Indeed, what would an encounter mean that was not initial and inaugural? However, is not the beginning of every encounter already lost, not because of a subsequent loss and forgetting, contingent and fortuitous, but because of an essential loss that is contemporaneous with its event?

In truth, an encounter is an event in which another irrupts into the world for the first time by reconfiguring its intrinsic possibilities. As *event*—even when it is "contrived"—it exceeds my initiatives and gives itself to me only *by excess*: "But certain it is that the going and the searching and the meeting belong in some manner to the mysteries of Eros. Certain it is that on our windy path we are not only propelled forward by our deeds but lured on continuously by something which seems to be continually waiting for us somewhere and is invariably veiled."[85] We not only await, we are awaited. What awaits us and attracts us is out of reach and beyond expectation for us—we are not its measure. An encounter is a prelude to nothing but itself. The event fills an expectation that it alone could have created.[86] This is why an encounter never arises from my doing or from my competence. Even though, as the poet says, encounters belong to the mystery of Eros and are "the decisive erotic pantomime," they are inseparable from a quest and an expectation, without which the out-of-reach could not even occur and, thus, reach us. Nevertheless, an encounter's occurrence is strictly *incommensurable* with this quest, nothing can prepare for it or anticipate it; instead, it gives itself in itself, by opening the playing field where it can happen, literally inaccessible by any other path than itself, itself conditioning its own access. The "leap toward another" or seeking for her can only prepare access to the inaccessible, opening the possibility of what happens only *per impossibile*. This "experience" of the ungraspable, which always precedes us and catches us by surprise, of the unforeseeable, which only occurs without warning, of what "continually wait[s] for us somewhere and is invariably veiled," is the undergoing of an "otherness" of which I am never the measure. This alterity is only exhibited as such in this event: the *event's* alterity that is incommensurable with us, perpetually precedes us, touches us only on its own initiative, and essentially escapes our own powers. Even in the case of a "contrived" encounter, where I make the first step in reaching out to another, what remains impossible to contrive ("unprovokable" and "unable to be stirred up") is always the *encounter* as such.

Experience of the ungraspable is therefore expressed in *being caught by surprise.* Poets have strongly and beautifully expressed the mix of almost sacred terror and astonishment that characterize it. Speaking of his encounter with Constance Dowling, Cesare Pavese repeatedly uses the oxymoron "the horror and wonder [*l'orrore e la meraviglia*]"[87] and writes to her: "I forgive you all this pain gnawing at my heart, yes, I welcome it. It's you, it's the true horror and wonder of you."[88] Horror and wonder, the appalling and the mystifying, astonishment and terror: all are experiences of being grasped by what cannot be grasped, by what, like surprise, overtakes us and suspends any grip, is never at our disposal, but has us at *its disposal* by exposing us to what cannot be experienced. For a genuine encounter can never be reduced to its actualization as a fact; it always happens in the secret and suspense of its latency such that we are never contemporary with it and never realize it until later, "too late," according to the essential—transcendental—a posteriori of a necessary retrospection, when the event of an encounter has *already* happened, has already reconfigured all our possibilities and the world. Granted, an exchange of looks, or the first words exchanged, happen as such in the datable present of *facts:* it could even be, completely contingently and fortuitously, that I can recall precisely "the first time" I saw someone in particular, and the circumstances of this "encounter"; it could also be that I have forgotten them, for here recollection or forgetting are equally contingent and just as unessential for understanding the encounter itself as event. For each genuine encounter has an *essential* nonsimultaneity and noncontemporaneousness, which distinguishes it from the *fact* of the actual introduction of two people, their factual being put in one another's presence in the world. There is never simultaneity, as in the *fact* of an actual introduction, never contemporaneousness between the actualization of an encounter and its reappropriation as event but instead a necessary temporal disparity, which belongs as such to its evential tenor. The very first time, the first instant of a love or a friendship, are always already lost, not by a contingent empirical "loss," an accidental weakness of memory, for the event of an encounter cannot be reduced to the actual introduction of two people, which could be the object (or not) of a "memory"; rather, an encounter happens always *on the margin* of its actualization. Strictly speaking, it "is" nothing other than the impersonal reconfiguration of the world that happens unknown to us, perhaps even against our will. Many "worldly" introductions are indeed not *encounters*, and, inversely, an encounter, if it is a genuine one, imposes itself on us with its own "evidence," such that it is not some "subjective sentiment" but rather the phenomenological meaning-character of the event in question that makes an encounter seem already to have taken place "long ago"; we seem to have known each other "for ever," even when we have only been together for a few hours.

However, this "evidence" of an encounter never occurs apart from the being caught by surprise that was described above and therefore can only be retrospective. Initially, an encounter is what shatters our familiarity with the former world and suspends all *settledness* in the world. It exposes me to the risk of an otherness that escapes any mastery or foresight. To this extent, it can only be adventurous, an experience *per impossibile*, where I put myself in play in my selfhood, where I always risk myself in the first person. The risk to which I am exposed here is not an inner-worldly danger but rather that of a radical upheaval of the world itself and a reconfiguration of its possibilities. By shattering our solitary world, by introducing eventualities to it that are in no way prefigured in it, an encounter always signifies the advent of a new world for an *advenant*—an advent that Kafka, echoing Pavese, strongly emphasizes ("my world is collapsing, my world is rebuilding itself")[89] as a genuine birth, in which joy and terror are mixed. An *impersonal* reconfiguration of my possibilities, and nevertheless one that is *addressed* and *assigned*, an encounter does not happen in the world but opens a world and exposes me to the raw light of outdoors, the too-intense radiance of birth, which is not a mere metaphor.[90] Indeed, like birth, the upheaval of my eventual possibilities in an encounter, by literally striking me with powerlessness ("my weak forces," writes Kafka) and opening a new world for me, transcends all experience in an empiricist sense and consequently all memory: not in the way that an innerworldly fact might when it has been secondarily forgotten, but to the extent that an essential "forgetting" happens here, which is not a deficient mode of memory but belongs exclusively to this event's eventuality. An encounter is neither "forgettable" nor "recallable" as is an empirical fact: we have already observed that the first moment of a love or a friendship is *always already lost*, just as is any genuine beginning. This is the same in the case of birth—though differently, since while the event of an encounter can *also* be experienced as a fact, this is certainly not the case with birth—where the upending of my possibilities precedes in principle any empirical recollection or forgetting and is instead prior to their distinction.

This is why an encounter is not so much a "presentation" (of two people) as a *futurition*. It has meaning only through the possibilities that it holds in reserve, which give it its future-loading. It is never a mere "presentation" because it cannot be reduced to a phenomenon of an instant, which would take place once and for all, in an achieved and definitive *present*. Instead, the event's "first time" is a "time" of *all times*, for though an encounter establishes a beginning, it is a genuine *encounter*—appearing as such in the "deferred view [*après-coup*]" of retrospection—only if it has a later destiny and is not exhausted in the initial face-to-face. Its evential character prevents it from occurring in the closed and achieved present of its actualization and from ever taking on the definitive character of a "fait accompli." Rather, it necessarily overflows the fact of its own actualization; it is a beginning that never ends and, because it constantly defers itself by opening ceaseless new possibilities, it essentially has the meaning of a *continuing encounter*. An approach that is always renewed and that is not becalmed in the harbor of possession.

Thus, only the event of an encounter opens the field of play of possibilities—the world—where another can appear to me with the meaning that is hers. The phenomenon of an encounter presumes, of course, that the other anticipates and precedes me, in an approach where she has the initiative. But this initiative itself, like my own initiative, is subordinated to and conditioned by the event's impersonal prevenience, which alone can strike me with powerlessness in the experience of being caught by surprise. An encounter takes place as event, in its unforeseeable and unanticipatable occurring, only where it radically precedes any projection by opening a playing field where it can happen incommensurably with me: the world. Nevertheless, the other conserves a kind of priority and precedence over me in this phenomenon. Even though "I would reach out to her" and do anything to bring about an encounter, the encounter can only occur as an event if the other, in her free approach, has already anticipated my own initiative and thus taken away my power. But is not this phenomenon *reversible*? Does not the other take away my prerogative as I paradoxically take away hers? There is a double dissymmetry here, where the free initiative of one "precedes" that of the other and vice versa: a reciprocity in dissymmetry of this double "prevenience" without which the field of play for an encounter would remain forever closed. Nevertheless, this "reciprocity" is never an initial phenomenon but always a secondary one, in the sense that it introduces the other's point of view, which is always concealed from me, by definition, in an encounter's inaugural instant; this double dissymmetry may well be reconstructed after the fact, but what is initially and originally given in every encounter is this preceding by the other and this "heteronomy" by which another is revealed to me as exceeding any grasp or hold, in the primary undergoing of my exposure to her.

But should we not rather say that it is the other who opens the space where an encounter becomes possible, since she seems precisely to precede me? Is it not more accurate to hold that it is from the other herself and not from the event that I receive the possibilities that determine our history? In one sense, it is indeed true that every encounter is an encounter with another, in the richness and diversity of her concrete features. But the *event* of another's revelation is not *the other* herself, such as she is revealed to me from this event. If another is *originally* manifested in the *impersonal* event of an encounter, she is not the *origin of this event*. It is not by chance that, in *Sentimental Education*, the encounter between Frédéric and Mme Arnoux is first expressed in the purely impersonal form of "taking place," "coming about," "there is." From the outset, the other is introduced under an impersonal regime, in that any genuine encounter is precisely a matter of an event:

> It was like an apparition:
>
> She was sitting in the middle of the bench, all alone; *or rather he could not see anybody* in the dazzling light which her eyes cast upon him. As he passed, she looked up; he bowed automatically; and when he had walked a little way along the deck, he looked back at her.[91]

Here, bedazzlement precedes the gaze and, exceeding it, carries it to encounter the visible. The impossibility of distinguishing anyone, the impersonal "it was" of the event, precedes and transcends the corporeal presence of the other—not through some sort of misapprehension of the other but because it is the condition of her appearing. In any encounter, the other is first hidden, without our knowing her—and nevertheless we recognize her by a kind of blind memory, with an infallible certainty and a faultless accuracy. As in Platonic recollection, this recognition is less a recalling of a mythical past that never took place than a preknowing of what we have never known, a premonition in which anteriority is the seal of the event itself in that it "forever" precedes us. Here, the event is an anonymous appearing, which opens the dimension in which and according to which another can herself appear and reveal herself to me on her own initiative, preceding me only to the extent *that it is the event itself that precedes me* and, by preceding me, exceeds my powers.

Consequently, if, as was asserted above, in every genuine encounter the other has already preceded me by her own initiative, in an approach that belongs to her alone, then it is no less the case that, for this to have a future and genuinely be an *encounter*, for it to open a later destiny in light of which it can take its meaning, this encounter cannot be exhausted in the initial "shock" of a face-to-face but must ceaselessly (and paradoxically) come about by happening to me from the future it opens and by making possible my eventual possibilities. Without this excess of eventual possibility over all actuality, an encounter would run dry—by exhausting its own possibilities—as soon as it began, and would never be pursued, prolonged and opened out in a common history. Just as every event is illuminated only in light of its posterity, an encounter necessarily comes about according to the event's transcendental deferral, by which it defers itself from its own origin: on this condition alone can another conserve her inexhaustible transcendence for me, even though I might believe, wrongly or rightly, to "know" her better and better. For this is not so much a matter of "knowing [*connaissance*]" another, which is always impossible in fact and problematic in principle, as of *co-birth* [*co-naissance*] to another, which is never exhausted in the initial face-to-face but only "becomes an event" if it also opens to a later destiny. The otherness of another is revealed here, in strict terms, as an "otherness" that is also temporal. This otherness is evident in the evential character of the encounter as continuing, as a "boundless movement of approach,"[92] in Erwin Straus's fine phrase. It is a movement that is never exhausted in possession or proximity, but, by "approaching" the other—by coming close *to* the other—paradoxically distances her (in the Heideggerian sense of *Entfernung*), restoring her inexhaustible transcendence to her.[93] Not a spatial distancing, but first of all a temporal one. I will never finish encountering the other and deepening this relationship that is not knowledge of her but co-birth with her, and that an encounter has unforeseeably and "for the first time" (even if this "time" is of all times and must constantly be achieved) made possible. To be born constantly and co-born to another [*naître constamment à autrui et le co-naître*] is thus to receive from an event the eventualities that articulate our shared history.

However, these considerations on the perpetually "deferred" character of an encounter do not mean that the friendship or love it makes possible—as well as hate, antipathy, sympathy in general—are never actual and achieved in themselves, as though they always had to be put off until later: they arc fully actual in the present but are never exhausted in the present, in that the other's alterity temporally transcends the present and, consequently, encounters always happen according to *eventuality's essential overflowing of any factual possibility.*

Something like a singular history of two people, which is not the sum of their individual histories, can only be conceived if an event (i.e., an encounter) makes possible the possible before any projection of mine. The earlier analyses of eventuality are here confirmed and deepened. If all eventual possibilities are "simply encountered," then every encounter is, inversely, a continuing advent of possibilities. Therefore, the possible here is neither what preexists its actualization for an *advenant* nor what he makes possible in a free projection; it is what is opened by an event and, because it is conferred on me *impersonally*, also connects me to the history of others, with whom my possibilities are intrinsically articulated in what must be called, eventually, the world. But how exactly should "world" be understood here? Have I not asserted earlier that an encounter introduces into my solitary world eventualities that are not prefigured in it—not only another, but strictly that other's world? But is there not *one single* world? How can we phenomenologically conceive of this reciprocal inclusion of our worlds, which is attested to as much by the phenomenon of bereavement as by that of encounters? If the world originates in each case in an event, does not its transcendental impersonality render inconsistent any attempt to speak of "my" world, or of "yours"?

Actually, the world's transcendental impersonality does not contradict the assertion that an encounter signifies the irruption of another world in an *advenant*'s own world. Indeed, this formulation rests on the thesis that the possibilities that articulate "my" world are not originally "mine," that they are such only by becoming mine, in my appropriating them and understanding myself in my singularity from them: they are originally impersonal, for they are born of an event, like the world they configure. As for the "other" world—the world of another—that is put forward in an encounter or, inversely, irremediably stripped from me in bereavement, it also is only configured or enworlded starting from inaugurating events for another, from which she understands herself, just as I understand myself, and which, consequently, punctuate her unsubstitutable adventure.

Some examples will perhaps make this clearer. I have said that any encounter gives us access to particular possibilities that happen only through it: striking up an acquaintance with someone, sharing time with her, little by little constructing friendship or love. Such possibilities are not mine from the outset; conferred by the event of an encounter, they only become mine if I make them mine by appropriating them, by redeploying them according to a unitary projection. At the same time, an encounter is not limited to introducing another into the world—world as transcendental *universum* of possibilities from which *I* understand myself as such and that is therefore also *my* world. It gives me access to another's world, to the unique way she has of appropriating the totality of possibility and redeploying it in a new world-projection. From this perspective, it is not impossible to assert simultaneously that an encounter, like any event, opens *the* world by reconfiguring its possibilities in another way, and that it gives me access to *another's* world, as it happens to her, according to the incomparable way she has of advening from what *makes history* in her adventure. These two assertions are situated on distinct planes and imply one another without being mutually contradictory.

Therefore, "my" world does not mean the solipsist world isolated in itself: it is the world that, because it is originally opened to me by events, can be appropriated in understanding. It is only by virtue of such an appropriation that the world in its transcendental impersonality can also be "my" world, with its constellation of singular possibilities, thus distinct from another's world. My world is articulated differently from another's in virtue of the unique constellation of possibilities, which befall me unsubstitutably from events and in which my ownmost projects are rooted. But there is actually only one and the same world, starting from which our worlds can differ, as so many ways of appropriating one and the same world-in-common starting from dissimilar and singular histories. Thus, it is always from an impersonal and common world that we acquire, as we determine ourselves in light of what happens to us, as we happen to ourselves in our singularity across events, a world of our own, individual and incomparable to any other.

§18 The *Advenant* and the Subject

The forgoing analyses of bereavement and encounters have brought to its term the exposition of the properly evential concept of selfhood. Selfhood, as responsibility with respect to what happens to us, has emerged as rooted in a number of eventials, from which it is inseparable. First, selfhood is dependent on birth: it is because an *advenant* comes into the world by being born that the world is an *evential*; that is, the world is opened to an *advenant* prior to any projection, so that he is never its origin. In being born, an *advenant* is opened to events in general, according to a *measureless* possibility, which is initially conferred on him by this protoevent; this possibility, as what befalls him *from* and *through* an event, is not a prior "condition" in a "subject"; rather, it is that from which a "subject" can advene to himself—precisely as *advenant*; it is an uncondition that is irreducible to any formal-ontological condition of possibility and unthinkable in terms of facticity. Selfhood is the capacity to hold open possibility's openness by holding oneself there: it signifies availability to events and the possibility of responding to them. Its counterpossibilities are terror and despair, where an *advenant* sinks into a bottomless anonymity that closes any possibility of his advening in the first person from the eventualities that events open and of welcoming these events by appropriating them. Second, selfhood is inseparable from world, as originating in its turn from events and, ultimately, from the original event of birth. To be a self is to be able to appropriate the possibilities that articulate the world by redeploying them in conformity with one's projections. Such a redeploying includes an understanding by which the meaning of events for an adventure is brought to light despite its initial obscurity. Here, understanding does not signify merely a particular cognitive grasp but rather a modality of adventure. By this modality, an *advenant* relates himself to the totality of meaning of the world, according to an orientation of his interpretative projection that is determined in each case. Third, this constitutive relation to the world's totality of meaning is that from which an *advenant* can also understand himself and can advene as himself in his singularity: that from which he can understand who he is in light of his history.

Thus, through the concept of selfhood, an *advenant*'s most fundamental characteristics are made clear in a synoptic way. But what happens once he is stripped of the possibility of facing what happens to him, as in terror or despair?

In sinking into despair's impersonal lucidity, where the world no longer enworlds for him, an *advenant*, absent from himself, observes his own suffering as if it were another's. No longer able to make the events that affect him his own, he relates himself to them as to mere facts occurring *to nobody*, facts that strike *himself* no more than the natural and impersonal spectacle of the rain. But is such an *advenant* still an *advenant*? Is he not dispossessed, not only of his selfhood but also of his ownmost phenomenal traits, to the point of no longer being able to be understood and referred to by this term? On numerous occasions above, an *advenant* reduced to this posture has been called a "subject." "Subject" must be understood literally here in the sense of subjection to what happens to us, to events, insofar as we cannot make them ours. Subject refers to an *advenant* insofar as selfhood is lacking to him, and, since selfhood refers to the fundamental dimension according to which events can make sense for an adventure, the term "subject" is only appropriate for an *advenant* inasmuch as he is stripped of himself. Of course, to be able to be a subject of assignation for a given event, an *advenant* must still possess an "egoity," must be given to himself as a factual ego, spatially "localized" in a body, etc.[94] But at the same time, to the extent that he is no longer himself, he can no longer *make* this assignation *his own* and *respond to it*. He is only the one *to whom* something happens if he is first of all *the one* to whom something happens: selfhood founds any possibility for him receiving [*accueil*] events, and an *advenant* only happens as pure "subject" when this possibility of reception [*accueil*] is altered and closed. In this respect, birth constitutes a kind of paradigm: it attests that this possibility of a deficiency in selfhood is not acquired by an *advenant* "along the way," so to speak, but dwells at the origin of the adventure to which he is born. At birth, I am indeed "subject," to the extent that I am never *capable* of it: "that" happens to me prior to any capacity for me to undergo it in the first person; my selfhood does not coincide with itself in the parousia of an origin but is itself determined by this original delay on itself that is constitutive of the "Self" itself.

At this point, there is an unavoidable question: Is the properly evential meaning of the term "subject" merely homonymous with its metaphysical meaning? Or, on the contrary, is it not possible, and even *necessary*, to reinterpret the latter in terms of the former? In other words, is not the metaphysical subject also fundamentally characterized by lacking the *advenant*'s principal characteristics, which we have just recalled? It must be emphasized that such a parallel could not be simply an identification. While despair indeed remains an *evential*, and as such still occurs *to an advenant* and thus still bears the negative imprint of his fundamental characteristics, the metaphysical subject on the contrary is characterized by a complete lack of these characteristics. Then it is perhaps possible to attempt *to make evident from the advenant and his principal eventials* the covering-over of his ownmost phenomenal features, which covering-over determines the metaphysical conception of the subject. This explicit phenomenological elucidation of the subject starting from the *advenant* should also show the sense in which the former presupposes the latter and receives its genuine meaning only from concealing this.

The modern subject, which is originally conceived as a substance, is established as such by a threefold covering-over: of events, of the world, and of understanding. Without entering into a detailed analysis of the historical forms that the subject has been able to take on since Descartes, it will suffice here to summarize three points briefly. (1) The covering-over of events: The subject is what stands under (*sub-jectum, hupo-keimenon*) everything that happens to him, that for which any event functions as a predicate, attribute, or accident. Immutable substratum for any predication and the ultimate ontological *fundamentum*, the subject is therefore characterized by an at least relative autarchy: a substance is "a thing capable of existing independently"[95] or "a thing existing in such a manner that it has need of no other thing in order to exist."[96] In virtue of this "*per se* character," all predicates are ordered to a substance, which sub-ordinates them by existing. For an event to "exist," it needs a substance as ultimate subject of attribution, in which it is realized. Here, subjectivity signifies the capacity not to be implicated oneself in what happens to us, to hold oneself always behind or under what comes to pass, by exercising an unlimited ontological prerogative over events. Therefore, passibility is foreign to such a subject; it has only passivity: a way of taking up what exceeds it by bringing it back to a mere subjective disposition. For if it always finds itself, and only itself, in what happens to it, this is precisely because it *is subject to it*, that is, submitted and passive. (2) Concealing of the world: The subject-substance of metaphysics is a-cosmic. This is not because of a "historical error" by Descartes (Husserl), where he interprets "*ego sum, ego existo*" as "*sum res cogitans*," that is, because of the mundane reification of the ego. Rather, the subject-substance is already a-cosmic by virtue of its interpretation as *subject*, that is, as immutable substratum of lived experiences. In fact, the covering-over of events that is at work in the characterization of the human being as "subject" implies a corresponding covering-over of the world in the evential sense, and its reduction—first to the rank of pure context in which objects and facts are presented for knowledge, and then to the rank of pure objective vis-à-vis for knowledge itself.[97] (3) Covering-over of understanding: What characterizes a subject is not the understanding in which the world's totality of meaning already necessarily gleams but rather knowledge as pure theoretical face-to-face with an object. Only to this extent can the "I" who grasps itself on knowledge's horizon have epistemological primacy and be considered as easier to know than any possible object.[98]

But what now for Heidegger's Dasein, since it appears, like the *advenant,* against the background of a phenomenological destruction of the traditional metaphysical concept of the subject? If this destruction, as was emphasized at the outset, is grounded first and foremost on a renewed understanding of Being in its verbal and transitive, *evental* sense—if, as Levinas asserts, there are no longer copulas in fundamental ontology— then does not Dasein provide the only real philosophical alternative to the traditional metaphysics of the subject, whose vocabulary Heidegger begins by deconstructing?

This question would have to be answered in the affirmative if access to Dasein, in *Being and Time*, did not first presume a reduction of events (*Ereignisse*). This reduction, in the phenomenological sense of the term, which alone allows Dasein to be brought to light as that being which "is primarily Being-possible,"[99] can be demonstrated from a 1920–1921 course on Pauline eschatology, in which the properly Heideggerian concept of ecstatic temporality is elaborated for the first time.[100] I will not repeat here my exposition of this argument[101] but will limit myself to re-stating its conclusions. Just as, in this course, the phenomenological eluci-dation of the temporality of factical experience in Christian life supposes a reduction of the eschatological event—a reduction framed in terms of an opposition between two temporalities, the one structured by expecta-tion of Christ's parousia as a future *event* (considered to be inauthentic by St. Paul) and the other consisting in the Christian's vigil before the immi-nence of a possible-at-any-instant (the only authentic temporality)—so, in *Being and Time*, the analysis of Being-toward-death repeats and radical-izes this previous approach. Here, through a reduction of the event of demise, the existential phenomenon of Dasein's mortality can emerge into the light as a singular (because "unrealizable") *possibility* of Being-in-the-world—full reduction this time, since death, by contrast with Christ's parousia, is no longer at all envisaged as a future event, but only *sub specie possibilitatis*: "On the other hand, if Being-towards-death has to disclose understandingly the possibility which we have characterized, and if it is to disclose it *as a possibility*, then in such Being-towards-death this possi-bility must not be weakened: it must be understood *as a possibility*, it must be cultivated as a possibility, and we must *put up with* it *as a possibility*, in the way we comport ourselves towards it."[102] The elucidation of the sin-gular meaning of the possibility that Dasein itself *is* is grounded on the reduction of death as an actual (*wirklich*) event. Inversely, only an inau-thentic understanding of death can convert the imminence of a possible-at-any-instant into a mere "certain fact [*gewissen "Tatsache"*]"[103] in virtue of an empirical certitude or into a mere "event which one encounters in one's environment [*umweltlich begegnendes Ereignis*]."[104] It should be em-phasized that this analysis of Dasein's mortality does not merely constitute one interpretation of its Being among others but is rather the focal point in which its principal existentials converge: anxiety, since "Being-towards-death is essentially anxiety";[105] but also care (*Sorge*), since if Being-in-the-world is founded on care (and not the contrary), the totality of this struc-tural whole is only evident in light of "the possibility of taking the *whole* of Dasein,"[106] and since only the anticipation of death can make possible "the whole of Dasein completely 'given' ";[107] and selfhood, above all, since "the non-relational character of death, as understood in anticipation, in-dividualizes Dasein down to itself [*auf es selbst*],"[108] and thus it is only from this singular possibility, Dasein's "ownmost" possibility, that the fundamental authenticity (*Eigentlichkeit*) of its Being can be seen. To die in the existential sense—that is, to bear with the possibility of one's im-possibility without covering it over and modifying it into a mere future event, without "realizing" it in a pure future actuality—is at the same time Dasein's ownmost possibility and the possibility of the authentic as such, the origin of all self-authenticity and all selfhood (*Selbstheit*).

This brings us to a genuine paradox. On the one hand, by conferring an evental sense on Being, Heidegger takes a decisive step beyond the limits of metaphysics and definitively puts an end to any thinking about the "subject" in terms of substance. On the other hand, Dasein, on the ground of which a phenomenological destruction of the "subject" becomes possible, is only accessible in its turn through a reduction of events (*Ereignisse*), which are thereby relegated to the level of mere facts (*Tatsache*), whose mode of Being is actuality (*Wirklichkeit*) or subsistence (*Vorhandenheit*). This reduction is achieved here for the sake of putting in relief a singular meaning for the possibility from which existence itself (*Existenz*) becomes conceivable. But is not this paradox untenable, nullifying the foregoing interpretation of *Being and Time*? On the contrary! Far from being mutually exclusive, the two operations we have pointed out are instead inseparable. It is because Heidegger restores its verbal sense to Being, as opposed to its substantive sense as copula, or, in other words, because he conceives Being as event, that he thereby reduces the multiplicity of events to *one alone*: *existing*, in a transitive sense. No other event happens to Dasein than that event which it *is* itself, insofar as it understands Being—insofar as it *is* itself understanding of Being, transcendence. The event of Being and the event of being are, for it, one and the same. This is why dying, where the totality of Being is made evident, as the totality of a potentiality-for-Being, is never an event, but only a way of Being: the meaning of Being itself is dying, and this is why anxiety, care (for oneself), and selfhood only appear concretely in light of this "primary" existential.

Heidegger's reduction of events in his fundamental ontology not only has the consequence of his misunderstanding the *evential* dimension of the human adventure and his incapacity to think about birth (or natality) as an existential,[109] to give it a status in the conceptual economy of *Being and Time*. It also makes any summary identification of Dasein and the *advenant* quite mistaken. Indeed, despite certain analogies, which can be grouped under three headings—(1) openness to the world, (2) primacy of understanding, and (3) thinking about the "Self" and selfhood as against thinking about "I" or egoity—evential hermeneutics is not set out on the same bases as Dasein-ontology but is rather prior to it. The questions that arise on the basis of the preceding analyses are the following: In being established as the "ontological" being (endowed with an understanding of Being) by means of a reduction of events, is Dasein entirely freed from the "subject" of metaphysics, in opposition to which it is conquered? If this subject is defined by the capacity always to step back behind events and not be implicated itself in its selfhood in what happens to it, is not Dasein still "subject" in its own way? Does not its closedness with respect to events in general reproduce *at another level* substance's radical autarchy?

To free these questions from the appearance of mere provocation that they may have at first glance, and to avoid excessively prolonging these analyses, it is possible to demonstrate the point by attending to three of Dasein's fundamental traits, which we have already identified: openness to the world, understanding, and selfhood. Despite a certain resemblance between these phenomenological characteristics of Dasein and the corresponding characteristics of the *advenant*, it is useful to explain not only the profound difference of meaning that separates the existentials from the eventials, but *the former's derived character with respect to the latter*. The ground for this difference can be briefly stated before being established in more detail: while the former are fundamentally understood from mortality, the latter are made clear in light of birth as original event. Now, this is not a matter of a secondary difference: the existentials in question only become possible against the background of a most profound *misunderstanding* of the *eventual* character of the human adventure, such that, while Heidegger's fundamental ontology may well be interpretable on the horizon of a hermeneutic of the *advenant*, the reverse is not true. Thus, it is apparent that eventual hermeneutics delves under the groundwork of Dasein-ontology, confirming its principal results but radicalizing its approach to the point of stealing its ground from under it.

First, what does it mean that Dasein is determined as "Being-in-the-world" in *Being and Time*? By existing, Dasein always already transcends entities in the direction of their Being, and thus understands it. In concern (*Besorgen*), it understands the Being of ready-to-hand (*zuhanden*) entities: readiness-to-hand (*Zuhandenheit*). This type of Being is characterized by a particular involvement (*Bewandtnis*), in the sense that every tool is a tool *for* a totality of equipment, which compose a utilitary complex in their mutual connection. The worldliness of the environment (*Umwelt*) can thus be brought to light starting from the characteristic feature of the way of Being of tools, as that in which the "look" proper to concern, circumspection, operates, in that it always has to do with the totality of references of a meaningful complex of equipment. Hence, the world is ontologically determinable as this totality of references of equipment, dubbed by Heidegger as "significance [*Bedeutsamkeit*]." As soon as Dasein understands the Being of ready-to-hand entities, a world is opened to it; or better, as soon as it exists, understanding Being, it exists as Being-in-the-world. The world is not something that is added to its existence, but an ontological constituent of that existence. As existence is determined by thrownness (facticity) and Being-ahead-of-oneself (existentiality), so the world also has these two characteristics. It appears as such only in the *Grundstimmung* of anxiety, where Dasein experiences its thrownness and where this thrownness, in that it is inseparable from a potentiality-for-Being, always means thrownness into a possibility of itself that cannot be overcome or annulled, thrownness into death. Therefore, the world's closedness is inseparable from the horizon of death as one's own death, death as *my death* ("death *is* just one's own"),[110] from dying as what still refers to a way of Being *towards* death, from dying as a modality of existing for-the-sake-of-oneself. Like death, the world *is There* in existence and therefore has a *mode of Being* for Dasein: "Dasein *is* its world existingly."[111] The world is always *my* world, like death is always *my* death, in that Being itself is constituted by mineness (*Jemeinigkeit*). It is "subjective," as Heidegger asserts, on the condition that the "subject" in question is itself conceived ontologically.[112]

This existential characterization of the world can be contrasted with an evential characterization trait by trait. Of course, an *advenant* is also "in the world," but here "the world" does not refer to an ontological a priori. Rather, the world is what befalls an *advenant* only inasmuch as he *is born* and originates in this *arch-event*. It is not an ontological constituent that belongs to the exemplary being independently of whether he exists factically or not. For an *advenant* is not an essence (*Wesen*) that is neutral with respect to every factical existent; his only "essence" is not having one: he is fundamentally determined as ex-per-ience.[113] Consequently, though the world may well be an a priori of his adventure, since it is the transcendental horizon of meaning from which every innerworldly fact can be understood as such—the world, as we have seen, has a hermeneutic structure—this a priori is nonetheless given a posteriori, such that this a-posteriority belongs to the meaning-character of its a-priority. The transcendental a-posteriority of every (evential) a priori is what attests to the original and irreducible character of birth for any understanding of the *advenant* and his eventials. Thus, to the extent that the world is what befalls an *advenant* from this primary event of his adventure—and is also what enworlds through the series of ensuing events—it follows that it cannot be originally determined by "mineness": rather, the world is that from which "I" advene to myself and that I can appropriate as such only according to the original disparity of originary and original, which belongs constitutively to the phenomenon of birth. The world is thus this array of possibilities that articulate my adventure on each occasion and that I can appropriate only inasmuch as I advene to myself: it is always given to me with a *transcendental impersonality.* By situating itself in this instant of world-virginity and impersonality that precedes the advent of a "Self," evential hermeneutics takes a further step *prior to* the analytic of Dasein, by bringing its presuppositions to light. By filling the absence of a conception about birth, it leads us to rethink Dasein's principal existentials.

The same holds for understanding. For Heidegger, understanding (*Verstehen*) is not a type of knowledge, but a "determination of existing."[114] Now, existence is essentially defined by mineness: Dasein is that being for which, in its very Being, Being is at stake. Therefore, for Dasein, understanding always means understanding itself in its potentiality-for-Being: "Understanding signifies one's projecting oneself upon one's current possibility of Being-in-the-world; that is to say, it signifies existing as this possibility."[115] If all understanding is potentiality-for-Being, where what it is at stake is essentially Dasein itself, then all understanding is a self-understanding of Dasein in its possibility. And, since no possibility is offered to this being except against the background of the possible impossibility of its existence—death—it follows that all understanding is a self-understanding of oneself as mortal (finite). This is why the meaning brought to light by understanding, "that wherein the understandability [*Verstehbarkeit*] of something maintains itself," "the 'upon which' [*das Woraufhin*] of the primary projection of understanding,"[116] always has Dasein's mode of Being (i.e., it exists): "That which we have such competence [*gekönnt*] over is not a 'what,' but Being as existing."[117] And so Heidegger can assert, in a formula that in a way summarizes all his analyses of this existential: "*only Dasein can be meaningful* [sinnvoll] *or meaningless* [sinnlos]."[118] There is no other meaning than that which articulates Dasein's Being, as an essentially finite being, and this is why the meaning of Being is finitude—that is, temporality. In other words, in understanding, where Dasein only ever has to do with itself and its Being, all meaning comes from the horizon of death, which closes existence back on itself and makes possible its totalization: only an understanding-Being-toward-death makes possible "the whole of Dasein completely 'given.'"[119] Any meaning that comes to light in existence is therefore essentially finite, in virtue of this ontological correlation of understanding and death.

It may be useful to point out again the distance that separates these analyses of Heidegger's and the ones I have undertaken, despite certain analogies. For an *advenant*, understanding is always marked by a kind of ex-centricity: understanding is always understanding something else—events—so that, through them, we can understand who we are. The interpretative possibilities from which an understanding-projection aimed at meaning becomes possible are not in our possession; they are allotted to us, in excess of any projection, by events themselves. This is what happens in the first of them, birth, by which a human adventure is opened to the excess of a meaning that goes beyond it. Understanding cannot make this meaning possible; rather, this meaning comes to understanding from elsewhere than the horizon that closes an adventure back on itself: my death. With birth, a human adventure is connected to a meaning that precedes it "from the outset," to a prepersonal history that overhangs it and that, by this very fact, confers a destiny on an *advenant*, who originally follows with a delay after his possibilities. Hence, birth gives understanding itself its delayed character: exceeded by the meaning of what is to be understood and plunged initially into incomprehension, understanding can bring meaning to light only by appropriating interpretative possibilities of which it is not the origin. This inexhaustible excess of meaning, as originally transcending, in that I am born, the horizon of my own finitude, is what pledges understanding itself to an in-finite task. I will never have finished the task of bringing to light the meaning of what is to be understood. First and foremost, this is because I am never contemporaneous with the a prioris that structure my own understanding. On the contrary, these a prioris are only arrayed for me according to the transcendental a posteriori of an irreducible legacy, with respect to which I am somehow always delayed. Hence, any possible meaning for an *advenant* does not come from his finite adventure, as it appears to him, closed on itself within the horizon of death; this meaning, by constitutively overflowing any mortal adventure, is by this very fact open to those who survive me: openness to the possibility of being taken up again by others, without which the task of understanding would be senseless for an *advenant*. In virtue of this inexhaustibility, the meaning of a human adventure eludes any possible totalization and can never be rendered entirely transparent (*durchsichtig*) in the instant of a resolution.

Only an analysis of birth and the perspectives it opens on our mortal adventure allows us to avoid what could be termed a certain "idealism of understanding" in *Being and Time*, according to which a meaning can only come to Dasein from Dasein itself, thereby confirming the latter's "closedness." This closedness—which is that of death—still plays a fundamental role in the existential characterization of selfhood. Heidegger observes: "In the 'ontology' of this entity [Dasein], the 'I' and the 'Self' have been conceived from the earliest times as the supporting ground [*tragende Grund*] (as substance or subject)."[120] From this arises the necessity of removing the phenomenon of selfhood from the self-exposition that everyday Dasein gives of itself, in saying all the more readily "I, I" the less it is *itself* in an existential sense—that is, having its Being dictated by the "they."[121] The question of the selfhood of this being gets its ontological start in the question of the authenticity (*Eigentlichkeit*) of its existence. This existence "is authentically and wholly what it can be, only as *anticipatory resoluteness.*"[122] Hence, it is in anticipating death that selfhood finds its existential ground: Dasein is authentically itself only when it resolutely relates to this possible impossibility of itself that is its potentiality-to-die. Indeed, death is an *unsubstitutable* possibility, which excludes any sharing or delegation: nobody can die in my place, and this is why death constitutes the genuine *principium individuationis* of my existence. It is from anticipating this ownmost and unsubstitutable possibility of Dasein that all the other possibilities that populate its existence receive their individuation. Resolute, Dasein "becomes free from the entertaining 'incidentals'"[123] and transmutes the possibilities that are offered to it by chance from the world and circumstances into destiny. Nevertheless, the unavoidable questions are the following: How can this unsubstitutable possibility of Dasein, the potentiality-to-die, confer individuality on existence, unless it has already received it from that existence? Cannot death only be determined as *my* ultimate and not-to-be-outstripped possibility if existence is already principally defined by mineness (*Jemeinigkeit*)? Here, there is a genuine circle, as Sartre emphasizes in *Being and Nothingness*.[124] For example, could one not maintain with equal right that selfhood is grounded in the possibility of being ill, since the event of illness is also one that no one can undergo in my place? But this circle is not so much a defect in reasoning as the explicit confirmation of the thesis that no event can occur to an existence other than this existence itself, and thus also the dying from which it is inseparable. The sole individualizing event for Heidegger is the very event of individuation: existing *as* dying. Heidegger would probably recognize that what he says about death holds just as much for any event: nobody can love in my place, be ill in my place, get married in my place, etc. But these events cannot have an existential status for him: the event of being, existing, is a dying—and this is the one and only event, stressed in different ways throughout his analysis of the various existentials. Nobody can be ill in my place, first and foremost, because I exist as mortal, and in some respect this unique event, attested to by resolution, makes possible all the others. Therefore, selfhood is based entirely on mortality as a *way of Being* (Seinsart) of Dasein.

But what are the consequences of such an analysis? If death—or rather, dying: anticipatory resolution—is what makes all other events possible, then *there are no more events* for Dasein. Its selfhood is never implicated in what happens to it, but is instead *formally* determined solely from the event of being, from existing as dying. Conceived entirely on the opposition between authentic and inauthentic, between two ways of Being-toward-death, selfhood in its existential sense remains entirely closed to any event: to this extent, it reproduces certain aporias of the traditional metaphysics of the subject, despite *Being and Time*'s "breakthrough" beyond that. This can be shown briefly. Existence's closedness on itself and Dasein's radical autarchy prohibit any evential conception of my history as what singularizes me. Far from determining myself in my singularity from the array of possibilities articulated in a world that are deployed for me in each event, I determine myself one time for all from one single and unique possibility: my death. Such a state of affairs derives, once again, from the fact that Heidegger's fundamental ontology absorbs all evential plurality into existing as dying. Thrown into this possibility that is not to be outstripped, resolute Dasein can take possession and mastery of its existence; it "can no longer be outstripped [*überholt*] by anything,"[125] not by any event, and it escapes all surprise, for example.[126] Conceiving selfhood existentially as "self-constancy [*Selbstständigkeit*]" of Oneself[127] excludes all otherness to oneself, all original difference with oneself, which would come to disturb the "Self-subsistence [*Selbstständigkeit*] of existence";[128] it is set against any self-renewal that might be possible from what happens to us. Dasein does not have to happen to itself starting from events; it is already and unconditionally itself in the enduring and supremely "transparent [*durchsichtig*]"[129] instant, where it is resolute and can embrace its existence in a single instant of vision (*Augen-blick*), gathering together death, birth, and what comes between them. Once it exists authentically, Dasein no longer loses its time nor loses itself in time by succumbing to the multiplication of the tasks of everydayness. It gathers itself together and unifies itself, eluding any dispersion. This is why selfhood is still defined here by the constancy or enduring of the Self in opposition to the scattering of the "they"—a "constancy" that is certainly not the permanence of a subject with subsistence (*Vorhandenheit*) as its mode of Being. This selfhood presumes a time that is essentially removed from any *loss*, from the "dispersal" of discontinuous nows, whose passage punctuates inauthentic time.[130]

By contrast, selfhood in its evential sense is not a formal condition of possibility for receiving [*accueil*] events but is an *uncondition*, according to which an *advenant* risks himself in what happens to him, himself advenes at the risk of himself, puts himself at stake in this risk, wherein he is himself the stakes. This sense of selfhood is inseparable from that self-transformation in undergoing what happens to us, by which singularity *happens* [advient] on each occasion. In this respect, it presupposes a time that is impossible to "hold," retain, or totalize, a time that an *advenant* ceaselessly gives and gives himself: time as pure "generosity," a continuing separation with oneself, which is also self-loss and rebirth. To appropriate an event by understanding oneself starting from it is at the same time, and on each occasion, to be transformed through undergoing it, to forget in a positive sense, to die to oneself and to others, to break away from a concluded past by opening oneself to a future that transcends any projection, to renounce all mastery or hold of one's adventure and of the temporality that events temporalize.

Such a selfhood, as possibility in play in every event to advene to myself as other through undergoing it, is not an object of knowledge. Nor can it be understood in the sense of a formal structure or a condition of possibility. It can only be undergone, in a nonempirical undergoing, through the events in which it is in play. Its possibility is only accessible from events, which put it to the test, and through which—at the risk of itself—it shows itself: what I will call *ex-per-ience.*

PART $\boxed{3}$

Experience

Every wound is a source.
—**Octavio Paz**, *Libertad bajo palabra*

A. The Primary Phenomenological Meaning of Experience

§19 Experience as Undergoing What Cannot Be Experienced

We have seen above that events as such cannot be experienced, if any experience, any *"empirie,"* is related exclusively to facts able to be explained within a world, a given evental context. As pure reconfiguration of possibilities, an event transcends any innerworldly fact and eludes any causal explanation. Neither causing anything itself nor being caused by anything, it is simply *origin* of the world. Origin inaccessible for any explanatory archeology and accessible only for an understanding that reveals its *meaning*.

But must not events at the same time be "experienced" in some way or other by the one to whom they occur? Is the empiricist concept of "experience," in terms of which events cannot be experienced, the only possible concept of "experience"? *In other words, is there not an experience that does justice to events in the evential sense?* Is there not, paradoxically, a nonempirical undergoing of what is, in itself, unable to be experienced? And, if so, how is this to be conceived?

a. The Problem of the Primary Phenomenological Meaning of "Experience"

What does "experience" signify? *Who* experiences? *What* is experienced? Before any attempt to answer these questions, we must first show their connection.

Undergoing [*faire*] an experience, *having* [*avoir*] experiences. In French, as in other languages (*Erfahrung machen*/*Erfahrung haben*), these two verbs govern thought about experience. The verb "to have" in the second formulation expresses the idea of possible accumulation, as if, by adding experiences to each other, they could give rise to acquisition or possession, a stable reserve that would be at the disposal of the *advenant* who we are. Experience is first of all knowledge, which grows over time; one who "has" experience is one who understands such and such a situation. One who is experienced is one who *has lived*: lived experience is expressed in German by *Erlebnis* (from *leben*: to live). It is not surprising that Husserlian phenomenology, which is motivated principally by a gnoseological problematic, has preferred *Erlebnis* to *Erfahrung* and has made it a key concept in its technical vocabulary. Each consciousness "has" its lived experiences: *Erlebnisse* are experiences of a consciousness inasmuch as that consciousness, appearing to itself, is able to describe them by setting out their pure a priori invariables. In order for this to happen, each lived experience must be able to give rise to a possible repetition, at least imaginary, which by varying the object's features brings forth its unvarying *eidos*. The experiences I have are repeated, and it is only on this condition that I can derive from them a stable knowledge that is valid beyond a singular experience.

Completely different is the idea suggested by the expression "undergo an experience." An experience that I undergo is that necessarily unique and unrepeatable ordeal, in which I am in play myself and from which I emerge changed on each occasion. The important thing here is not the idea of acquisition but, on the contrary, the idea of being put to the test, which is at the same time a transformation: I can only *undergo* an experience because it happens to me unsubstitutably, by allowing me to advene to myself, always anew, differently, unforeseeably. Heidegger specifies this point remarkably in *On the Way to Language*:

> to undergo an experience [*eine Erfahrung machen*] with something—be it a thing, a human being, or a god—means that this something befalls us [*es uns widerfährt*], strikes us, comes over us [*über uns kommt*], overwhelms and transforms us. When we talk of "undergoing" an experience, we mean specifically that the experience is not of our own making; to undergo [*durchmachen*] here

means that we endure it [*erleiden*], suffer it [*annehmen*], receive [*accueillir*] it as it strikes us [*das uns Treffende vernehmend*] and submit to it.[1]

To experience is to let ourselves be struck by what befalls us (*er-fahr-en ist vernehmen was uns wider-fährt*): here, Heidegger follows the German language very closely, insisting on -*far*- as the root for *Erfahrung*, in which the sense of traversal is present; *faran* in old high German, from which come *fahren*, to travel, and *führen*, to lead. Experience is a traversal, which presumes an intervening distance and a passing from self to self, which alone allows us to receive [*accueillir*] what happens to us by happening to ourselves as *other*. This is what etymology first teaches us: "experience" comes, in fact, from the Latin *experiri*, to put to the test. The radical is *periri*, in which can be seen the Indo-European root -*per*-, across, one of the richest in our languages.[2] Undefinable in itself, this root is present in a multitude of lexical forms, whose meanings at first seem to be foreign to one another. (1) "Enemy" (Sanskrit: *pára-h*) and, by derivation, "danger," which is found in the Latin *periculum*. (2) "Traversal" or "passage," which is clearly evident in Greek: *peirō*, to traverse; *peraō*, to pass through, to pierce, like an arrow; *perainō*, to go through to the end. In each case, *per* expresses a tension toward something that is beyond (Greek: *pera*, beyond), on the other side, and reached by a traversal (whence *peras*, limit; *poros*, ford; and *peratēs*, traveler, emigrant). But this cluster of meanings is not as disparate as it might first appear: every traversal is a danger; an enemy (Sanskrit: *pára-h*) is at the same time one who is far away, on the other side; in German, the meaning of *Erfahrung* is arranged along the same two axes as the Greek *empeiria*: on the one hand "traversal" and on the other "endangering" (*Gefahr*, danger, derived from the old high German *far(a)*; and *gefährden*, endanger), exposure, ordeal. As Roger Munier emphasizes: "On an etymological and semantic level, the idea of experience as traversal is difficult to separate from that of risk. From the outset, and probably fundamentally, experience is a putting-in-danger."[3]

But what kind of danger is this? It is such that I put myself at risk in it in the first person, en-gage myself in it, put myself literally at stake [*en gage*] or in play in what constitutes me essentially as such: in my selfhood. Experience is this risk of exposure to what touches me in the depths of my heart: to events, which alone, by being addressed to me unsubstitutably, allow me to advene to myself. "Event" must be understood here strictly: not as an innerworldly fact but as what, by reconfiguring all my essential possibilities, opens a world to me that is beyond any projection. If experience is henceforth understood in this radical sense of traversal and risk, where I am in play myself at the risk of losing myself, there will be no experience in the proper sense other than of events. The three questions posed at the start of this section thus begin to be clarified. Experience is that traversal toward oneself, at the risk of oneself, inasmuch as it is exposure to that which is altogether other: to events.

Which of these two concepts of experience (*having* experiences or *undergoing* them) is the primary phenomenological concept, from which the other could be derived, in a way that is still to be determined? The first concept, which I have attempted to expound by following language as a guiding concept, is the one that has become predominant philosophically in empiricism. As for the second, I will attempt to bring its original character to light, and will thus begin with it.

b. Ex-per-ience as Traversal and Danger

Experience, in the primary sense, is what profoundly modifies us by putting us in play ourselves, so that *after* having passed through, endured, and traversed, we will no longer be the *same:* to undergo illness, bereavement, or joy; to love, journey, write a book, or paint: these are "experiences" in this primary phenomenological sense, very simple, but not trivial. Indeed, in each example, the "vis-à-vis" of experience, that of which experience is an experience and to which it comes back, is always an *event,* for it is only by being exposed to an event that I am in play *myself,* in such a way that I can emerge transformed by the ordeal it serves on me unsubstitutably: to love, journey, etc., are fundamental events for an *advenant,* structuring his possibilities articulated in a world and determining his relation to others, with whom he shares these possibilities and this world that befall him. In this respect it matters little, when speaking of experience in general, that the event in question be "external," happening to me unplanned, in a radical "unpreparation," like a "twist of fate," an "accident," or an illness. The most "internal" events, for which I am the most "prepared" (a decision taken well in advance, the writing of a book that I have planned for a long time), are just as much the source of an *experience,* where the "traversing" from self to self is inseparable from risk and transformation and is possible *only* as this very "transformation"—a transformation that is not a change of state for a "subject" who remains identical in its alterations but is rather *the advent of self to self, in absolute difference with itself,* starting from an event's primary-surge [*prime-saut*] (*Ur-sprung*), the origin that is always already noncoinciding and deferred by the suspended bursting-forth of the present. Consequently, it matters little whether an event is "internal" or "external"—

presuming that this distinction is relevant for thinking about the event in question. On the contrary, as an event that opens a world, it is, like the world itself, at the same time more internal to me than any "interiority" and more external to me than any "exteriority."

What matters for determining the primary sense of experience is that every event, no matter how "prepared," has a "first time" character (*Erstmaligkeit*), which leaves us entirely exposed and as though naked before its radical novelty. While an innerworldly fact recurs, even if it undergoes empirical "variations," an event is always necessarily unique, that which will never be seen again; and because experience, in its primary phenomenological sense, is fundamentally experience of *events*, their first-time character belongs to it necessarily; it is new each time and forever incomparable. Contrary to any empiricist thesis, experience is not what recurs and would give rise to knowledge through its repetition, for experience is not fundamentally experience of *facts* and so cannot give rise to "facts of experience." In its properly human, evential, dimension, all experience is experience of the first time and for the first time: this is most apparent in the case of death, an experience that has never been undergone, that one does for the first and last time—the first being also the last—and that is thus "experience" in a singular and founding sense.[4] But in fact this holds for *any* experience, in that it is essentially a matter of *events*.

This primary characterization of experience leads us to reassert: since ex-per-ience, in its original sense, is not the knowledge of a *repeatable* innerworldly fact but rather the absolutely unique undergoing of what will never be seen again, ex-per-ience *teaches nothing*, in the sense that it would make possible the acquisition and accumulation of empirical knowledge. First, it is always *my* unsubstitutable experience, without common measure to another's; second, like events, unique and singular on each occasion, experience is always new and incomparable, signifying nothing other than the transformation of oneself, at the risk of oneself, starting from events. In this respect, nobody can teach their experience to another, for the experience they teach is always *their own*. Only events "teach" in the strict sense, nevertheless without transmitting any "knowledge": they *teach us about ourselves* by allowing us to *understand* ourselves. Ex-per-ience instead obliges me to "learn" at each instant *ex novo*, to undo myself and to distrust all my prior knowledge. Its role is fundamentally *negative*, as Hegel saw in *Phenomenology of Spirit*, in that it only "teaches" us to *unlearn*, to undo our prior knowledge and certitudes, by holding ourselves ready to learn anew from events themselves, by *transforming* ourselves to respond to their impersonal injunction.

If ex-per-ience teaches nothing, in the sense of making knowledge available, this is because it is not itself "knowledge" but is rather a *way of understanding oneself.* More precisely, it is *a way of understanding* events in their singularity and of thereby understanding oneself according to a hermeneutic circle that belongs to all understanding: events receive their individuation from the singularity of the one to whom they happen and vice versa. Thus, our failed loves teach us nothing, for love must be started again and relearned in each new love; it is an ex-per-ience that is only possible, paradoxically, if it is achieved *each time* "for the first time." Not that we could be as though new, and virgin of any past, in each singular experience; rather, experience, precisely to be ex-per-ience, must put us in play ourselves, such that the "risk" encountered there, of a measureless exposure to what happens to us, is the very one that gives its name to any genuine *adventure.*

All the same, if ex-per-ience is a way of understanding, then, inversely, understanding, in its properly eviential dimension, is always ex-per-ience, to the extent that it is inseparable from a transformation of the one who understands through events, which he understands, and from which he understands himself. Ex-per-ience is the eviential sense of understanding, in that this is inseparable from transformation and "distance" of self from self, or rather from putting at a distance: distanciation. To undergo an ex-per-ience is to understand oneself otherwise, in light of what happens to us, to accomplish a "traversal," at one's "peril." But if every ex-per-ience is *traversal*, it presumes an intervening distance and a passing through from self to self, through which we can receive [*accueillir*] what happens to us by happening ourselves as another. Ex-per-ience can only be a traversal if it puts past events at a distance, and so it is inseparable from a transformation of an *advenant* himself. To understand oneself in the eviential sense is always to understand oneself as *other*, as the one I have *become.*

If ex-per-ience, understood in the above sense, is not capable of delivering any empirical knowledge and does not allow anything whatsoever to be explained, this is because the understanding that is laid out there is, fundamentally, understanding of the unexplainable; its dimension is that of meaning, and resists every etiology. Even if I could explain an illness, for example—by setting out all its bacteriological, genetic, or allergenic causes—even if I could precisely date its beginning, determine all its stages, survey all the facts, symptoms, and psychological reactions that it brings about in the sick one, in spite of all that, I would never have shown the properly evential tenor of this phenomenon, nor would I have understood *the meaning* of such an experience for the one who suffers it. For, strictly speaking, an event is *nothing* of all this: it is only the reconfiguration of my adventure and of the world. And the *ex-per-ience* that I have undergone of it, this traversal of specific psychological lived experiences (*Erlebnisse*)—bodily suffering, feelings of fear, anxiety, and abandon—cannot itself be reduced to any of them. Just as "undergoing an experience" does not mean "having some lived experiences," so indeed the transformation, which is inseparable here from understanding, does not mean the passage from one "lived experience" to another within a particular "subject." Rather, it is what makes me able to say, after the fact, that this illness has changed me, has allowed me to *understand otherwise* the world, others, and myself. It is what makes it so that, having suffered and endured it, *I will never again be the same*. If there is an "alteration," this is not about lived experiences, but only about the *meaning* they can have for an *advenant*: it is solely about an *advenant*'s understanding of himself and of the world.

It follows that understanding here is not what comes "after" experience, as its "result" or consequence. On the contrary, it is nothing other than *its innermost movement*. Indeed, ex-per-ience, as "traversal" from self to self, is an *advenant*'s putting himself at a distance from what has taken place. It is through this distance that the *meaning* of past events is opened to him and that he is thus able to *understand* them. To understand a past event is just as much to understand what separates me from it, to understand what, *through a movement of ex-per-ience itself in itself*, has taken on a particular *meaning* for me, from the fissure that the event has introduced into my own adventure. Ex-per-ience is this evential understanding of oneself, inseparable from transformation—an understanding by which an *advenant* grasps himself again in his distance and strangeness from himself and thus understands himself in light of the events that befall him, without entirely recognizing himself. I only understand an event fully, in the original delay of its happening-in-suspense, when I no longer *undergo* it as such in the present, when I can submit it to a process of interpretation starting from that strangeness to myself that ex-per-ience has introduced into my own adventure. But how are we to conceive more precisely of this constitutive disparity and delay, which are at play in all understanding, in that understanding is never contemporary with the meaning of what it has to understand but is rather arrayed on each occasion according to the temporal distance of events themselves in their happening-in-suspense, such that they take place as a *sui generis* event only essentially "after the fact," in the transcendental a posteriori of their own temporalization?

§20 Understanding and Experience

a. The Problem of Preunderstanding

We have seen that all understanding is circular. Projection in the direction of meaning is always accomplished from a prior understanding and returns to deepen and possibly modify this preunderstanding in light of the meaning it brings to light. Classically, this "circle" has been called the "hermeneutic circle." The notion of the hermeneutic circle was initially used in the hermeneutic of *texts* (especially by Schleiermacher and Dilthey), designating the to-and-fro movement from part to whole and from whole to parts characteristic of a philologist's practice, where the whole is only understood by understanding the parts and vice versa. As one moves around the circle, understanding is modified and deepened; the circle of understanding never returns exactly to its starting point but is rather a spiral movement. This notion of a "hermeneutic circle" can be extended to all understanding in general (textual understanding, but also the understanding of phenomena in the broadest sense), on condition of a particular modification in its meaning. Here, it is no longer a matter of the to-and-fro, from part to whole and whole to parts, but of the movement between a particular prior understanding and the meaning actually brought to light by an interpretative projection. This extended meaning of the expression was legitimated in the framework of Heidegger's fundamental ontology and by Gadamer's project of a general hermeneutics. However, the status of this preunderstanding remains problematic: Is it entirely a priori or does it come down to a historical given fact? The interpretation of what "understanding" itself means is played out starting from this alternative.

At the risk of simplifying the problem, it is possible initially to attribute the first of the above two options to Heidegger. According to this theory, a preunderstanding of Being belongs to Dasein by the very fact that it exists, or essentially maintains a relation of Being to its Being. This preontological understanding of Being, as Heidegger also calls it, is the condition for any explicit ontological understanding, any conceptual elaboration of the categories and existentials that allow the apprehension of Being as such, in its difference from beings. Here, preunderstanding refers to a genuine (ontological)[5] a priori of Dasein, which belongs to it in that it exists. This a-priority of preunderstanding guarantees the universality of any understanding of Being. However, it raises the problem of knowing how this understanding arises *in fact*, since the tradition cannot provide any support here, being always connected to Dasein's fallenness, where Being is covered over in favor of beings.[6] In other words, it is the very event of understanding that becomes aporetic.

But it would be possible to maintain, against Heidegger's ontologization of understanding, that the preunderstandings that orient every interpretative projection come from a legacy and a tradition: they are characterized first of all by being historically rooted. And so, preunderstanding can be initially understood in the sense of a "prejudice" or collection of prejudices, belonging to a historical time or situation, and consequently belonging to a particular *facticity*. It is the multiplicity of factical preunderstandings that prevents an interpretation from ever illuminating these presuppositions to the point of rendering them entirely transparent. But it must be emphasized that this impossibility is a matter *of fact* rather than a matter of principle; it depends on a historical facticity from which understanding can never be freed. Interpretation's task of making explicit the prejudices that orient understanding can never be completely realized, because the "filtering" of prejudices cannot be achieved *in fact*: "The discovery of the true meaning of a text or work of art is never finished; it is in fact an infinite process. Not only are fresh sources of error constantly excluded, so that the true meaning has filtered out of it all kinds of things that obscure it, but there emerge continually new sources of understanding which reveal unsuspected elements of meaning."[7] By thus placing the emphasis on understanding's being rooted in the facticity of a historical legacy of which it is a tributary, this thesis of Gadamer's is much more capable than the previous one of accounting for the factical arising of understanding from the prejudices that orient it. On the other hand, what becomes problematic here is the universality of understanding: if the prejudices from which I understand are purely a mere factual given of my historical existence, it is difficult to see how it would be possible to escape a certain relativism. It is difficult to see how understanding could be set free from the relativity of its being historically embedded, so as to be valid beyond its contingent situation.

Before examining in what sense each of these conceptions is insufficient from an evential point of view, it is useful to return briefly to the simplification that underlies this presentation. It could rightly be objected that the recognition of the factical historical prejudices that orient understanding is so far from being incompatible with an ontology of understanding as developed in *Being and Time*, that Heidegger himself makes facticity an a-priori-ontological characteristic of Dasein. The thesis of ontological understanding's a-priority appears instead *inseparable* from the thesis of factical prejudices deposited in a tradition, prejudices that obscure under-standing and that consequently must be "destroyed" to reach the meaning of what is to be understood. From this perspective, the opposition sketched out between Heidegger and Gadamer could well be reduced to a mere difference of emphasis. This objection is certainly justified. How-ever, it is perhaps tangential to what is essential. Indeed, if understanding is an *evential*, it is the givens of the problem that need to be reconsidered. In what sense?

As we know, understanding can take on two forms: evental, if it has to do with innerworldly facts, which are able to be explained; or evential, if it relates to events where an *advenant* is in play himself in his selfhood. It is only the latter sense of understanding that is envisaged here: the one where what is at issue for an *advenant* is always himself in his adventure. Envisaged in this respect, understanding is an evential, a modality of the human adventure such as it is arrayed around events. Now, if all under-standing, in this sense, is a matter of *events*, preunderstanding has a partic-ular status here. Indeed, from one angle, it must in some way "precede" an event itself, for the latter to be understood and interpreted in its event-dimension: it is, if one wishes, an a priori of the human adventure. In this respect, it is indeed an understanding of events *in general*, without which any *universal* evential hermeneutics would not be possible. However, from another angle, preunderstanding could not precede the events whose meaning it has to interpret, as some sort of ontological-formal a priori: understanding events in general is possible only if I have undergone an event at least once and if in fact I myself only advene to myself from an event that inaugurates my own adventure (birth), the condition of all other events. In other words, far from the a priori of understanding being a condition of any evential understanding, it *is itself made possible by an event*, such that it is always given in some way a posteriori, according to an original delay, in which all subsequent understanding is set in its turn. For, as we have seen, understanding events is always apprehending them on a horizon of meaning that they have opened themselves, in that they are strictly nonunderstandable in the light of their explanatory context. Any evential understanding is inscribed in this delay, which runs through the adventure into which we are born from end to end, preventing any totalization of itself or of its meaning.

How, then, is the status of this preunderstanding to be conceived? If it can be defined neither as an ontological a priori of Dasein nor as a historical given fact—that is, as the horizon of all the historically dated prejudices deposited in a tradition and bequeathed by it, which articulate a given context—how is it to be interpreted? Clearly, preunderstanding is a priori, in the sense that an *advenant* must be fundamentally opened to events in general in order to be able to advene to himself freely from what happens to him. Nevertheless, this a priori is necessarily arrayed a posteriori, such that its a-posteriority belongs to the evential meaning-character of its a-priority. Such a preunderstanding no longer has, and can no longer have, the status of an ontological a priori, which thematic understanding would be limited to explicating; as such, it is never at an *advenant*'s disposal, with the result that he can never coincide with it in the full presence of an origin. Shaped at its core by this deferral, which runs through the adventure into which we are born and which confers its belated character on understanding, preunderstanding is rather a task; that is, it is an a priori that is constituted a priori by its very delay, indefinitely a posteriori, ceaselessly deferring its a-priority, or, in yet other terms, inseparable from the movement of understanding itself, in that it is arrayed, historically, as ex-per-ience. It is a task that, because it is infinite in principle or, rather, because it is the very movement of its infinitization, is also a "task" in a paradoxical sense, irreducible to any *telos* and to any teleology. In all understanding, I am exceeded by the excess of meaning that precedes me immemorially from my birth, which is arrayed on each and every occasion starting from interpretative possibilities that are not made possible by me, and which makes all appropriation an infinite task, transcending the horizon of death and my own finitude. But is there not also a finitude of understanding? To what extent can this finitude be reconciled with understanding's character as unlimited and nondefinitive? Is it not inseparable from the intrinsically *experiential* character of understanding?

b. The Finitude of Understanding and the Infinity of Meaning

What becomes of the problem of understanding's unlimited character, according to the perspective sketched out here? On the one hand, it is important to reject the ideal that *Being and Time* continues to maintain: that of a full and complete understanding in which the meaning of existence would be made entirely transparent for Dasein in the instant of resolution, where it reaches its total potentiality-for-Being. On the other hand, neither is it possible to reduce understanding's unlimited character to a simple historical facticity, as if this facticity were itself a *factical* characteristic of understanding, as if the impossibility of reaching a total meaning were due only to presuppositions, prejudices, etc., that "encumber" understanding and from which it would first need to be freed. On the contrary, if there is a *finitude* of understanding, which prevents it from ever entirely appropriating the meaning of what is to be understood, if understanding is thereby consigned an inexhaustible task, this finitude is not due to any historical "facticity," of which understanding would itself be the tributary; rather, it is due to understanding's intrinsic constitution. The delay with which any interpretation can appropriate a meaning that constitutively precedes and exceeds it does not arise from a supposed historical "facticity" but instead belongs to the a-priori-evential character of its meaning. This evential character depends, in turn, on the *advenant* being basically characterized by the event of his advent in the world, birth, as absolute nonground, *irreducible to any "facticity."*

The finitude of understanding should not be conceived starting from Dasein's Being-toward-death, but rather starting from birth. In the precursor and inaugural event of its coming into the world, a human adventure is open to a nonground that an *advenant* does not himself make possible. It is solely starting from this nonground that any making-possible and any subsequent event can happen. In virtue of this inborn fissure, which runs through an adventure-as-projection and sets it in relation to an absolute nonground that it does not make possible but is instead that from which any possibility befalls it, our possibilities do not arise from a free projection toward death, but transcend any projection and originate in events: they are, literally, *eventualities.* It is the same here for my interpretative possibilities. That fissure that is found in the adventure into which we are born as such is what makes all projection derivative, and consequently also all projections of understanding: these are preceded and exceeded by the interpretative possibilities addressed to an *advenant* before any of his projections, which interpretative possibilities he must instead appropriate, according to an original delay. Preunderstanding is not originally in his possession; rather, he must always appropriate it by understanding in the original rupture from any origin—a rupture established by the very event of *birth.* This is why preunderstanding can only be grasped after the fact, on the background of a primary and fundamental incomprehension, just as selfhood only happens to an *advenant* starting from an initial irreducible anonymity.

Indeed, no understanding can happen without incomprehension: understanding a text, a phenomenon, or an event always wrenches it away from an initial incomprehension, and it is only in relation to this incomprehension that *meaning* [sens] can be conquered and drawn out from non-sense. As we have seen, this is not a matter of incomprehensibility *in fact*, which would be the impossibility of clarifying and making entirely transparent the set of presuppositions that orient any projection of understanding. *For there is no understanding that is not confronted from the outset by the incomprehensible.* It is only *where the incomprehensible is found,* and in the name of this incomprehensible, that it is possible to question the preunderstandings that form the legacy and tradition that orient comprehension, by revoking these preunderstandings in classing them as misunderstandings. Any understanding is possible only as a progression beyond an initial incomprehension from which it is inseparable. It is because an *advenant*'s birth has always taken place; because he is never contemporary with the first event of *his advent* in the world, which he undergoes as long as he happens, but always as deferred; because, consequently, this initial event has always conferred possibilities (including interpretative possibilities) on him with a constitutive delay, before he can appropriate them—it is because of all this that incomprehension is necessarily *primary*, such that the inexhaustible meaning addressed to an *advenant* from the nonground of birth is revealed as a bottomless source of incomprehensibility, a *nonsense*,[8] through which alone understanding can come to light.

However, this "non-sense," this "incomprehension"—like the nonground of adventure—does not signify something primarily *negative*. In fact, it refers to a positive phenomenon: namely, *the absolute excess of meaning in general* over all appropriative understanding. The "non-sense" in question is *a modality of meaning*, in its inexhaustible excess over all interpretation. From the inaugural event of birth onward, a human adventure is open to *the infinity of a meaning that does not originate in me*—inexhaustible in principle rather than *in fact*. Here, the inexhaustibility of *meaning* is the inexhaustibility of interpretative possibilities, which, because they are opened to me starting from the nonground of birth, do not close over with death either. I will never exhaust the meaning that is given to me to understand starting from my birth, not only through a language that is assigned to me without being made for me, a language that I have to appropriate with the infinity of possibilities of speech that it holds in reserve, even though this infinity remains irreducible to this appropriation *in principle* (because it radically transcends any singular attempt at speech), but also through the inexhaustibility of historical possibilities, which are bequeathed to me by a transpersonal history that is radically *unable to be taken over*, for it surpasses any possibility of appropriation but is the sole ground—ground that is also *nonground*—on which I can grasp myself. Thus, the *original delay* of all understanding arises from the fact that, far from being an a priori structure of existence, understanding is structured by an original delay; it is essentially belated and therefore *necessarily* a posteriori, with an a posteriori that is not empirical but rather *transcendental*.

Hence, one can better understand the assertion that understanding is inseparable from an ex-per-ience, understood in a different sense from that of empiricism: here, ex-per-ience is nothing other than *the a-priority of this a-posteriority*, which belongs to comprehension as such. If ex-per-ience is a way for an *advenant* to understand himself, understanding itself is only possible according to the transcendental a priori of ex-per-ience. Indeed, to understand an event is no longer to recognize ourselves in what we were; it is to undergo a radical foreign-ness to oneself and an incommensurability with oneself established by the event, in its happening *outside anything that can be measured* against ourselves. If understanding an event is to understand oneself starting from it, by measuring the incommensurable gap with oneself to which it gives rise, then this is to understand oneself *as no longer being able to understand entirely what we were before undergoing it.* This incomprehension, which lies at the heart of ex-per-ience, is not only the result of undergoing an event but is also what precedes it and makes it possible from the outset. Events are precisely what opens this fissure and distance of ex-per-ience in an adventure, allowing not only the acquisition of a new orientation for projection (i.e., understanding *differently*) but also allowing a *better* understanding.

But what does "better" mean here? It signifies the more powerful character of an interpretation that is able to account for a greater number of phenomena than the preceding, weaker, interpretations. However, I can only understand "better" on the condition of never understanding *everything.* Any better understanding, which is consequently conquest over a misunderstanding, can only account better for the phenomena it interprets if it is also conscious of its inherent finitude, that is, conquest over the non-sense that runs through a human adventure from end to end, in that an *advenant* comes into this by being born. Because he must necessarily be born, an *advenant* is handed over to the opacity of a meaning that prohibits in principle any self-transparency for comprehension. Consequently, the "best" understanding rests on an incomprehension that precedes it just as much as does the weakest, and it is solely on the grounds—the *nonground*—of this incomprehension that either understanding can be grasped. All understanding is an advance on misunderstanding, but at the ground of both (as their nonground) lies a more radical incomprehension, which arises from the irremediable excess of meaning over any appropriative understanding. At the very moment of understanding, I realize all that is to be understood and that I do not understand. I can only understand "something" because I cannot understand *everything.* And nevertheless, all understanding, to be able to be "better," must have a global aim, even if it can never claim to bring to light the totality of meaning, which is necessarily and in principle *inexhaustible*. Understanding is always a singular event and can only be "global" according to an orientation directed on the phenomenon in question, through which a meaning comes to light that is itself determinate. Understanding can claim a universality only through the singularity of its projection of understanding.

But how are these two dimensions to be properly articulated: the singularity of every act of understanding in its historical relativity, and the universality at which it does and must aim if it wishes to escape relativism? In fact, this question is identical to the one put to the properly evential meaning of ex-per-ience: for there the universal cannot be given as a *terminus a quo*, an ontological a priori, for example; it is necessarily a *terminus ad quem*, the "term" of a passing from self to self as being exposed to events—wholly inseparable from ex-per-ience, which is arrayed as history.

By happening, every event introduces a meaning into the adventure into which we are born, which that adventure did not carry with it but which it must instead appropriate: the *meaning* here being that which has always anticipated any understanding, by opening it to its inexhaustible excess, to the incomprehensible. Now, this appropriation is itself possible only by the *advenant*'s transformation and his becoming foreign to the past: only such a distance with respect to the past allows him to bring about new projections of understanding, which were not heralded by the past. Understanding, defined as appropriative understanding, according to a determinate interpretative projection, of a meaning introduced by events, as opening to its own inexhaustible excess—to the incomprehensible—is identical to the nonempiricist sense of ex-per-ience. This becoming-foreign by and through undergoing an event, as appropriative understanding, according to a determinate projection and a definite orientation of comprehension, of the irremediably excessive (inexhaustible) meaning that the event introduces into a human adventure—an adventure that cannot be totalized in a self-projection in understanding—this is, precisely, "ex-per-ience."

§21 Experience as a Fundamental Characteristic of Humanity, and the Question of Transcendental Empiricism

In a vague and nontechnical sense, each human being "knows [*connaît*]"[9] experiences throughout their life. However, neither the anthropological concept of "human being" nor the biological concept of "life" suffices for grasping the meaning of these phenomena. Moreover, "knowing" does not signify here a "human being" having a "theoretical" relation to an "object" of experience. For in no way is an event an *ob-ject* in the sense of something *ob-stant*, standing before us as the vis-à-vis (*Gegen-stand*) of a "subject." To "know" an event is *to undergo* it in a nonempirical way, to be transformed by and through it, to cross the interval from self to self that is necessary for any ex-per-ience. Events carve out the distance of this interval from birth, by opening an adventure to the boundless gaping of an absolute nonground, to a "meaning" that does not come from itself, to the excess of a possibility that it does not make possible, and by setting this adventure in relation to a past earlier than any past that can be re-called. In this respect, ex-per-ience is not something that is at a human being's disposal (as is suggested by the misleading expression "having ex-periences"): he does not make ex-per-ience but is instead made by it; it is only in and through ex-per-ience that he has access to his humanity. Here, his "humanity" means nothing other than measureless exposure to events—according to which alone he can *advene to himself* as such (a human being). *Ex-per-ience* is not determinable from a prior concept of "human being," as one of his "faculties." Rather, the humanity of the human being is characterized in principle in terms of ex-per-ience: to be a human being is to be exposed beyond measure to events and thereby *to be capable of ex-per-ience*. Only a human being is capable of experience in this sense, as only he can be in a relation to events such that he is in play *himself* in them. No doubt, an animal *has* experiences, but no animal "knows" the original phenomenon of ex-per-ience, lacking the power to grasp themselves in ex-per-ience, lacking also the power to lose themselves entirely in it by risking themselves in the first person.

But what does it mean, more precisely, for the humanity of the human being to be fundamentally characterized as ex-per-ience? Ex-per-ience only happens singularly, since it originates in events on each occasion. Moreover, in its original sense, it signifies the becoming-singular of an *advenant* through undergoing what happens to him: his *singularization*. However, to the contrary: Is not humanity that supraempirical generality in light of which differences can be unified in a common essence? How can humanity in its generic universality be identical to ex-per-ience, that is, identical to the singular undergoing of events, in their irreducible sin-gularity, through which I singularize myself? These objections only make sense, however, if the singular and universal are conceived apart from each other: if, on the one hand, the universality in question is understood in the sense of the impersonal and empty generality of a genus, which can only subsume differences by holding itself above them, and if, on the other hand, the singularity of ex-per-ience is conceived simply in the sense of a straightforward particularity, resistant to any generalization—in short, only if the singularity of ex-per-ience is interpreted in the sense of an empirical particularity and if the universality of the human is interpreted in the sense of a supraempirical generality. But does not such an opposition burst apart under the constraints of the "things themselves"? Have not the preceding analyses put us on the path of a different understanding of the singular-universal relation, such that the opposition suggested here betrays its own inadequacy?

What is universal in humanity is precisely this capacity to singularize oneself through what happens to us, which I am calling "ex-per-ience." Humanity is not given as a generic, transempirical, and transindividual essence, apart from singular men and women. It is only arrayed across the irreducible singularity of ex-per-ience, as what singularizes *me*. Humanity *happens* on each occasion only as singular. This assertion should not be interpreted as a nominalist thesis supporting the nonexistence of universals: it is not a metaphysical thesis bearing on the status of certain "entities" as either mental or real. On the contrary, refusing to give human universality the status of an essence in the traditional sense and insisting that humanity is arrayed as ex-per-ience still entails a thesis about essence: namely, that the essence of the human being is not to have one. Or, to put it more exactly: the human "essence" is ex-per-ience, the capacity to advene to ourselves singularly through what happens to us, and consequently to be irreducible to any generic essence. For ex-per-ience is not that from which knowledge about the human being *in general* can be acquired. It is, on the contrary, what allows me to learn each time *ex novo*, to hold myself in the joyful or sorrowful novelty of an event and thereby welcome new experiences in their incomparable singularity; it is something whose role is essentially negative, since it first of all teaches us to unlearn, to rid ourselves of our prior knowledge, so as to hold ourselves open to what happens to us, that is, to be ourselves in the face of events. This is why ex-per-ience, in singularizing us, *opens us to the irreducible singularity of each human being*. Far from abstractly revealing an impersonal generality—through "induction," for example—the movement of ex-per-ience is entirely oriented to the possibility of singularly learning the unique, not only the unique as it is assigned to me through events but also the unique as it is given to me to "know" in a singular encounter with another. If the human is essentially what is given to us to understand in all ex-per-ience, this comes not under the guise of an abstract generality, but in the face turned to us by another. In other words, experience gives us something of the human "in general" to understand only by opening us to another in his uniqueness, such that if there is "knowledge" here at all, it is not of a generic essence but of an ex-per-ience that is on each occasion singular. This singularity of ex-per-ience is the condition of possibility for any elevation of comprehension to universality. If the universality of humanity is only accessible through singular ex-per-ience, this is because *humanity itself (the universal) is ex-per-ience, that is, the capacity to become ourselves (a singular) through undergoing what happens to us.* Thus, if humanity is accessible to us, it is not only *from* ex-per-ience but *as* this ex-per-ience itself, insofar as it singularizes us. It is in becoming myself that I understand humanity in me and outside of me, not in the sense of a theoretical knowledge, exterior to its object, but in the sense of an understanding that is *given* only through undergoing, as the traversing and enduring of the human: ex-per-ience in its first and primary sense.

In virtue of his ex-per-ience itself, every human being is everyman, universal *by virtue of* being singular. The humanity of a human being is ex-per-ience, the capacity to singularize oneself, formally synonymous with selfhood in its evential sense. To be a human being is to be capable of becoming oneself, and to be a self is to be capable of becoming a human being, of appropriating one's own by becoming it, in an irreducibly unique way. This amounts to saying that being a human being is being able to be a self, to have selfhood. All these assertions converge and complete one another. Through them, we can better understand the sense in which characterizing a human being as "*advenant*" is not simply an arbitrary substitution of one term for another. This substitution can claim legitimacy first of all because, as we saw earlier,[10] evential hermeneutics does not operate at the same level as empirical-factual sciences (anthropology, ethnology, psychology, sociology, etc., which aim to explain facts from their causes); it is the sole approach that grapples with the question of *the origin of meaning* for a human adventure. Moreover, as is now clearly apparent, this substitution can also claim legitimacy because humanity only *happens* [advient] as singular; that is, humanity in its properly *evential* dimension signifies the very capacity to advene as oneself (singular). Thus, "humanity" is a synonym for "selfhood," in being a fundamental characteristic of an *advenant* in his adventure.

Thus, from an evential perspective, being human is not participating in a universal genus: to be "human" is to undergo the unsubstitutable ordeal of what is given to be understood in the event of *birth* as such. Such an understanding only really approaches universality to the extent that it immerses itself in singular ex-per-ience. For the universality that it attains is not the empty generality of something that is valid in a totally undifferentiated way for anyone at any time, like a mathematical theorem, for instance. To the generality of mathematical theorems must be opposed a thoroughly *experiential* understanding, which only rises to a universal by drawing on the unique. It is only through ex-per-ience that I can undergo being human, and "know" this as identical to ex-per-ience in its original sense. This nonempirical sense of ex-per-ience, along with the nongnoseo-logical sense of "knowing," upon which I have been attempting to shed light, are by no means "novel" senses, introduced for the sake of the argu-ment, drawing on a technical vocabulary that is abstract and foreign to common sense. Greek tragedy, for example, understands the humanity of the human being starting from this fundamental dimension. Aeschylus's famous phrase *"to pathei mathos* [knowledge through undergoing]"[11] evokes this constitutive dimension of humanity. To be human is to un-dergo experience in suffering, to suffer what one is given to undergo in the very event of *being born human, and being only human.* A human being is not himself through an understanding of his essence, as though it were at his disposal, nor by virtue of an understanding of *Being* that would allow him to understand himself as a being who has an ontological consti-tution of one kind or another (Da-sein). For such an understanding of oneself and of humanity remains *theoretical*, to the extent that, here, "knowing [*connaître*]" oneself as such does not signify co-birth [*co-naître*] to oneself in a continuing self-undergoing: unsubstitutably undergoing this ex-per-ience.

However, holding that a human being only "knows" in undergoing or, in more precise terms, that *the humanity of a human being, in the evential sense, is ex-per-ience*, does not imply that the human being has no "es-sence," in that his existence "precedes" his essence and he must constantly choose himself (Sartre): such a characterization still specifies an essence in the traditional sense; it simply amounts to holding that freedom, as an undetermined potentiality to choose oneself, is the essence of a human being, in the sense of a common genus. By contrast, asserting that the humanity of a human being, interpreted in the evential sense, is ex-per-ience, signifies that a human being's humanity is never a "given," a ge-neric essence that transcends individuals, but is what is reached with great struggle at the price of an ordeal. There is no such thing as a nontemporal essence of a human being, which could be our measure. Rather, our hu-manity is something we are exposed to beyond measure and that befalls us in the constantly suspended event through which, from birth, we un-derstand it and understand ourselves in it, by becoming ourselves (singular).

A human being does not have experiences; ex-per-ience is rather what makes it possible to conceive of her in her humanity. Experience must itself be thought in terms of this essential inversion: it is not "experience" of some innerworldly fact but exposure to the very *event* of advening to oneself as a human being that befalls us from our birth, and the continuing undergoing of which is time. Such ex-per-ience can only do justice to events, as occurring beyond its measure, if it does not refer to any prior structure of a "subject," to any structure of "reception [*accueil*]" rooted in that subject's transcendental constitution. Rather, ex-per-ience is the playing field and reception [*accueil*] space opened to an *advenant* by each event itself—in and through its arising. Consequently, ex-per-ience, conceived in terms of events, is the possibility of allowing an event to cross over us, to happen in its unexperienceable occurring, to transform us by irrupting in our human adventure from the nonground of its initial advent. Far from being a subjective "faculty," a transcendental condition of reception [*accueil*], ex-per-ience is the very way in which an *advenant* advenes to himself—a passing from self to self, at the risk of oneself, by being exposed to the totally other: to events. Thus, it is events themselves that provide the "condition" for ex-per-ience and that alone can hold a "transcendental" status. It is only from events, according to an *essential delay*, that we are given the possibility of "knowing" ourselves (in a non-gnoseological sense: "knowing [*connaître*]" signifying here only co-birth [*co-naître*] with events, being transformed by undergoing their ordeal) by understanding what happens to us and by understanding *the one to whom* that happens as being precisely ourselves.

Thus, ex-per-ience in its original phenomenological sense is the milieu for all understanding, in that it is a matter of events. Such an ex-per-ience is not the "experience" of empiricism, which is concerned with inner-worldly facts, which are repeatable and able to be foreseen in some way through the regularities they demonstrate. While experience as understood by empiricism can serve as a starting point for the transcendental question that bears on the conditions of its possibility, the ex-per-ience we are discussing *is the genuine transcendental* from which the humanity of a human being can be understood and characterized. But is it not an extraordinary paradox to say that ex-per-ience itself, in its nonempiricist sense, is *the very instance of the transcendental*? No doubt. But before asserting this, we need to clarify the sense this assertion could have.

Classically, "transcendental" can have two distinct meanings: first, in its scholastic sense, it is that which has a universality transcending any generic universality (thus, there are three transcendentals: *ens, unum (bonum),* and *verum*); second, in a modern sense, it means the instance of "conditions of possibility": the transcendental subject fills the role of epistemological *fundamentum*—whether one asserts, with Kant, the impossibility of experiencing this *fundamentum* or admits, with Husserl, the possibility of such an experience by means of a phenomenological *epoché*.

The assertion above that ex-per-ience in its original sense is itself the instance of the transcendental should be understood strictly in terms of the two semantic axes illustrated in the traditions just cited. First, ex-per-ience is the most *universal* characteristic of the human being, radically transcending the pure generality of a genus; what is at stake here is his own humanity, insofar as that fundamentally signifies the capacity to advene to himself *singularly* and, consequently, to have a history. Indeed, *the most universal* trait of the human being is the possibility that he is given of advening to himself and thereby acquiring a singularity. This most universal characteristic is such that it precedes any essential characteristic, in the sense of a genus that would subsume all individuals, and is irreducible to that essence. The characteristic feature of ex-per-ience is precisely that it dissolves any generic essence, and the unique "essence" of a human being is not to have one.

Second, ex-per-ience indeed refers to the instance of the transcendental: not in the sense of a formal condition of possibility, of course, but in the sense of always being an issue of an event. It refers to the dimension of play in which an *advenant* is himself at stake and of which he is himself the stakes—a dimension that does not precede events but is opened by them, as a condition (without condition) of its own advent. The "condition of possibility" in question here should therefore not be understood in the sense of a formal condition in the subject, at the core of a hypothetical regress (Kant), but rather in the sense of a *making-possible* by events. In fact, ex-per-ience cannot be understood and characterized in reference to innerworldly facts: it has no "vis-à-vis" other than *the transcendental itself*, what escapes in principle any empirical experienceableness and any *empirie* in general: *event* as world-configuring. This is the sole transcendental for any *advenant*.

Thus, "transcendental" can be said, in the first place, of ex-per-ience itself as *the most universal* characteristic of a human being: the capacity to advene oneself as singular through a history. But, second, "transcendental" can also be said even more originally of events, and only afterward of ex-per-ience, in that there is only ex-per-ience of events, which are the "condition of possibility"—themselves unconditioned—for the advent of something such as an "*advenant*."

To the extent that ex-per-ience becomes the instance of the transcendental, the hermeneutic phenomenology with the task of presenting its modalities and meaning can be called *transcendental empiricism*. Such an "empiricism" is satisfied neither with the naïve empiricist thesis, according to which the "facts of experience" lie at the origin of all knowledge, nor with the naïve realist thesis, according to which facts themselves are "reality." It is therefore situated outside the classic alternative of realism and idealism, empiricism and rationalism. Indeed, it conceives the transcendental starting from the signal transcendence of event as such with respect to any state of affairs and innerworldly fact. Such an empiricism is also—if one wishes—a "realism" to the extent that events, which are more "exterior" to an *advenant* than any fact in the world, are also that starting from which all self-intimacy and "interiority" is constituted. More "foreign" to an *advenant* than any state of affairs, events are the condition, for him, of any advent to himself: they are as real and even "more real" than empiricism's facts.

§22 Experience and Speech

The relation between the meaning of a phenomenon brought to light in comprehension and the *speech* by which in turn this meaning becomes apparent for another cannot merely be one of "explication [*Auslegung*]," as *Being and Time* still suggests. For if all understanding is articulated by means of speech, which gives it voice and body in the world, the inverse is also true: speech is not limited to explicating an understanding that is self-transparent and self-sufficient, of which it would be a secondary and derivative incarnation, as though words were joined to meaning externally and without necessity. On the contrary, far from being the pure reflection of a preexisting meaning, speech *puts understanding to the test*, such that understanding cannot be fully grasped as such prior to its advent-event as speech. It is speech alone that allows me to learn what I *wish to say*, making me understand for myself and for others what would remain unarticulated without it. This apprenticeship *of* speech (in the sense of both an objective and a subjective genitive) is, strictly, an *ex-per-ience*. To undergo an ex-per-ience with speech is, literally, to understand what I wish to say by learning it [*l'apprenant*] from speech, that is, by *taking* speech up [*la prenant*]. *To take up speech*, an inaugural event, whose status and meaning we will have to describe, is not a neutral act by which I would limit myself to bringing to pass in a preexisting language an intended meaning that would be wholly independent. The "intertwining" of thought and speech, on which Merleau-Ponty meditates, foils any simple interpretation of an act of speech in relation to a fund of language from which it would draw *words*, on the one hand, and, on the other, an understanding and intended meaning whose *meaning* it would articulate. On the contrary, a *speech event* is irreducible to any "attainment" or prior possession (any "linguistic competence," any intended meaning articulated according to a meaning that understanding alone would give rise to), and this very irreducibility is precisely what makes it possible as an act of speech: a speech event in which signified and signifier arise together, a condition of possibility for the advent of a "speaking subject"—and not the reverse. *In an act of speech, the advent of speech and the event of meaning are one and the same.*

What does "taking up speech" signify? What is in play in such an event? Not less than the possibility of articulating comprehension as such and putting it to work. But this possibility is itself irreducible to any prior condition. *Indeed, annulling any prior "possibility" is the "condition" of that which escapes any condition (of possibility): events as such.* Henceforth, an act of speech can be inaugural only if it is irreducible to its own "conditions." Of course, an "intended meaning" and a language must "precede" an act of speech, which would be impossible without them. However, speech, like an *event*, is irreducible to its own "conditions" and annuls them in arising. Taking up speech is always an initiation to speech; it has no prior "attainment" at its disposal, no "linguistic competence," as capacity to put a given language's system of syntaxic and morphological rules to work, nor, consequently, a "language" that is already given and available and by this fact reduced to the rank of a mere tool. For though it is indeed possible, after the fact, to formulate these rules, they do not explain an act of speech itself nor allow us to trace its genesis. Nor does speech have available a self-transparent intended meaning, whose sense it would articulate. *Because there is no such thing as a pure "intended meaning" prior to a speech event, neither is there a given language that would provide this "intended meaning" with a fund from which it could draw its words, by adapting them to a prior signification.*

Indeed, if we can "take up speech," this is because speech is not in our possession at the outset, like some item of property we could *use*: speaking is not a matter of *using symbols*, "adapting" them to a meaning that is already self-transparent in our comprehension. Conversely, language can be considered as a tool that is at our disposal only if we presuppose the autonomy of a signification that would be given to us in understanding prior to being articulated as speech. As a result, language is in no way at the disposal of the one who speaks: speaking never consists in merely *applying* syntactical or morphological rules that we have progressively learned and "integrated," nor in drawing on a lexicon, for speech is more original than language, which only acquires its meaning and status in being put to work as speech. Though we may well be able to reconstruct and analyze a language's rules after the fact, as a kind of "code," in no way does this *explain* the *event* of speech, or, at the limit, it gives only a semblance of explanation. "Signification" itself is not "engendered" by the application of a language's rules, considered here as a code; rather, it *happens* in the event of speech and is, consequently, irreducible to these rules.

So, *taking up speech* is never a simple act, like picking up a hammer or opening a door: this "action" cannot be phenomenologically interpreted in terms of a hierarchically ordered set of means and ends, according to the scheme of goals that applies to a tool. Indeed, in a sense that Heidegger profoundly meditated on in *On the Way to Language*, it is not we who have speech at our disposal but speech that has us at its disposal—and this is so insofar as an act of speech must be interpreted originally as an *event*. To take up speech is to situate oneself in that inaugural instant where I am one with the *saying* of speech, with its own *energeia*, in being one with its very arising. This is what is attempted by poets, for whom nothing "exists" before being named. As Hölderlin says, prior to the poetic act, neither the poet, nor the world, nor the language for expressing it has yet begun to be:

> Namely, in that the poet feels himself comprehended in his entire inner and outer life by the pure tone of his primordial sensation and looks around in his world, this is as new and unfamiliar to him; the sum of all his experience, of his knowledge, of his intuition, of his thinking, art and nature, as they present themselves within him and outside of him, everything exists, as it were, for the first time and for that reason is uncomprehended, undetermined, dissolved into pure matter and life, present to him; and *it is especially important that at this instant he takes nothing for granted, proceeds from nothing positive, that nature and art, as he comes to know them and sees them, speak not until there exists a language for him . . .* for if, prior to the reflection on the infinite subject matter and the infinite form, there exists for him some language of nature and art in specific form, then he would to that extent not be in his sphere of effect; he would step outside of his creation.[12]

The event of poetic speech—though all inaugural speech, which as such is an event, can only be "poetic" to the extent that it coincides with its own *energeia*[13]—is that by which a language "is there" for a poet, as Hölderlin says: the former does not preexist the latter, as linguists suggest. Indeed, to follow linguists in beginning from Saussure's distinction between "language" and "speech"[14] would be to render the *event* of speech strictly incomprehensible, as it arises inaugurally in poetic speech; it would be to make speech a simple *product* of language, wholly determined by the application of its rules and the actualization of its lexicon; now, the disjunction between "language" and "speech" only applies in the instant where speech, raised to its poetic power, establishes a real beginning, the event of a meaning that annuls all preexisting understanding, the event from which alone I appropriate to myself the "language" in which this speech can be pronounced. For it is the event itself (*Er-eignis*) that grounds the appropriation of one's own—and thus also of one's own language. In such an event, says Hölderlin, neither the former world, the "language of nature," nor the language of art any longer has anything to say to us. It is against the background of collapse and cataclysm, when language itself, nature and the world, show themselves to the poet "dissolved into pure matter and life," as not understood and undetermined, as though they were being presented to him for the first time, that a new speech can arise that no longer draws its resources from a common language but on the contrary raises this language to its poetic potential. In this cataclysm of language, without which speech's arising would itself be impossible, the well understood becomes for us nonunderstood. We must unlearn language, its lexicon and syntax, its "idiomatic" expressions, and all the past that it carries with it, so as to allow speech to speak in its joyfully arising novelty and to happen as an event. At the same time, we must agree to learn everything from it, by placing ourselves in that instant of "the virginity of the world," as Cézanne puts it. We must agree to learn everything from the renewed understanding that comes to light through the event-advent of speech, that is, strictly, *to undergo an ex-per-ience with it.*

Here, ex-per-ience signifies comprehension's primary exposure to the inaugural power of speech, to its poetic event-advent, which means that I can only understand what I say when I let "speech speak," so as to grasp, in the *after-the-fact* of understanding itself, the irreducibly new meaning that comes to light through speech. Understanding always already *traversed* and *saturated* by the event of speech, unable to reach a "pure" meaning, which would be open *before* the event of speaking, a pure "intended meaning," which would declare itself apart from the act of speech. Thus, understanding can only be articulated in speech if it is the *very ex-per-ience* of that speech setting itself forth: traversing speech as exposure to its poetic event-advent, through which a meaning is opened up, wrenched from non-sense.

It is only from this perspective that Rilke can declare, in *The Notebooks of Malte Laurids Brigge*, that "poetry is not sentiment, it is experience."[15] The "experience" at issue cannot be taken in its empiricist sense, as if poetry could be limited to relating experiences, as if it were necessary to travel first, or to know mankind, etc., to be able to write a single verse. Rather, what Rilke wants to say is that without a primary exposure to the very event of speech setting itself forth, without that opening to the new and ungraspable possibilities that grasp us in each speech by disarming our powers over it, without that risk, consubstantial with any genuine speech, of sinking into silence and inability to speak, it would be impossible for the poet to write a single verse.

For any poetic speech, like any genuine ex-per-ience, has something adventurous about it: *it is only possible as such at the risk of its own impossibility*, when, any prior possession of a language having collapsed, and any "linguistic competence" having failed to say what has not yet received a name, a poet has no other possibility than throwing himself into the new eventual possibility of a speech that has never been spoken or heard and that can therefore only be conquered on the margins of silence. It is by breaking with the uninterrupted chatter that everyday language constantly proffers without our knowing it, by making a silence in oneself, that a poetic, new speech can burst forth. This initial speech is exposed to the danger of falling back into the silence that gave rise to it in the first place and that accompanies it throughout as its shadow. Indeed, such a silence is not the opposite of speech, but what echoes in it and accompanies it as its most intimate risk, and that into which it could be plunged at any instant. In fact, there are two silences here, with different though not unrelated phenomenological statuses: a silence before speech, which, by silencing common chatter, is the condition of speech's advent and constantly echoes in poetic speech, and a silence after speech, an inability to speak, the risk of mutism, which speech overcomes in each instance. Just as an *advenant* only grasps himself in his selfhood on the edge of the fissure of his own collapse, so poetic speech perpetuates itself only by perpetuating its own welling up that is a conquest over silence, which nevertheless echoes in it as its most intimate and omnipresent risk.

Constantly perpetuating its own origin, speech happens only as traversed and penetrated by silence, a ubiquitous silence that is like its second power and that only really belongs to it where it is maintained at the level of a pure beginning. Now it is by refusing any mastery over the "already made [*tout fait*]" language that a poet has at his disposal and that we have in common with him, by nurturing the adventurous character of speech, and its most intimate risk—not the contrary of speech, but its double that echoes in it at every instant: silence—that the poetic act can establish a genuine beginning in language:

> Trying to learn to use words, and every attempt
> Is wholly a new start, and a different kind of failure

Because one has only learnt to get the better of words
For the thing one no longer has to say, or the way in which
One is no longer disposed to say it.[16]

What the poet calls "failure" here—and that could be splendid suc-cess—consists in that relation to words where *every attempt is wholly a new start*," an absolute beginning without any concession to old words, to words sedimented and worn out by language, to "words of the tribe" (Mallarmé), and the possibility of such a beginning lies precisely in re-nouncing any mastery of speech, for this mastery could only ever reach an already made and dead language that is stripped of its poetic power and always arrives too late to say anything or, at the limit, would only speak of things about which there is no longer anything to be said, and in a way that no longer speaks of them. Unless it always begins anew, the poetic act falls back into a fund of language that conceals it from itself and strips it of its powers. But beginning presumes here that one actively disarms oneself of any "power," in favor of speech, that one renounces any mas-tery over it, and thereby accepts the risk of *failure*: for mastery is only possible over the old, and never over the new in its radical novelty. In this respect, failure is probably as inseparable from a *work* as silence is from speech. As Malraux writes, and this probably holds for any genuine work: "The work speaks on one day a language it will never speak again, that of its birth."[17] In this, he reiterates Rilke's admirable question: "Whence should art proceed, if not from this joy and excitement of endless begin-ning!?"[18] In the inaugural act of poetry as such, there is a rigor in holding oneself at the level of a beginning, a demand that is also a risk and at the same time the only help in face of the latent powers of silence. For a be-ginning is assuredly what is most difficult: "For five years, since I finished *Malte*, I have remained as a beginner and, actually, as someone who does not begin."[19] This inability to begin is said again and again by Rilke, re-curring throughout his work: "To start anything requires an enormous effort. I can't *start*. I'm simply jumping over what should have been the beginning. Nothing is so strong as silence. If each one of us were not born into the midst of speech, silence would never have been interrupted."[20]

Nothing precedes speech; it is always announced in advance of itself, such that to take up speech is to leave it to itself, to allow to speak that in it which is assigned to us before any initiative of speaking and whose ori-ginarity is perpetuated by such an initiative. To let speech speak is first to listen to what is addressed to us with it, and such listening demands si-lence. By beginning absolutely in each proffered speech, speech merely perpetuates the act of its birth: its truth consists in holding itself on the brink of beginning, exposed to the risk of silence and to another more insidious and banal risk, in the face of which it nevertheless constantly reaches itself: that of falling back into a dead and utilitarian language, incapable of *speech*. It is in the inaugural act of speech that the disjunction between language and speech occurs. The latter cannot be mastered, and it is assigned to us without us being able to enclose it in the circle of any projection, possibility that exceeds all our powers, and that is given to us as excess, adventurous possibility that is only perpetuated by its exposure to the risk of falling back into silence, the former being what is progressively learned, integrated, and mastered as "linguistic competence." An abstraction reconstructed after the fact, language *explains* nothing about the welling up of speech. Or, rather, the language I use, possess, and have at my disposal is merely a theoretical construction: the only "language" that *happens* in the event of taking up speech is one that, because it precedes me immemorially in multiple acts of speech, is removed from any mastery, and that I can allow to speak only by setting myself to listen to it—hence it is a language that is irreducible to Saussure's distinction. A "language" that is a homonym to the one mentioned earlier, which only "exists" as actualized in singular speaking and is not the "system" familiar to linguists, but speaks, to put it this way, in all inaugural speech.

Consequently, the polar disjunction between speech and language originates in *the event* of speech that, like any genuine origin, is an arising of itself and in itself, a pure bursting forth from itself—that is, from nothing, thus opening to itself the instant's nothing. Before any act of speech, before any beginning for it, there is nothing, and it is only starting from speech that the world, poetry, and poets are able to be. In the opening of poetic speech, not only speech but also the world are always *in statu nascendi*: "We cease to recognize reality," writes Boris Pasternak. "It appears to us in a totally new category, which seems to us as its own state, not ours. Apart from that state, everything in the world has been labeled. Only this is new and unlabeled. We try to give it a name. We get art. The clearest, most memorable and important feature of art is how it arises, and in their telling of the most varied things, the finest works in the world in fact all tell us of their own birth."[21] To understand language as a tool, a *medium* that is not productive of meaning,[22] a vector of communication, which I have at my disposal and over which I exercise mastery, is to misunderstand *speech* by overlooking its *evential* meaning from the outset. Inversely, it is because an act of speech does not have at its disposal any prior attainment or "linguistic competence" or mastery of language that speech is neither the *expression* of meaning nor *communication*, that it is never a *means* or a tool, that it signifies nothing, is not made up of *symbols* that signify *other things*, but *signifies itself* in setting itself forth. As Hugo von Hofmannsthal writes: "Poetry never *puts one thing in the place of another*, for poetry is just the zealous endeavor to put forward the thing itself, with a quite different energy from dull everyday language."[23] The essence of the "symbolic" lies in such a *substitution*, the *sumbolon* being, etymologically, nothing other than that sign which "takes the place of" a thing, substituting for its presence; the "energy" that belongs to speech consists instead in doing without symbols. This is the case for the swans in Hebbel's poem: "*On dark billows / Downward drawn on / Two shimmering swans, they glide away.*"[24] Clemens, one of the interlocutors in Hofmannsthal's *Dialogue*, asks: "And these swans? Are they a symbol? They signify—"[25] At this, Gabriel interjects: "Let me interrupt you. Yes, they signify, but they do not state what it is they signify: whatever you wanted to say would be incorrect. *They signify nothing other than themselves: swans. Swans, but seen without inhibition, with the eyes of poetry, that each time sees each thing for the first time.*"[26] If "poetry never puts one thing in the place of another,"[27] this is because it perpetuates the inaugural gesture by which speech dawns to itself, signifies itself, and thus summons a thing to its own manifestation.

In this respect, all speech is poetic. It can only be "used" where it no longer resonates as *speech*; it is only reduced to the rank of a neutral *medium* of meaning, instrument for "communication," where *the inaugural event of its own arising* is covered over. Like any genuine event, the event of meaning that comes to light through speech puts the world itself in play: a poetic act always has to do in some way with the birth of the world. Speech resounds as poem only if it is inaugural, and it can be this perpetually inchoate speech only if in it the world itself is brought to appearance in a renewed light. Consequently, if speech *signifies itself*, as an irreducible event of meaning, it is neither "expression" nor "communication." It is not *expression*, because the very idea of "expression" encompasses the idea of an autonomous signification that would precede an act of speech in the purity of an intended meaning, entirely self-transparent in an act of understanding; meaning only *happens* in an act of speech, with it, and is only given to be understood as such starting from its event-advent *as* speech. Nor is speech *communication*, for, as with the idea of "expression," the idea of "communication" fundamentally presumes a scheme of utility: language would be the neutral *medium* between me and another, the vector of a signification that had to be "passed" or "transmitted" from one interiority to the other. Language would have the task of "communicating experiences" (in the empiricist sense). Communicating would mean exchanging experiences by the intermediary of a language-tool, and "expressing" a signification through a neutral *medium* would be the only appropriate means of achieving this "end."

In fact, it is strictly to the extent that it escapes any "expression" and any "communication," understood in the above sense, that *speech* establishes a much stronger and deeper "link" between "speakers": a common belonging to the event of speech. Indeed, it is in and through this event that an *advenant* is able to discover this common belonging to speech, which immemorially connects him to other "speaking subjects," in common with whom, by being born, speech is bestowed on him. Thus, the "speaking subject" of linguistics, along with a "language," a set of rules, assimilated as a "competence" and lexical resource on which this subject draws, is only an inadequate abstraction for *understanding* the *inexplicable* (according to the rules of a given language): the event of speech. A "speaking subject" and language are only given after the fact, starting from the event-advent of speech, and the codifications of grammar, the cataloguing of a lexicon are derived from this event. It is because speech alone is original, as also being a perpetual "birth" to oneself (Boris Pasternak), and because we are "born into the midst of speech" (Rilke), that we were able to break silence for the first time, according to an event that was "prepared" by nothing and that is its own measure.

Thus, an *in-fans advenant* does not possess speech as a possibility that is already his own; he can only come to speech by taking it up. This seeming truism means that an "*in-fans*," plunged in the heart of speech and always already preceded by the anticipatory speech of a naming that took place for him without him being able to take it on himself or take it over, must break this initial silence, even before possessing a "linguistic competence" or mastering a language; otherwise there would be no *sense* in him speaking. *The "sense" in him speaking lies solely in the possibility for the "speaker" of making sense happen.*[28] Each subsequent speech prolongs and perpetuates this original speech, conquered at the risk of itself and adventurous, which in order to say the unsaid, must ceaselessly measure itself against the unsayable. Such a speech transcends the resources of an already made language, and exceeds in principle any *usage* of language. It endeavors to promote a new meaning that is not already present in language as it "is spoken." It is only on this "condition" that speech can be "taken up"; that is, be *left* to itself and resound as speech, signify itself in its poetic event by summoning things to their own manifestation. It is only on this "condition" that there is "sense" in speaking. We will never have finished with speech, because all speech is initial and perpetuates the original, by breaking a silence, which otherwise "would never have been interrupted" (Rilke).

Now, the limitation of most theories of language, which misunderstand the event of speech and only attribute to it an expressive "function," lies in the fact that, for them, there is strictly no *sense* in speaking, because there is no meaning to make happen. An *in-fans* does not take up speech for the sake of determinate ends but in order to experience his own speech resources, so as to raise speech to its proper power and let it happen freely and be laid out as speech. To believe that an *in-fans* takes up speech in order to "express" thoughts or "representations" is to succumb to the naïve instrumentalization of language, which makes its welling up strictly incomprehensible. For, by what strange "translation" procedure could an *advenant*, who does not yet "possess" language, move from mute representations to their linguistic equivalent? It is a very different matter if a linguistic act is conceived as undergoing speech and its resources, which undergoing requires no "translation" of originally mute thoughts but rather is situated from the outset in the element of meaning. For meaning is precisely what *happens* in any speech.

Only the one who reaches speech by *taking it up* can also genuinely *lose* it. This loss of speech, mutism, is particularly evident in despair, and even more in the case of post-traumatic aphasia. Mutism is not silence, for to be silent one must also have the possibility of speaking. An *advenant* who falls short of speech, and who loses it in losing himself, is no longer capable even of silence. A mute, on the contrary, who "speaks" with his hands, can also remain silent. Strictly speaking, he is not struck with mutism; mutism is falling short of speech by one who "possesses" speech, one who has appropriated it by taking it up.

§23 Experience at the Limits: Suffering, Death

"The humanity of the human being is eventually characterized as ex-per-ience; an *advenant* can only advene to himself starting from this fundamental dimension of his adventure, where he is in play himself in his selfhood." If these theses have a phenomenological meaning and pertinence, we still need to reflect on two ex-per-iences in particular. First, suffering, which is not only one ex-per-ience among others but, in a way that is still to be understood, an ex-per-ience in a singular and privileged sense. Second, death, which is the archetype for ex-per-ience in general and, since this latter defines the human being's humanity, an inalienable mark of being human. According to distinct modalities and to differing degrees, both allow us to deepen our analysis of the evential meaning of ex-per-ience, by carrying this analysis to its limit; for both are *limit ex-per-iences*, in which an *advenant* is submerged by an event that upends him and strips away the possibilities from which he advenes to himself. However, this happens differently in trauma and despair, because these limit ex-per-iences, which are always a matter of the limits of ex-per-ience, still have to do with an *advenant* himself in his selfhood. We are still able to respond to them, though with a response that is already broken and faltering, from a self-ex-per-ience at the limits where the Self, on the point of succumbing, nevertheless continues to advene, for example, in the broken speech of a moan, where a suffering *advenant* only bears witness to the impossibility of bearing witness.

a. Suffering

Like most Indo-European languages, French and English have two words for suffering: suffering [*souffrance*] and pain [*douleur*]. While the first suggests a primarily moral or psychic origin, the second tends to evoke a physical one. Is it possible to begin from this duality of terms in order to appreciate the phenomenological meaning of pain? Such an opposition seems fragile from the outset: there is no intense and prolonged pain that is not also suffering, nor is there intimate undergoing of suffering that is not accompanied by pain. I always suffer "in my flesh," even when it is from a vexation, humiliation, or abandonment. In the end, the phenomenon of suffering casts a legitimate suspicion on the very distinction between "psychic" and "physical." For this reason, in the following pages, both terms will be used without any distinction of meaning.

All suffering, like all ex-per-ience, has to do with myself in my selfhood. Only an *advenant* can suffer in this sense. An animal "suffers," but its mute suffering moves us like a voiceless prayer; such is not an ex-per-ience that is a matter of selfhood, and thus speech, even when that speech is profoundly altered or broken and transformed into a moan, for even in extreme moral or physical collapse I can still respond to what happens to me. If there is a properly human meaning of suffering, it depends on there first being a properly *evential* meaning of ex-per-ience, as laid out according to a dimension of meaning that the occurring of events has alone been able to open.

Whatever the event from which an *advenant* suffers—bereavement, abandonment, illness, etc.—undergoing suffering is not only a factual or "empirical" experience of the psychological and physiological modifications that occur to him; rather, it is the undergoing of the upending of his possibilities as a totality. With the irruption of suffering, a human adventure as a whole suffers a *crisis* and is submitted to a metamorphosis. An *advenant* not only "senses" painful *lived experiences* but is traversed by the event of an impersonal and ubiquitous suffering, which transforms him through and through by making him falter on his foundations and run aground on the breakwater of his essential projections. As Hegel saw with unequalled insight, all experience, considered from the point of view of finite consciousness—i.e., immediate Spirit—as alteration, transformation, becoming-foreign to oneself (*Entfremdung*),[29] is an undergoing of a tearing: "[Spirit] wins its truth only when, in utter dismemberment, it finds itself."[30] This is why the principal signification of experience for consciousness is *negative*: it is consciousness' itinerary for coming to absolute knowledge, where it is confronted by the nullity of its prior knowledge and its object; this path can be regarded "as the pathway of *doubt* [Zweifel], or more precisely as the way of despair [*Verzweiflung*]."[31] Thus, experience can be understood for Hegel as having the essentially negative role of stripping consciousness of its constitutive illusions through a long and arduous path, where this wrenching and loss is undergone in pain. From here, in keeping with the tragic dictum "suffer in order to understand [*tō pathei mathos*],"[32] any truth can only be conquered *at the price* of experience: it is fundamentally *truth in suffering* [en souffrance: in waiting],[33] that is, at the same time truth suffered at the price of pain and a "violence"[34] consciousness inflicts on itself—painful truth—and truth *pending* its own advent. Heidegger emphasized this point in a 1942 lecture course: "Hegel always conceives of suffering [*Schmerz*] metaphysically; that is, as a mode of 'consciousness,' as consciousness of being-other, of laceration, of negativity. The experience of consciousness is always, as transcendental-dialectical experience, 'bad [*böse*]' experience, in which that which is conscious is manifested differently on each occasion, in the way that it first appears on each occasion. Experience is the transcendental suffering of consciousness."[35] This is why, to the extent that Hegel understands Concept as knowledge of the Absolute reflected in itself, experience, as "transcendental suffering of consciousness," can also be characterized as "conceptual labor [*die Arbeit des Begriffes*]," where "labor" is not so much productive activity in view of an end as it is the suffering of giving birth.

Thus, as Hegel profoundly saw, suffering is not one experience among others, but is the fundamental ex-per-ience, the "archetype" of all experience. It is the lacerating ordeal of an irreducible alterity to oneself, of an irremediable conflict where the stakes are the "Self" itself. However, though by distinguishing the point of view of the Absolute from that of finite consciousness in the Spirit's odyssey of returning to itself across various dialectic figures of consciousness, Hegel can limit suffering to the finite point of view (since it is only from such a point of view, which misunderstands the immanence of the Absolute in each dialectic moment, that experience appears essentially *negative*), suffering understood eventially, by contrast, escapes all possible dialectic, because of its intrinsically irreducible character. For, to take up one of Kafka's spoken but carefully considered remarks, "the only definite thing is suffering"[36]—not in the sense that suffering is irremediable, but in the sense that all endured suffering is definitive and cannot be annulled by anything. Hasty consolations mock suffering's gravity. Any compensation for it is impossible, either in this life or in "eternity." *What makes the evential meaning of suffering is precisely its irremissibility.*

The relation between suffering and time is fundamental here, and conditions the phenomenological meaning-character of this phenomenon. Passion more "passive" than any passivity, and whose *pathos* is time itself, suffering leaves us deprived of all initiative, constrained to endure through and through, right to the end. For though there are analgesics for purely "physical" pain, suffering is something that in itself cannot be eluded, abridged, or dodged by the one who suffers, and nobody can take it on himself or endure it in another's place. This unsubstitutability is of the same order as in death; it pertains to any ex-per-ience in general. But in what sense is time the *pathos* of pain? In one of Tolstoy's major works, "The Death of Ivan Ilyich," it is not only the recurrence of suffering that appears to be monotonous, but its irruption into the character's socially conforming and well-arranged life, which renders everything monotonous, so that it becomes impossible to separate the ordeal of suffering from a certain ordeal of time: still and amorphous time, without beginning or end, endlessly displaying the impossibility of any beginning, where instants no longer burst forth in their incomparable novelty; time of always, where nothing comes to pass or passes away, mere backwash of living time, without projections, expectations, or any genuine future. When pain wells up, with its unavoidable character, each present appears empty, because it is emptied: emptied of its meaning as soon as it happens, expelled from itself. For Ivan Ilyich, time no longer temporalizes, in the sense that, for him, the very event of *temporalization* no longer occurs in its bursting forth from the contrast of different, nontotalizable, and radically dia-chronic times: "Whether it was morning or evening, Friday or Sunday, made no difference, it was all just the same: the gnawing, unmitigated, agonizing pain, never ceasing for an instant, the consciousness of life inexorably waning. . . . What were days, weeks, hours, in such a case?"[37] Days, hours, and minutes are born already old; the present, without incidence or opening to a future, arises as already past, in that indefinitely synchronous time of sinking into oneself, where selfhood is turned away from its projections and twists in on itself in an eternal recurrence. Sinking into oneself, prostration, and the broken speech of moaning are the *pathos* of pain-time; time, writes Tolstoy, "did not exist for [Ivan Ilyich]."[38] An admirable and terrible text of Cesare Pavese makes clear that not only is there a time proper to pain, but that pain itself, from an evential point of view, is nothing except this detemporalized time of sinking and falling back into oneself, punctuated only by monotonous alternation, by temporal spasms of hope and despair, moans and giving up, battle and abdication, like a game that pain plays with itself:

> Suffering is a fierce, bestial thing, commonplace, uncalled for, natural as air. It is intangible; no one can grasp it or fight against it; it dwells in time—is the same thing as time; if it comes in fits and starts, that is only so as to leave the sufferer more defenseless during the moments that follow, those long moments when one re-lives the last bout of torture [*strazio*] and waits for the next. These starts and tremors are not pain, accurately speaking; they are moments of nervous vitality that make us feel the *duration* of real pain, the tedious, exasperating infinity of the time pain lasts. The sufferer is always in a state of waiting for the next attack [*sussulto*], and the next. The moment comes when the screaming crisis seems preferable to that waiting. The moment comes when he screams needlessly, just to break the flow of time, to feel that *something* is happening, that the endless spell of bestial suffering is for an instant broken, even though that makes it worse.
>
> Sometimes there comes the suspicion that death and hell will consist of pain like this, flowing on with no change, *no moments*, through all time and all eternity, ceaseless as the flow of blood in a body that will never die again.[39]

The jolts and lurches of pain are like the unfurling of successive waves that attack us, wearing down our resistance: the alternation of incessant battles and capitulations is what defines suffering and the infinite recurrence of its temporality. Moans and inarticulate cries are still human testimonies to the impossibility of giving witness to what remains beyond speech—this *limit* experience, which is not a pure limit for ex-per-ience. For if all suffering is properly agonic and is inseparable from an *âgon* and battle, then though selfhood is broken, overwhelmed, and crushed, it does not succumb completely: an *advenant* still grasps *himself* in what crushes him, in the alternation of his abdications and renewed lurches. This is quite different from despair, where, at its peak, suffering becomes *painless* and there is no longer anything to fight against or triumph over, *no more ex-per-ience* in the proper sense, since selfhood as such collapses in a world that has become pure "spectacle," where any implication of an *advenant* in what happens to him is suddenly annihilated. Any plea or possible call for help, like any possibility of testimony, even to the impossibility of testifying, are thus stripped from him.

Hence, suffering, as an experience at the limit and of the limit, is nevertheless defined as an ex-per-ience, where an *advenant* is implicated in what happens to him, even there where a painful event, along with the suffering to which it gives rise, leaves him as though broken and unable to react: for suffering is still *mine*, it always has to do with my unsubstitutable selfhood. It is in this respect that it is still an ex-per-ience, even if it leads to the limits of the latter. Indeed, suffering is what renders me unable to recognize myself by equating me to all others, in their extreme banality, in *making* me *banal:* not only because of the truism that we are all equal before suffering, but more profoundly because intimately endured suffering ends up erasing everything that belongs to my social and public persona, everything that makes me externally recognizable and identifiable by others. Thus, in Tolstoy's novel, the brilliant official Ivan Ilyich, struck by the event of an incurable illness and increasing suffering, progressively becomes a nobody, unrecognizable, not only externally, for others, due to the bodily changes following his illness, but also for himself. By equalizing all people, suffering and illness, like death, make the question "*Who. . .?*", the question of selfhood, more acute and agonizing. This question alone is what occupies Ivan Ilyich's final hours, his frequent recollections of his childhood and the decisive moments of his life, the statement without appeal of his failure: "His professional duties and the whole arrangement of his life and of his family, and all his social and official interests, might all have been false."[40] Thus, the event of suffering's irruption in the existence "without change"[41] of the official Ivan Ilyich introduces an upending such that he will never again be the same: an administrator satisfied with his social success and preoccupied solely with his career. Moreover, by reconfiguring his possibilities articulated in a world, the event of suffering impoverishes Ivan Ilyich's existence to the point of making it infinitely common and banal, and solely on this condition can it also reveal what is essential to him: the depth of his failure. With suffering's intrusion into an existence that is entirely motivated by ambition, Tolstoy describes an emptiness and chill that are always greater, which invade not only the character but also his world, all that surrounds him, and even the dazzling sun, which lacerates him, scrapes him to the bone, and pierces his flesh by gathering all the joys that have not been accomplished and all the promises that have not been fulfilled by his life itself.

Pain is always banal. Like death, it *makes* an *advenant banal* by rendering him unrecognizable for himself and for others: one who is suffering is no longer distinguishable in any way from others who suffer in a similar way. In suffering, we commune with suffering humanity in its entirety, to be brought ourselves to banality in its fullness. Everything that makes selfhood, all our projections in a world, are erased by the gaping and growing emptiness of an experience at the limit, which robs them of any signification by robbing an *advenant* of his incomparable singularity. Infinitely banal, anonymous, and faceless, we suffer with an immemorial, universal, and common suffering, which we can only experience as *ours* in the rare lurches of a battle that is continued but always on the point of being abandoned. Suffering is "bestial," says Pavese, and, indeed, suffering is what *strikes* us *down*, literally throwing us to the ground. In this respect, it is not insignificant that when pain strikes a human being, who stands upright, naturally holding himself erect, elevating his whole body, it throws him to the ground and casts him down. "The upright position, tearing away from the earth"[42] is the first thing that pain's irruption assails, confining us to bed, but in a way that only a human being can undergo, in that he alone is able to hold himself with an open face and serene gaze, facing the stars:

> Os homini sublime dedit caelumque tueri
> Jussit et erectos ad sidera tollere vultus.
> [He gave to man an upright face, told him to look upon
> The sky and raise his face aloft toward the stars.][43]

To this sublime description of the human being contrasts the decline into which pain casts him, the extreme banality and faceless anonymity that is emphasized by Rilke in the last poem he wrote before his death:

> Come, then you the last thing, which I acknowledge,
> Unholy agony in the fleshly weave; . . .
> Without plan, completely pure, free of future
> I mounted suffering's tangled pyre
> So sure of nowhere buying times to come
> For this heart, its store so mute.
> Is it still I, burning here beyond recognition?
> I will not drag memories inside.
> O life, life: externality.
> And I in flame. No one knowing me.[44]

It is this extreme banality of suffering, where I no longer recognize myself nor am recognized by others, which makes it a limit experience where selfhood itself, though holding itself, teeters on the brink of the abyss of its collapse. In this extreme banality, the experience of suffering decisively approaches that other ex-per-ience at the limit: death.

b. Death

Only the ex-per-ience of death, which I have deferred considering until now, makes it possible to comprehend an *advenant* in his adventure, according to the fullness of his phenomenal features. Indeed, the principal eventials that have been brought to light above are coordinated and articulated by this *singular* ex-per-ience. Along with birth, death is the privileged eventual, starting from which an *advenant* is characterized strictly as such. What, then, is the meaning of death as an *event*, and as an event par excellence? Can we speak of an ex-per-ience of such an event, and in what sense? Does not ex-per-ience, in confronting its limits here, at the same time also reveal its most original meaning?

In what sense can death be described as an event? Folded back and closed in on itself, it seems to elude our grasp, since at the very moment when it occurs, it is already too late to undergo it: "We know just nothing of this going hence / that so excludes us," writes Rilke in his poem "Death Experienced."[45] However, this incapacity to experience death signifies the empirical impossibility of experiencing it as an innerworldly *fact*. The event of death, in its *eventital* sense, *never* occurs as a fact: a fact "takes place" in the world, but an event as such *does not take place*, it is pure making-possible and opening of the world, it *comes to pass* [ad-vient] in all facts, in that these facts are assigned to me and reconfigure my eventual possibilities. *It is the "taking-place" of a fact that itself never takes "place" in the world*, but is the pure making-possible of my possibilities and of the world that articulates them. Now, this *transcendence* of an event with respect to innerworldly facts, according to which its occurrence can never realize it, since by definition its eventness transcends any possible actualization, this transcendence of the *pure transcendental*, from which an *advenant* can be understood and characterized in his adventure, is what is revealed in a singular way in the event of death.

First of all, in the event of the death of others: we remain strangers and radically external to this death, and if we attempt, all the same, to grasp it as a fact in the world, we can only gain access to its bodily signs—and precisely to *nothing* else: *nothing* has happened, nothing that can be experienced as a fact in the world, and this "nothing" is death. However, if death is radically unexperienceable as the ultimate event undergone by another, in another sense it can indeed be experienced by those who survive: this ex-per-ience of death is *bereavement*. The primary ex-per-ience of death is always the death of others: first not only *contingently*—the "first" experience *in fact*—but first in principle, primordial and original. Not only is it mistaken to maintain, as Heidegger does, that another's death can teach me nothing about my own, but, on the contrary, from an evential perspective, others' deaths are so intimately linked to mine that they are inseparable from each other in the ex-per-ience of bereavement. This ex-per-ience of another's death is not a "representation" of an event that is in itself *unrepresentable*, where I would "speculate" about the experience that another has undergone, imaginatively putting myself "in his place," etc. On the contrary, bereavement is intimately undergoing—beyond any "representation"—*my own dying to another and, consequently, to myself*. It follows that in such a dying my selfhood is always put in play. Undergoing of what is unsubstitutably assigned to me in the literally unexperienceable and unrepresentable event of another's death, *death to another, and death to myself*, as loss of our compossibles, bereavement is a metaempirical undergoing of another's death, which strikes me in the depths of my heart—at the heart of my possibilities and the world. The primary ex-per-ience of death is therefore that of another's death. It is not by chance that Rilke's poem "Death Experienced," whose first verses were cited above, does not deal with the poet's own death but with the death of the one to whom it is addressed.

However, it is not only the undergoing of another's death that shows in a remarkable way this event's transcendence with respect to any fact; it is also the ex-per-ience of my death. Indeed, there is an ex-per-ience of my own death, a limit experience that is as such *an ex-per-ience of the limits of experience itself*. Any transformation from self to self originates in an event: it does not occur within a world, in the way a fact does. It never "happens" in the sense of something *actual*, but it *comes to pass* [ad-vient] *as a pure making-possible that opens the world for an advenant*. Here, the ex-per-ience of an event means nothing other than this transformation of an *advenant* through the metamorphosis of his world. But in the case of my own death, in what sense can we still speak of "ex-per-ience" and "event"? Of course, to the extent that death is never realized or experienced as a fact, it appears, in one sense, as an event par excellence: about death, about my death, I can never say that it has occurred, in the sense of a *fait accompli*, because as soon as it is actual, I lose any possibility of being there and undergoing it. Death is the event par excellence precisely to the extent that its accomplishment can never realize it; its eventness transcends its factual actualization. However, in another sense, can we still speak of an "event" where there is no possible ex-per-ience of it, where the world is not trans-formed or re-configured but simply lost, where experiencing the end entirely coincides with the end of experiencing? Can we still speak of an "event" where the making-possible does not so much "open" a world as close it over, by closing over an adventure? But does not putting the problem this way presume that it is already solved? Is it self-evident that death is only closure? As a *mystery*, is not death an opening par excellence, as one says that a question remains open when a solution cannot be provided to it: a puzzle without a key, an unresolvable enigma? In fact, the event of death, if it is truly a singular *event*, since it differs absolutely from every innerworldly fact, is not what happens with every fact insofar as that fact reconfigures my possibilities, but is that which, like birth, can never "take place" as a fact, and does allow for an ex-per-ience, but in a modified sense: a limit experience that we must now attempt to understand.

If ex-per-ience signifies, eventially, this passage and traversal at the risk of oneself, as exposure to the totally other, to the *nothing* of the event, to the extent that an event occurs on the margin of any fact and in *reserve* of any actualization, then one can say that undergoing death is the ex-per-ience par excellence: ex-per-ience that at the same time deprives us of the possibility of any ex-per-ience. Indeed, though death is a passage and traversal, it is a traversal of the untraversable (what the Greeks called *apeiron*), a traversal that reaches no destination or goal, a "passage" that is not a transition of something toward something but rather one where *the destination is abolished in the passage and is nothing other than the passage itself*. If this is a matter of a trans-formation, it is not in the sense of a passage from one form to another, but of a "form" that founders and "falls to the ground [*zugrunde geht*]," as Hegel says,[46] and is abolished in its passage. In such a "passage" *I* am no longer there to experience "what passes away," but instead what *comes to pass* is the only "passage." In no sense is this a passage *from something to something*, a trans-formation, but rather a complete change, a *passage "from everything to everything* [du tout au tout]."[47] All these expressions, which are not so much obscure as deliberately paradoxical, attempt to indicate the *sui generis* nature of this ex-per-ience—what precisely makes it a *limit* experience.

But this limit experience is indeed still an ex-per-ience to the extent that it conserves the principal phenomenological traits of the latter. First, like all genuine ex-per-ience, it is an experience that has never been had before and is had for the first and last time, the first time being also the last and, therefore, only time. This is true of experience in general, in that it is related to the one and only time of an event in its radical individua-tion, to this "first time" that is also, because of that, its only time. Second, the ex-per-ience of death is such that it puts selfhood in play, as does all experience in general, where an *advenant* is implicated himself *as* himself in what happens to him. Finally, this singular and privileged ex-per-ience shares the adventurous character of all other experience: ex-per-ience is fundamentally ad-venture, that is, *opening to the ad-vent of what happens to us* [ouverture à ce qui nous ad-vient]. In this traversal without return, the destination is not assigned in advance: one only knows where one is going by going there, like in all genuine adventures. If all worldly adven-ture is intimately related to death, this is because death as such is the origi-nal ad-venture. Ad-venture that is not an odyssey but rather a departure without return: for here death is not the "destination" of the journey; or rather, if it is a "destination," its characteristic feature is precisely not to let itself be assigned, captured, or represented in advance. Death is not the "end" of life, for any intra-temporal end is always *at the same time* an end *and* a beginning: the end of one time and the beginning of another. By contrast, death is only thinkable in the origin-instant where the scheme of time as "passage" is abolished.[48] Like birth, it is the event of its own advent, which happens in an instant and is removed from any linear and successive duration. It cannot be understood in terms of passage unless it is a "passage" without destination, abolishing and reabsorbing its own conditions in itself. As an event exempt from any actualization, pure mak-ing possible of a human adventure, death, as death that is undergone, is also the ex-per-ience par excellence: self-undergoing at the point of noth-ing, traversal of the untraversable, where it is not we who go anywhere but, rather, where the future comes to us, falls on us from above and sub-merges us: absolute catastrophe.

To understand this limit experience requires that we stop envisaging death as the ultimate turning-point from "being" to "non-being," which would be the "end" of the first and the "start" of the second. For this would surreptitiously bring us back again to conceiving it as a *fact* within the world, assigning it a content in advance, and considering it from the point of view of Being (as a nothing or negation) and not in itself, as absolute event. Ultimate event, parallel to no other, in which the very meaning of our adventure is at play, without us ever being able to capture this meaning in advance by a resolute anticipation. Of course, as soon as we are born, death accompanies us as one of our inner possibilities, which we can anticipate in free projections and that confers on our projections their adventurous coherence. But this death that is represented as one of our possibilities is not death itself as the ultimate event. Death in this respect is closest to us—"For, nearing death, one perceives death no longer" (Rilke)[49]—not only in the suspended imminence of a possibility-at-any-instant (Heidegger),[50] but as what comes upon us without coming from us, happens to us in the impersonal mode of an event, since when I think I have grasped it, in fact it has grasped me by undoing my grip on myself and delivering me over to the ungraspable. This death, in its transcendental impersonality as an event, always happens to me out of a future that is radically yet to come, without possible coincidence with my present—a future toward which I cannot anticipatively launch myself, for as Blanchot writes so well: "In it *I* do not die, I have fallen from the power to die. In it *they* die; they do not cease, and they do not finish dying."[51] Event par excellence that, when it happens to me, is never brought about for me as a realized fact, and when it is realized, no longer happens *to me*, since it deposes the "I" itself. Essentially anonymous death, whose essential anonymity is not that of the "they" in its fallenness but rather that of *events*, which never occur as facts but *happen* out of the future by exceeding any potentiality-for-Being, any resolution, any possible totalization of an adventure over itself.

As an event, death is what absolutely prohibits conceiving any self-totalization of finite existence, "the whole of Dasein completely 'given.'"[52] It removes itself in principle from any "horizonality" and from any horizon-structure in general. It is not the horizon of any possible meaning for Dasein, according to the enclosure of meaning, which is a necessary feature of finite existence and which means that this existence can only receive its meaning—or be deprived of meaning—from the perspective of its end. Death no longer signifies that singular possibility that closes Dasein's resolute existence in on itself, but it is much rather that which comes to open Dasein from the outside and confer a meaning on it that it has not projected, a *meaning* that is open to being taken up by others than itself, thus transcending the "horizon" of its finitude. Understood eventially, death is much rather this "escape [*échappée*]"[53] beyond any horizon of a meaning that eludes any possible totalization, since on this event, whose meaning constitutively escapes me, also depends necessarily the very meaning of my adventure. Therefore, *the necessary excentricity of the meaning of any destiny* for the one to whom it befalls appears thanks to this ultimate event: by leaving this meaning open, the event of death prohibits an *advenant* having any exclusive privilege for understanding his own adventure and opens this adventure to an understanding that is endless by right, in the charge of those who survive it. Each of us can have a history only on the condition of entering by death into a history that exceeds him, on the condition of abdicating any overseeing position with regard to his own adventure: it is only ever *for others* that his history acquires a complete and self-enclosed meaning. By his death, an *advenant* is caught in a spiral that drives him out of himself, dispossesses him of his centrality, and prohibits him from establishing himself as an autonomous *subject* who would be the source of meaning in general and who would always discover himself to be "behind" or "beneath" what happened to him.

Therefore, this death that comes "from outside," from an absolute outside, belonging to events, is not merely a modality of my *Being* that is characterized by mineness. Elusive and omnipresent, it belongs, on the contrary, from the outset to the adventure into which we are born, insofar as it is intrinsically arrayed as ex-per-ience, that is, insofar as it is constituted in itself by that opening to other than self, to events in their radical alterity.[54] And since we are *born into* this adventure through and through, death cannot be separated from birth. Because an adventure is fundamentally open to a nonground that it does not make possible, to the first and original event, it is also mortal, constitutively structured by the coming of the event that overhangs it and that it cannot appropriate: the radical *advent* of death. Suspended death, on which an *advenant* never gets a grip, which he can never make his own, transcending, like birth, any position of selfhood, inaccessible to any pro-jection by which an *advenant* would relate to his end and attain a certain "autonomy of existence," irreducible to any facticity, which Heidegger still conceives as what Dasein *renders possible* by taking it over through a resolute anticipation of its end. Opened only to an ex-per-ience that, because it carries with it the risk of the "Self" itself, is the sole one to do justice to death's alterity.

Thus, an *advenant* can never circumscribe the adventure into which he is born by enclosing it as an accomplished whole that has its meaning in itself and is entirely understood on the horizon of his death, for death is precisely an *event*. Now, an event *is only ever announced on its own "horizon"; it is that which opens to itself by canceling any prior condition* and consequently escapes from any idealist philosophy of *representation*, which conceives experience precisely in terms of a "horizon" and "conditions of possibility." On the contrary, what death, in its evential sense, reveals, *in its escape* [échappée] *beyond any horizon*, is that the adventure into which I am born has its meaning essentially *outside itself*, that I am never the measure of this meaning by resolutely anticipating my "end." This meaning, which always remains opaque to me, is literally in-com-prehensible for me, impossible to embrace in a projection of understanding, in virtue of the intimate articulation of birth and death. *Birth*, which, as the precursor and inaugural event of my advent to the world as *advenant*, opens me to a possibility that I do not make possible, that is not first of all "mine," and to an inexhaustible meaning, which precedes and exceeds any projection of understanding and delivers understanding to what exceeds it—the incomprehensible—which it can neither embrace nor circumscribe. *Death*, which rather than closing an adventure in on itself, hands over the task of interpreting it to those who survive it—an adventure deprived of "horizon," because it is necessarily excentric.

Now, if death, understood in its evential sense, does not make possible "an exhaustive 'givenness' of Dasein in its entirety," it can no longer serve as the *principium individuationis* for an *advenant*. In the impersonal event of death, which always happens to me from an ab-solute future that is irreducible to any projection, and the ex-per-ience of which I undergo as long as I ad-vene to myself, what is striking above all is its utter *banality*, as is also the case in extreme suffering: nothing is more banal than death, for as Maurice Blanchot says, death is always neutral, always "undistinguished death."[55] The radical individuation of *this* event does not contradict its impersonal character: death equates us, making each *advenant* an "undistinguished *advenant*," in that we are all equal before it, so that even though each of us only experiences his own death, death in itself is by contrast the absolutely *banal*. We always already have a fraternal bond with someone who is suffering or dying, for it is *this same death*, in its ungraspability as an impersonal event, *that befalls them and that befalls us.* Death is essentially *impersonal* and is not one of *my* possibilities to which I could therefore resolve myself. The essential anonymity of death effaces faces, but is not the anonymity of the "they" in its fallenness. As Blanchot writes again: "*They die*: he who dies is anonymous . . . whoever experiences this suffers an anonymous, impersonal force, the force of an event which, being the dissolution of every event, is starting over not only now . . . [because] from the instant 'they die,' the instant is revoked."[56] It is not by anticipating death that we will find an answer to selfhood's question of "Who?"

This is why death is more fundamentally related to despair than to Heideggerian anxiety. Anxiety is that *Grundstimmung*, that fundamental and singular mood of Dasein, which makes it possible for Dasein to be given phenomenally as a whole and thus prepares the "ground" for Dasein to be fundamentally characterized in its Being as care. Anxiety brings together in itself the two structural moments of existence and facticity: "That in the face of which we have anxiety is thrown Being-in-the-world; that which we have anxiety about is our potentiality-for-Being-in-the-world."[57] But since "Being-thrown in the world" more fundamentally signifies Being-thrown toward death (in the possibility of no longer Being-in-the-world), and since potentiality-for-Being signifies taking over the singular possibility that is not to be outstripped of my own impossibility, then the phenomenon of anxiety is not fundamentally distinguished from the existential phenomenon of *dying*, "as thrown Being towards its own-most potentiality-for-Being, which is non-relational and not to be out-stripped,"[58] such that "Being-towards-death is essentially anxiety."[59]

Now, what anxiety is anxious about is still always *a possibility* of a Being-in-the-world: the possibility of no-longer-Being-in-the-world. "Death," in the existential sense, is not a factical "event [*Ereignis*]" but rather a *mode of Being* of Dasein, in which it anticipates its "end" and relates itself to this end in the first person: "The 'ending' which we have in view when we speak of death, does not signify Dasein's Being-at-an-end [*Zu-Ende-sein*], but a *Being-towards-the-end* [Sein zum Ende] of this entity."[60] What anxiety is anxious about is therefore still a *representation* of death *as possible*—the representation of a possible loss of Being-in-the-world. Being-in-the-world is an ontological structure of Dasein, defined by "mineness": *it is this mineness of Being that anchors existential ontology in a philosophy of representation.* By attempting to remove death from all factuality by representing it as pure possibility that is only possibility, Hei-degger still *represents* it as a characteristic that belongs to Dasein's Being, as a mode of Being, and thereby overlooks its *eventful* character. Granted, speaking of "representation" here is not consistent with *Being and Time*'s terminology; however, it indicates that death is only envisaged there *sub specie possibilitatis* and *never as an event*, which is, from the instant I am born, as "unavoidable" as birth. To fix a *content* for death ("the possibility of my impossibility") is still to try to capture it, assign a meaning to it in advance, and cover over what is in play in such an event. To conceive death on the horizon of Being-in-the-world, with what might be inade-quate in this "idealist" conceptualization and the notion of "conditions of possibility," where events alone reign in their "transcendental" purity, is still to give a *representation* of it and surreptitiously reduce it to a *fact* that can be characterized in some manner or other ("the loss of Being-in-the-world"), just as Socrates represents it to his disciples as a return to the gods, who are wiser and better. Un-representable, death is without assignable "content," *pure event* and *nothing else*. It is only if this event that is radically unable to be anticipated, because parallel to no other, is covered over that I can *anticipate* it as *a future possibility of myself* and, consequently, also *resolve myself to it*.

Very different and more original is the relation between despair and death: in despair, the world's collapse and transformation into pure "spec-tacle," in which an *advenant himself* is no longer implicated in what hap-pens to him, lets the profound anonymity of death be made visible. Death is not one of *my* "possibilities," which can be freely re-presented, but rather the continued ordeal of an *impersonal* event that hangs over me from birth out of a radically unpresentable future. In despair, the world and selfhood are shipwrecked, *I* can no longer *face* what happens to me, I experience myself as *already dead*: I undergo that impersonal death, which accompanies and haunts my adventure from its first arising—that "great death which each one has within."[61] There is no contradiction here between death's interiority or intimacy and its "exteriority" as event: for an *advenant*, fundamentally determinable as ex-per-ience, is constituted in his most intimate intimacy by his openness to an exteriority: to the *transcendental* for any experience. Nor is there a contradiction between the radically future character of this event and the fact that it is inexorable from the instant of my birth, structuring my adventure through and through. On the contrary, death gestures toward a prepersonal dimension of adventure—precisely the one that despair reaches when an *advenant* is stripped of all power and selfhood, abandoned to an essential anonymity and an impersonal vigilance that henceforth haunts the collapsed world. Despair is this continuing death, this primordial ex-per-ience of death, which is no longer even an ex-per-ience, where I am stripped of my capacity-to-die and can neither anticipate death nor resolve myself to it. For anticipating death and resolving myself to it are existential attitudes, which presume that death is *my possibility*, which it assuredly is not, or is no longer, in despair. As in suffering, which is always private and mine, at the same time radically incommunicable and supremely banal, so despair is the continuing undergoing of an impersonal death that is inseparable from me and is nonetheless "other," absolutely private and incommunicable and nonetheless prior to my selfhood: muffled as the pulsing of my blood, united with my flesh, erasing even the features of my face.

Thus, in despair's bottomless anonymity a more intimate relation to death emerges than in anxiety, a relation to death as that impersonal *event*, which, welling up from an ab-solute future, is not a configuration of my present, and consequently cannot be anticipated, because it has no relation to that present. While one who is anxious is afraid of *his* death as something that is possible-at-any-instant, a possibility that is nothing but possibility, as Heidegger says, a *representation* he projects ahead of himself as a future possibility of himself (and this is why he can still be "afraid" of it, even if this is a metaempirical fear),[62] one who despairs is not afraid of death but instead, stripped of his capacity-to-die and unable to resolve himself to it, experiences himself as *already dead* and dully undergoes the anonymity of an obscure, diffuse, and incomprehensible death, which runs through his adventure from end to end, an "undistinguished death," infinitely banal, *common between others and himself;* he has a relation with this event that is so intimate that *it escapes the order of representation.* Being *already dead,* he neither dreads death nor anticipates it but is content to welcome it, for it is from and through it that the world is offered to him as "pure spectacle," in which he longer participates and is no longer implicated, in which ex-per-ience does not subsist, only this anonymous vigilance and impersonal lucidity: he is there without being there, *that* suffers without anyone to suffer or to testify to this suffering in a moan, in silence, or by crying out.

Despair thus reveals the prepersonal dimension of all ex-per-ience,[63] in which death is first "sensed," where *something* happens without happening to me, where I can no longer face what happens to me nor really respond to it. An ex-per-ience at the limit, of the limit, in intimacy with death, in the very impossibility of sharing what this ex-per-ience comes down to, in an intimacy that is more intimate than any "Oneself" of a "Self" lacking selfhood—a *fraternity in death* with all others, since through it I reach complete banality. Indeed, if there can be intimacy and proximity with death that is not merely proximity to oneself, this is because death is always "other": you and I both die with the same death, an anonymous death, an impersonal event—which, far from *distinguishing* me from every other, reveals an immemorial fraternity between us. This "great death" that each one bears in himself, inscribed on his face, in the fragility of his features, is *a common, immense, banal, and indistinct death.* As Hugo von Hofmannsthal writes, it is that "great, never articulated afterthought, steady, visible in good faces, which like a signpost through the confusion of life points to death and beyond death, and without which a face is not a hieroglyph, or is a distorted, diffused, faded one."[64] A vast and unique "afterthought," which shines out in every face and which is not a thought at all, as if the face were the sign of the soul, its code that could be decoded. The face is an undecipherable hieroglyph in its proximity to the impersonal death that dwells in it, its exposed fragility, its vastness and unsoundable depth; the gravity of death that haunts every face, even when it shines with life, like the once-living smiles in old photographs.

B. THE CONCEALING AND DOWNGRADING OF THE ORIGINAL MEANING OF EX-PER-IENCE: EMPIRICISM

If the evential meaning of ex-per-ience is its *original* meaning for a human adventure, we still need to understand why this meaning has been constantly covered over and stifled by the philosophical tradition running from Aristotle to the present under the general heading of "empiricism." We still need to understand how experience in the empiricist sense can be derived from the original evential concept of ex-per-ience—"rationalists," who oppose empiricists without genuinely questioning their concept of "experience," falling into this same broad class of empiricism, which we are concerned with justifying here.

§24 The Genesis of Empiricism

a. Experience and Knowledge

Experience in the evential sense is inseparable from the events from which an *advenant* can advene to himself in his selfhood. Inversely, it is only if I no longer understand events by understanding *myself* in them, if I no longer understand them as assigned [*destiné*] to me and thereby as fateful [*destinal*], as having a future for the one who undergoes them, and thus as offering themselves to an undergoing that is itself *unsubstitutable*, that I can understand them as innerworldly *facts* deprived of any specific assignation. Then, experience is no longer that in which an *advenant* is himself in play at the risk of himself; it becomes instead the experience of a fact in which I no longer have to "recognize" myself, a fact that simply occurs in the world and that is presented in the present as the pure vis-à-vis of *knowledge*. The profound mutation happening here at the heart of the concept of "experience"—and this, as we will see, from Aristotle on— consists in the concealment of its full evential character or, in other words, of the phenomenological trait of my being singularly in play in each singular experience such that my singularity itself is only possible by my being implicated in ex-per-ience as unsubstitutable.

Indeed, "knowing [*connaître*]" experiences does not originally signify relating to them in a theoretical way. In the tragic formula *tō pathei mathos*, self-knowledge in and through an ordeal is not the "result" of what is undergone, but rather it is what is inseparable from it, because an ordeal or ex-per-ience is not one way among others for an *advenant* to understand himself in his selfhood but the one and only way. Now, Aristotle interprets this expression in a psychological way—twisting it from its original meaning and distorting its evential tenor—in that he applies it in the *Poetics* to emotions, which belong to a *psuchē* and which can undergo purification (*katharsis*) by tragedy: "A tragedy, then, is the imitation of an action that is noble . . . in dramatic, not in narrative form; with incidents arousing pity and fear, wherewith to accomplish its catharsis of such emotions."[65] Emotion, as feeling, is not understood from ex-per-ience in its evential tenor,[66] but rather tragic experience is understood as a purification of emotions that are themselves simply modifications of a *psuchē*. From the outset, this psychological approach confines experience's meaning and import to the theoretical sphere of "knowledge"—a correlation of psychologism and theoreticism that recurs in modern empiricism. Hence, it is not by chance that Aristotle examines experience (*empeiria*) mainly in book 1 of the *Metaphysics*, which begins with the crucial declaration: "*Pantes anthrōpoi tou eidenai oregontai phusei* [All men by nature desire to know]." In-*sight* [*sa*-voir, knowledge] has the literal sense here of "have-in-view," in a "theoretical" consideration, which means a consideration characterized by *theōrein*, "sight." The analysis of experience takes off and develops from this gnoseological context. Indeed, human experience is approached within the horizon of a psychological faculty on which it essentially depends—memory: "*gignetai d'ek tēs mnēmēs empeiria tois anthrōpois* [from memory experience is produced in men]."[67] Characterized thus in relation to a psychological faculty that conditions it and on which it depends, experience thereby receives a theoretical meaning: it is "knowledge of individuals [*empeiria tōn kath'hekaston esti gnōsis*],"[68] while *technē* is knowledge of a universal.[69] Modern developments in empiricism have been made possible precisely thanks to this conjunction of a double orientation, psychological and gnoseological, from which Locke and his successors understand "experience." If the fundamental thesis of modern empiricism is that *all knowledge derives from experience*, then experience as a whole must be characterized from the perspective of *knowledge*. Whether the human mind is defined as a *tabula rasa* (Locke) or as "a kind of theatre" (Hume),[70] in each case the interpretation of knowledge is inseparable from a psychology of the faculties, in which the crucial element for Hume—who is undoubtedly the most radical and coherent of the empiricists—is the imagination in its linking and connection to habit.

b. The Downgrading of Events to Innerworldly Facts, and the Problem of the Correlate of Experience

In experience understood in this way, as the "experience" of empiricism, no longer essentially at stake are events as what open the dimension in which an ex-per-ience, in the evential sense, is possible, where an *advenant* is himself implicated in his selfhood. On the contrary, what defines the experience of empiricists is that it has to do with *facts* that simply occur in the world, without upending the world's intrinsic possibilities, and that are as such able to *be repeated*.

For Aristotle, in book 1 of the *Metaphysics*, experience is of course defined, in its properly and exclusively human dimension, beginning from its essential relation with competence (*technē*) and science, which are unique to the human being—and even determine him in his humanity. This is why, as properly *human* experience, *empeiria* is never completely separated from technical competence and science, which bear on the universal and which are acquired by means of the former: "science and art come to men *through* experience; for 'experience made art,' as Polus says, 'but inexperience luck.'"[71] However, what eidetically differentiates *empeiria*, on the one hand, from competence and science, on the other, is that the *cause* of what it apprehends is not clear to experience, while knowing the cause and principle is what makes the latter two knowledge to a higher degree: "*hoi men gar empeiroi to hoti men isasi, dioti d'ouk isasin; hoi de to dioti kai tēn aitian gnōrizousin:* for men of experience know that the thing is *so* [the '*Das*,' the *hoti*], but do not know why [*dioti*], while others [who have a *technē*] know the 'why' and the cause."[72] Experience is therefore limited to observing *that* this is the case: it has to do with facts and not with causes; only a technical competence has the faculty of comprehending (*to epaiein*) *why* it is the case. For example, experience teaches that when Callias took some particular medicine, he was relieved; it does not allow extending to *all* similar cases the universal judgment that this medicine is appropriate to the illness nor, a fortiori, explaining *why* this treatment has succeeded. But if experience is nevertheless capable of teaching us something, and of even rivaling in practice technical competence,[73] this is because the *facts* on which it bears are able to *be repeated*. What characterizes innerworldly facts, by contrast with events, is their unlimited iterability. Thus, in the most radical formulation about experience that we find in book 1 of the *Metaphysics*, what seems to be fundamental is precisely the idea of a possible repetition of the similar, from which experience arises and is generated: "*hai gar pollai mnēmai tou autou pragmatos mias empeirias dunamin apotelousin* [for many memories *of the same thing* produce finally the capacity for a single experience]."[74] It is the repetition of similar (if not identical) facts that, through memory, alone is able to generate experience, with the cohesion and unity that belong to it. So little is this element of identity in the repetition of a manifold of similar cases contingent or fortuitous that its eidetic necessity for experience is reaffirmed with force in the *Posterior Analytics*: "From perception there comes memory, as we call it, and from memory (when it occurs often in connection with the same thing), experience; for memories that are many in number form a single experience."[75] Of course, the element of identity here is not yet the universality of an idea, since experience does not reach the recognition of the universal in the particular: it is only knowledge of the particular as such. But can there be repetition of the *same* memory, repetition of the *identical*, without a universal concept being generated in the soul, thus allowing it to pick out identity in repetition? It is to this very extent that experience is never completely separated from technical competence and science, with their knowledge of universals, which belong to the human being and to him alone.[76]

That experience is essentially related to *facts*, and to *repeatable* facts, is what makes a tight connection between Hume's empiricism and Aristotle's theses. And yet, what separates them is that Hume no longer restricts experience to facts alone, since it is the constant conjunction of many similar facts that leads to the possibility of deriving the idea of cause—in other words, of uniting what Aristotle endeavored to separate: *hoti* and *dioti*.

Indeed, for Hume experience first of all signifies the succession of similar facts as they are presented for observation: "The mind is a kind of theatre,"[77] he says, a stage on which no performances [*représentations*] are played out, but only mere "rehearsals [*répétitions*]." Under the stage lights of this internal theater, the same "actors" follow one another in an unchanging order: the same successions of experiences, of impressions, perceptions, and images, play out their invariable script. Thus, what characterizes experience as it is offered at first glance to simple observation is its tendency to form observable constants, its propensity to repeat itself. Experience is a rule-governed repetition of similar facts, or the iteration of similar conjunctions between facts: if I put my hand in a flame, a sensation of burning follows; as many times as I repeat the experience, so many times will I observe a similar succession of phenomena. This repetition, for which the human mind is the theater, changes nothing about what is repeated, but it generates a qualitative modification in the mind itself. It could be described as a repetition that *does not amount to the same* but rather instills a difference in the very heart of identity. Because my mind is itself passively altered and modified by the playing out of similarities, an experience can be born and develop. Thus, we have arrived at a second concept of experience: "experience" in its second sense.

According to its first sense, "experience is a principle, which instructs me in the several conjunctions of objects for the past";[78] but this first level of experience, the observation of a succession of facts with their regularities, is not sufficient to constitute a rule-governed experience, in which I am no longer content to notice what played out in the past but can also *anticipate* what will happen in the future. For repetition in the past of similar experiences presupposes *the experience of this repetition*: but this is only possible if the repetitions, which modify nothing in the object itself, at least modify the subject who perceives them, in whom they are passively coordinated and organized. To understand this modification of the subject by which mere repetition of the similar is raised to the status of experience that is organized and governed in a constant way (the second concept of "experience"), we must add to observation, the first principle of human nature, habit as a distinct principle: "Habit is another principle, which determines me to expect the same for the future."[79] Habit, the principle of anticipation, is nothing other than experience in its second sense.[80] This is why custom can be defined in the *Enquiry* as "the great guide of human life. It is that principle alone," adds Hume, "which renders our experience useful to us, and makes us expect, for the future, a similar train of events with those which have appeared in the past."[81] The semantic slide that is constantly at work here between "expect . . . a *similar* train of events" (*Enquiry*)[82] and "to expect *the same* for the future" (*Treatise*)[83] is actually without consequence—or rather, is the direct consequence of Hume's radical empiricism. Indeed, though sensible impressions are never *the same*, but similar to each other at most, the ideas arising from these impressions, and only differing from them in their lesser force and vivacity[84]—e.g., the ideas of flame and heat—are at the base of the association that allows me to expect *the same* in the future. Repetition, fashioned by habit, constrains my imagination. Observation teaches us the conjunction of similar facts in the past; imagination draws a rule of association from this by its customary transition from one idea to another. Hume calls this process of passing from an already observed repetition of similar cases in the past to an anticipation of future events "inference." This is actually located in the passive faculty of habit and requires no reasoning (an infant is capable of it even before being able to reason). Habit, this natural tendency to pass from one idea to another without any use of reasoning, is thus linked to imagination (and not to "reason") as the principle of the association of ideas; according to another definition, it is that "easy transition of the imagination"[85] from one idea to another.

Consequently, it is at the very heart of experience, and as though by a continuous transition, that the passage from the *hoti* to *dioti* comes about, the two sides of human knowledge that Aristotle set himself to distinguish. For noticing the repetition in the past not only of isolated similar facts but also of their unvarying constellations or conjunctions, along with anticipating their future repetition (by means of associative imagination of ideas and habit as imagination's indispensable complement), is what produces a natural "inference" in the passive theater of the mind, leading it to form the idea of *cause*. This is indeed a matter of a "fiction" of the imagination, as Hume declares, but this fiction is so firmly rooted in our mind by belief that it is practically impossible not to take it to be a "force" inherent in phenomena themselves, or a *necessary connection* between facts. Without causality, experience would dissolve into a chaos of sensations: on this point, Hume completely agrees with Kant. But this causality is itself only a product of experience, inasmuch as it is a passive and customary association of ideas itself rooted in a fundamental belief that evokes Husserl's *Urdoxa*. Thus, it is through *experience* (in its first sense: the observation of *similar* facts in the past, the *hoti*) being *overcome* by *experience itself* (in its second sense: a repetition that has become habitual, by the intermediary of an association of ideas, engendering the anticipation of the *same* succession of facts in the future) that the idea of causality (the *dioti*) can be generated within experience, without any source other than the latter.

From this, it is clear that the decisive element in Hume's attempt at radical empiricism is the conjunction of two essential theses: (1) a thesis deriving from Aristotle, that all experience is experience of facts (it has to do with the *hoti* alone) which can be repeated—these "facts" are impressions or perceptions in their raw state; and (2) that the regularity of such experience comes from the useful "fiction" of causality, such that *without causality*—without a customary conjunction of *ideas* corresponding to impressions, united by imagination and consolidated by belief—*there would be no "experience" in the strict sense*. This second thesis is radically anti-Aristotelian and prefigures Kant's fundamental position.

But is not Hume's radical empiricism weakened—and, on examination, made untenable—by its very attempt to reconcile these two theses? The leading question of Hume's enterprise, if it can be summarily formulated, is the following: *How are these constant phenomenal conjunctions and constellations formed, which we call "causes" and which govern all experience?* Now, this question, which endeavors to derive the very idea of "cause" from experience itself, *is nothing other than a question about explanation and cause*, a question that tries to *take account* of the *fact* of causality, and to do this precisely by means of a causal explanation. In other words, it is a question about the *cause*, rooted in what Hume calls "human nature," of the very idea of causality. The circular nature of Hume's empiricism is clear here, in that it cannot give an account of the genesis of the notion of cause without resorting to explanations of a causal nature and consequently cannot itself be formulated without contradiction. Hume is aware of this, and he presents his empiricism as a school of modesty: "To explain the ultimate causes of our mental actions is impossible. 'Tis sufficient, if we give any satisfactory account of them from experience and analogy."[86] But can one propose an *explanation* at all? The empiricist project runs aground here in its attempt to advance beyond the simple *fact* of causality and understand its *why*, for this advance is only possible by means of the idea of causality that it is setting out to derive. If this latter idea is only a useful "fiction," then all empiricism's constructions and, more significantly, its very project (of examining habit and imagination to find the "principles" of experience; i.e., its first *causes*), are shown to be entirely *fictive*.

However, it is this strictly untenable paradox that also reveals the most brilliant trait of Hume's radical empiricism. The paradox lies in the fact that human nature, which is referred to as a principle (e.g., of the laws of association), is actually always also a product. Moreover, it is a principle *only if it is produced in principle* and to the very extent that it is *produced*. That is to say, it is a *fiction*: for Hume, to give everything to experience is necessarily to consign everything to fiction. The more radical the empiricism, the more general is the fiction, that is, the more experience is reduced to an illusion. Hume's philosophical strength is to hold fast to this paradox to the point of pushing it to absurdity. As a consequence, Hume can only derive the Cartesian subject, characterized by self-identity, by grasping its genesis, but the subject that is to be derived himself appears, through this genesis, as a mere fiction: he "is" only his generation through experience; that is, strictly speaking, he is *nothing*. Thus, what allows Hume to "deconstruct" the Cartesian subject is not the attribution to it of new psychological properties (memory, habit, the principle of association) but on the contrary the acknowledgment that in the end it has none: we have thus, in some fashion, a subject "without qualities," which is nothing other in its "essence" than a process of subjectification. But the real limit of this empiricism is the impossibility of expressing itself with such radicality and its constant collapse into a psychologism that contradicts its own project and thereby renders it untenable.

Whatever the internal contradictions of this empiricism may be, and in fact of any consequent, radical empiricism, what fundamental features of experience are set forth in Hume's analyses?

1. *All experience is experience of something that repeats itself*, without this repetition, there would be no such thing as rule-governed "experience," in the empiricist sense. Now, only an innerworldly fact can repeat itself, in a strict sense. Empiricism rests entirely on a reduction of events in their evential sense—that which never occurs twice—to mere facts coming about in a world. We will see that such a reduction is inseparable from a *de-worlding* of these facts: "*empirie*" can be conceived as the mere reception of *sense data*.[87]

2. *All experience fundamentally puts causality between phenomena in play.* Experience in the empiricist sense, experience of a fact, is therefore inseparable from an explanatory archeology. Now events, in their anarchic welling up, are in principle excepted from such an archeology and cannot be reduced to something like a causal explanation. An event is its own origin, that is, the origin of a meaning that, welling up for an *advenant*, is offered only to *understanding*: an origin that is ruptured from itself, originally differing from itself, as pure temporalization.

It remains to be shown that "empiricism," in the broad sense in which I am attempting to conceive it, exceeds the limits of a particular philosophical movement; in their critique of empiricism, "rationalists" rely on a concept of "experience" that they borrow, in broad outline, from their adversaries; they still remain "empiricists" in this broader sense. Without claiming to be historically exhaustive, I will limit myself here to a few examples.

Kant probably provides his most rigorous characterization of experience in section 18 of his *Prolegomena*, which sets out for the first time the opposition of two kinds of judgment: "*Empirical judgments, insofar as they have objective validity,* are *judgments of experience*; those which are *only subjectively valid* I call mere *judgments of perception.* The latter do not need a pure concept of the understanding but only the logical connection of perception in a thinking subject."[88] What does Kant gain here by this distinction? In what sense does it clarify his characterization of experience? Let us leave aside the difficulty internal to Kant's thought, of knowing in what sense one can speak of *judgment* where there is no category but only a succession of perceptions in a thinking subject.[89] For Kant, judgments of experience differ from judgments of perception in that they bear the imprint of objective a priori necessity, which the latter lack. There is a "judgment of experience" where particular perceptions are subsumed under a pure a priori concept of the understanding, which Kant calls a "category" and which confers universal validity on the judgment. But can every category play this role indifferently? Is there not rather a privileged category? It is not by chance that in all Kant's examples it is the category of causality that makes possible the transition from a simple judgment of perception to a judgment of experience: only the connection, in an act of judgment, of an empirical intuition (perception) and the pure a priori concept of cause, confers universal validity on judgments of perception, so that they are transformed into judgments of experience. Experience (*Erfahrung*), in Kant's sense, always signifies experience that is *governed* by the objective laws of *causality*. He specifies this immediately in an important note: "For an easier example, take the following. When the sun shines on the stone, it grows warm. This judgment is a mere judgment of perception and contains no necessity, no matter how often I and others have perceived this; the perceptions are only usually found conjoined in this way."[90] What Kant calls "perception" in this text is precisely what Aristotle calls *empeiria*, which refers only to the fact itself (to the *hoti*), without putting into play its cause (the *dioti*). Such a judgment of perception—expressed in terms of "*wenn . . . dann . . .* [when . . . then . . .]"—only has to do with a fact in its complete contingency; it cannot generate the idea of *cause* by means of repetition and habit, as Hume thinks, since according to Kant the idea of cause presupposes a *necessary* and objectively valid relation between two phenomena. In a judgment of experience, the factual relation expressed by the adverbs "*wenn . . . dann . . .*" ("*when* the sun shines on a stone, it grows warm") must therefore give way to a necessary relation: *if* the sun shines on a stone, *then* it grows warm ("*wenn . . . so . . .*") or, in other words: the stone grows warm *because* the sun shines on it ("*weil*"). The synthetic judgment that unites these two terms becomes universally and objectively valid by introducing the a priori concept of cause, "that must precede the turning of perception into experience."[91] For here "experience" signifies the concatenation of perceptions insofar as it is governed by universal laws: "Experience is an empirical cognition, i.e., a cognition that determines an object through perceptions. It is therefore a synthesis of perceptions, which is not itself contained in perception but contains the synthetic unity of the manifold of perception in one's consciousness, which constitutes what is essential in a cognition of *objects* of the senses, i.e., of experience."[92] Now, such a *synthetic unity* of perceptions requires not only the presentation (*Darstellung*) of a category in the intuition (in the analogies of experience, it is a matter of the categories of substance, causality, and reciprocal action, successively) but also the synthetic unity of apperception by which this empirical knowledge is related to the *subject* of experience, and it can provide knowledge of an *object* only on this double condition.

Consequently, though Kant rejects any empirical genesis of the idea of causality, so as to make it an a priori concept of the understanding, he nonetheless sets up Hume's two characteristics of experience as fundamental characteristics of causality. (1) Experience is always experience of something that is repeated: of phenomena insofar as their concatenation exhibits regularity and constancy. (2) What is at issue is always the conditions of possibility for such constancy and regularity in the linking together of phenomena, according to which it must be possible for the repetition of similar facts to be elevated to universality, whether by the *subjective* constraint of habit or by resorting to the *a priori* category of cause. Thus, while Hume understands causality as arising from merely subjective and contingent principles, Kant regards it as belonging to objective and necessary principles, but what at first glance appears to be an opposition between these empiricist and rationalist theses masks the essential proximity in their characterization of *experience* as such.

It is no different with Husserl, whose greatest innovation over Hume and Kant consists, first, in extending the concept of "experience" via the concept of "intuition" beyond the sensible domain to the "categorial" domain and to the domain of idealities in general (sixth *Logical Investigation*) and, second, in the elaboration of a descriptive science of phenomena, which, by means of the phenomenological epoché, show the residual naivety that belongs to the question of the empirical (Hume) or transcendental (Kant) genesis of experience. In fact, it is only by bracketing every question bearing on the real-actual genesis of the world that transcendental phenomenology can ask the question of its *constitution*, which, as Husserl notes in a letter to Hocking, never equates to such a real genesis: "The expression that recurs so often, that 'objects' are 'constituted' in an act, always refers to the act's property of *rendering an object representable*; it is not a matter of 'constituting' in the proper sense."[93] Any question bearing on the real genesis of the world only has meaning in the horizon of the world, still remains a "psychological" question, and therefore appears naïve from the point of view of the transcendental epoché. However, despite these essential differences between the phenomenological approach and the doctrines that precede it, experience remains characterized for Husserl as *the totality of universal legalities that govern the concatenations of lived experiences for a consciousness in general*: "*Experienceableness* [Erfahrbarkeit] *never means a mere logical possibility*, but rather a possibility *motivated* in the concatenations of experience. This concatenation itself is, through and through, one of 'motivation.'"[94] Hence, "the real world exists, only on the continually delineated presumption that experience will go on continually in the same constitutional style."[95] Here, experience is not the unrepeatable undergoing of an event in its absolute singularity but the concatenation of motivation that connects the lived experiences of a consciousness according to the material or formal a priori that governs the thematic domain of the objectness under consideration, prescribing to it its own constitutive style. Experience, as the coherent unity of a subject's lived experiences, unfolds in the element of *repetition*; the unvarying eidetic features that structure experience can only be extracted from this repetition. This experience, whose essential features are regularity and constancy, not only concerns the domain of sensible intuition in general but also extends to the domain of logico-mathematical idealities, to the domain of signification (formal ontology, pure grammar of signification). Husserl radicalizes the empiricist concept of experience by extending it to all possible domains of reality. It is for good reason that Paul Ricœur defines Husserlian phenomenology as "hyper-empricism."[96]

c. Empirie *as Experience-Without-World*

As we have seen, the obscuring of the evential meaning of experience is inseparable from characterizing experience's correlate as *innerworldly facts.* But empiricism strips innerworldly facts, in their turn, of their proper phenomenological traits, and of the following characteristic in particular: every fact announces itself as such within a signifying context, on the horizon of a "world." Empiricism misunderstands the innerworldly character of facts when it interprets the correlate of experience as a mere "given" without world—and then interprets this "given" as a "sensible" given. Experience, stripped of its relation as a totality to the world, which belongs to it constitutively, is thereby reduced to the reception of sense data: it is this sensible given that, in its ultimate concretion and particularity, constitutes the origin of all knowledge. I will call such experience, stripped of all relation to the world, *"empirie,"* as pure reception of a sensible given. Hume calls this latter "sensation," "impression," or "perception," but such a characterization of the correlate of experience as a pure "sensible given" is no less dominant in Kant, in the transcendental aesthetics, which deals explicitly with a "chaos" or "jumble" of sensations before they are given intuitive form by means of the a priori forms of sensibility; it is no less present in Husserl: does he not declare, in a manuscript given as an appendix to *First Philosophy*, that "it is perfectly correct that Hume begins from impressions and ideas, even if he does not clearly explain the reasons that justify such a starting point. Any theory of knowledge must begin with the given, which is represented exclusively by immediate lived experiences"?[97] The vestiges of such empiricism will resurface in the ambiguous phenomenological concept of *hylè*.[98]

§25 The De-worlding of Events and Information

Yet, aside from empiricism, and independent of any philosophical option, isn't there a more insidious and more common de-worlding of events at work in the way that our age, more than any other, relates to events in general by means of a technical apparatus: information? While empiricism reduces ex-per-ience, in its original sense, to mere knowledge of facts, and ultimately by de-worlding these facts themselves, to reception of sense data, the apparatus of information, embedded in the modern communication network, gives access to every event by grasping it as something that can be the object of an *informative* transfer—foremost guise under which our age allows an event to be grasped and put on display. This historic guise, which is dominant today, conceals events in their properly phenomenal characteristics, downgrading ex-per-ience to *empirie* by the destruction of the world from which it is inseparable. Analyzing this historic situation, which shapes the way our age has access to events, will allow me to show the way in which information constitutes the extreme culmination of a tendency that was already at work or, rather, whose roots lie in the historical forms of empiricism.

a. Journalistic Events as the Correlate of Degraded Ex-per-ience

Events are not limited to what I can experience myself in the first person; they are also what can be reported to me through a narrative. The dominant historic trait of our age is that it most often avoids a narrative mode (mythological, epic, novelistic, . . .) for reporting events that have taken place, instead using the form of a journalistic account, in a style that one might call, more generally, *information*. Hence, enquiring about the meaning of journalism is no longer only enquiring about one way among others in which events are "treated" and "transmitted" each day, but rather, it is endeavoring to identify the fundamental understanding of events that governs our time, so as to discover the historic trait that dominates the current obscuring of ex-per-ience, whose meaning is what we are seeking to recover.

No other age before ours has offered such refined technical means for being informed about events happening in almost any place on the planet, no matter where we happen to be ourselves. No age before ours has known such powerful upheavals. No age in the history of humanity has been marked by such terrible events as the Shoah, which defies description. However, probably no age could have so much held in check the upending power of the events that have profoundly determined its configuration and destiny. Today, information is the way in which events as such are "held in respect," that is, covered over in their proper meaning-character.

As *advenant*s subject to the information age, we are not exposed only to events that we undergo unsubstitutably; each day also brings its stock of "news" on events that happen to others, of which, strictly speaking, we have no experience of our own: a great statesman dies, an earthquake occurs, a famine or civil war breaks out in a distant country. In each case, these are certainly events in an evential sense: death is not only incomparable for the one who suffers it but also for those who are close and undergo bereavement; the death of a statesman is also an event for the professional historian, but it is, in truth, an event for every human being whose individual destiny is so inseparably linked to the destiny of humanity as a whole that no one can prevent such an event from striking him intimately as an upheaval. The same is true for poverty, civil wars, and earthquakes, which, in the first place, strike those who are actively involved or victims, but cannot leave our consciousness in peace.

However, the primary phenomenological mode in which events show themselves to us in and of themselves is not that of "consciousness raising." Even less is it that of ex-per-ience, where though we are not directly touched by these events, we are nonetheless implicated in them, in that on a historic level our own destiny is inseparable from that of humanity as a whole. Reported by the written or audiovisual press, transmitted in the form of "information," these events appear, on the contrary, as deprived of any specific assignation: they are addressed to each and every human being, which is to say, strictly to *nobody*—to a generic "everybody" that fundamentally signifies "nobody in particular." They seem to float, so to speak, above particular individuals, in the ether of an anonymous history, without real agents and without anyone being responsible. A public event is one wherein my selfhood is not an issue, and which I do not have to appropriate by means of an ex-per-ience. Indeed, the distinguishing feature of information is that it dispossesses us of our own ex-per-ience by putting every event at a distance from us: thus it determines our historic situation. The drama that strikes human adventures is no longer any different from a comet's fall in a summer sky. By juxtaposing heterogeneous "events," information levels out their differences and presents only a profusion of "events" that are addressed to nobody and uprooted from the world in which they occur. Far from allowing the gathering of the world around the meaning they set forth, they appear as fragments of a *broken-up* world deprived of any possible unity.

What journalistic communication of events levels out and alters is precisely the following two phenomenal traits: (1) the *addressed* character of the event—in which an *advenant*'s selfhood is in play—and (2) the possibility of an *ex-per-ience* of events, as an adventurous undergoing of that upheaval of the world that reconfigures an *advenant*'s intrinsic possibilities articulated among themselves: his world. By contrast, a journalistic event is an uprooted event that has no world, a de-worlded event. Walter Benjamin writes:

> If it were the intention of the press to have the reader assimilate the information it supplies as part of his own experience, it would not achieve its purpose. But its intention is just the opposite, and it is achieved: to isolate events from the realm in which they could affect the experience of the reader. The principles of journalistic information (newness, brevity, clarity, and, above all, lack of connection between the individual news items) contribute as much to this as the layout of the pages and the style of writing.[99]

A journalistic event is uprooted, floating so to speak in the air, without any constitutive relation to other events: it does not order the world around a meaning but announces itself as a fragment of a broken-up world, which is nobody's world; it is at the same time impossible for me to take over, unable to be assimilated to my ex-per-ience, and incomprehensible, if all understanding presumes a necessarily total unitary projection, according to which alone an event can be interpreted.

First, the mass media speaks for nobody in particular; the events it conveys have no addressee: at best, its "addressee" can only be an impersonal collection, an amorphous and indistinct mass, "public opinion." The events are not addressed to me in my selfhood but to the worker, administrator, citizen, or voter "in me"; they always strike me obliquely, through a contingent feature of mine, as an exemplar of a class, collection, or group. But must we not at least concede that the information is addressed to a certain "experience" in me, to the experience of a unionized worker, for instance, or to that of a citizen, if the event in question belongs to the economic (retrenchments in my company) or political (elections in my country) order? However, such a conjecture amounts to envisaging experience itself as if it could be compartmentalized into "sectors" that are completely separate from each other, as already sundered or broken up on the inside: such a conception of human experience is precisely the consequence of the de-worlding of events that is already at work in journalistic information and whose meaning we will shortly need to consider in more depth. It is not ex-per-ience in the evential sense, as traversing from self to self, where I am in play myself as such, in my unicity—the ex-per-ience that confers unity on my history.

Second, events that are publicly communicated are addressed to a "public" of disengaged observers, they dismiss any possible integration to an experience, they consecrate the breaking up of experience itself, as cataclysm of modernity. Once information extends its network, becoming generalized and globalized, it takes the form of a mass organization for the mass diffusion of information, and events are no more than one "mass-produced article"[100] among others, available to anyone yet closed to everyone.

But what, more precisely, are the features of the journalistic event, which we have thus far only summarily described?

The characteristic feature of information is to aim first at "novelty," what happens "day by day," what is new each day, like Heraclitus's sun: each morning brings its quota of *news*, whose main "interest" is precisely its *novelty*-character. As technical means develop for obtaining information, the mode in which it is transmitted is also modified: radio and television offer continuous information, so as to be the first to announce and spread the "latest" news. But far from bringing to light the novelty of events, this acceleration of information instead covers over and obscures their essential novelty. I noted earlier that the "first-time" characteristic (*Erstmaligkeit*) of events is one in which this first time is also the one and only time (*Einmaligkeit*). By contrast, journalistic events have no genuine novelty: the regularity of daily, weekly, or monthly publication takes no account of the temporality proper to events but instead subordinates it to external constraints. Events fill up a predefined temporal frame of a repetitive chronology that holds no surprises. Moreover, this borrowed and sham novelty of journalistic events depends on their essential novelty being always already covered over, held at a distance and attenuated in its wounding or joyous violence, its upending and critical originality, by the filter of a commentary. This commentary is not a casual addition but belongs in principle to the way in which information makes events accessible by "communicating" them through the press. Despite being informed about the news of the world each morning, we are poor in events. As Walter Benjamin remarks: "This is because no event any longer comes to us without already being shot through with explanation."[101] Information imposes the accompaniment of an explanatory commentary on events and so neutralizes their radical novelty. Explanation and commentary, which triumph in journalism, are precisely those modes of comprehension *that do not do justice to events in their eventness*, that do not regard them as *origins of meaning*, but instead as links in a causal chain, thereby degrading them to mere innerworldly *facts*. Information does not aim at *understanding* events, and it would not succeed if it did, given the means that it uses. It regards events only as "elements" within a system, the information system, with its multiple written and audiovisual networks and the technical apparatus that is subordinated to them. By contrast with ex-per-ience, which is understanding, in which events are regarded and grasped in their historic meaning—always overflowing and inexhaustible—with a constitutive and irreducible delay, information, which makes events accessible as "news," is characterized by its posture of *contemporaneousness*. It claims to be able to "account for" events "day by day," *at the same time* as they occur, and thereby, rather than *understanding* them, it is limited to explaining them by a more or less arbitrary analysis of their *causes*. Information substitutes immediate causal explanation for the long mediations of hermeneutic understanding, inseparable from ex-per-ience, which grasps an event, in its evential *meaning*-character, *after the fact*, according to an essential disparity and suspension, as an origin without reason.

The sham novelty of the news results in a second phenomenological trait: its *actuality* [actualité]. This claim of actuality is inseparable from the information process and characterizes it as such. Journalistic events, the "news," are synonymous in French with "actualities [*actualités*]." What is "actual" is what is presented in the present as accomplished and definitive. Actuality [*ef-fectivité*] was characterized above as the original phenomenological characteristic of *facts* in their innerworldly actualization [*ef-fectuation*] on the horizon of a causal context. Events, on the other hand, in their suspended occurring, are strictly irreducible to their actualization as facts. They transcend the present of their actualization by the load of possibilities that they keep in reserve and by their future-loading; as pure *making-possible*, they are precisely the essentially *inactual*. To this extent, the actuality [*actualité*] claimed by information serves only to hold us at a distance from and to warn us of the properly evential tenor of the events it communicates, just as the so-called novelty of news tends to eclipse the genuine novelty, the "first-time" character that belongs to *events* alone. Far from making them apparent in their constantly suspended occurring and according to their own temporality, information only delivers "actualities [*actualités*, news]" that are essentially *ephemeral*: crumbs of events coming one after the other, fading as soon as they appear, immediately replaced by other news. Moreover, this haste with which events disappear in journalistic chronicles is accompanied by a multiplication *of external signs* (memorials, anniversaries, celebrations, etc.), which can only accentuate the weakness of memory rather than offering it a remedy; they are as ephemeral in their turn as the events they commemorate.

Finally, while events shake our settledness and *upend* us, information is limited to *striking* us, and it touches us less deeply the more "shocking" its appearance. Events as such are separated from journalistic events by the difference between an intimate upending of the world and a superficial traumatism that leaves the settledness of our world unshaken. Indeed, news that is communicated as information is not given with that distance that I have insisted is the condition *sine qua non* for any understanding, in that understanding's retrospective projection is always already oriented by the perspective of the present, aims at grasping the inexhaustible evential meaning-character of events, and consequently can never be contemporary to them. Events are opened to ex-per-ience precisely by distance, for at the same time that ex-per-ience signifies belonging to events and full engagement by an *advenant* in what happens to him, it also signifies being foreign to what has become, henceforth, something past. Now, the pseudoexperience of news entirely lacks distance of any kind, and in particular the distance that is inseparable from understanding. Events that communicate information—by means of photos, "untouched" images, testimonies, and "live" broadcasts—only offer a head-on "experience" of shock without any step back being possible, a catastrophic "experience" that is supposed to upend us but actually upends us less with the event's escape from ex-per-ience in the proper sense. Thus, the less profoundly public events affect us, the less they shake our settledness in the world, and the more they have an appearance of "shock" and trauma: behind these simulated traumas is concealed a growing disinterest for events that tend to the *spectacular*, a disimplication of the *advenant* in his selfhood, who is no longer concerned with what "happens," the basic clear conscience that finds in "bad conscience" a pretext for inaction.

What defines the "experience" of shock is its instantaneous brevity deprived of any proper duration and its unlimitedly repeatable character: in the repeated "traumatism" of journalistic events, all distance is abolished and all genuine proximity along with it, all possibility of being touched or intimately upended by what "happens." An *advenant* "has before him only a storm that holds nothing new, neither teaching nor suffering."[102] Indeed, we have seen that there is an irreducible difference of meaning between traumatism and upheaval. In the former case, as happens for those suffering from aphasia and only able to repeat a single phrase, we see an incapacity to assimilate a traumatizing event to one's own experience: leaving the event outside it, this incapacity thus impoverishes experience in such a way as to generate, at the level of speech, the monotony of constant recurrence. Very different from this is the upheaval that is only possible through the integration of an event into one's own experience, or rather through the undergoing and traversing of an event, at the risk of oneself, that I have characterized phenomenologically as ex-per-ience. The catastrophic "experience" of information is thus a catastrophe of the experience itself, which is reduced to a shock that has more impact the less deeply, and therefore more ephemerally, it touches us. An event that strikes us in a newspaper's headline is unable to be inscribed in the "long term" of an ex-per-ience; it falls short of its own temporalization; it is no more than an instant and ephemeral shock, therefore endlessly reproducible, just like any other mass-produced object. A new edition is printed each morning and has to be "filled." This periodicity that is decreed in advance only indicates that the journalistic apparatus has stripped events of their own temporality. The characteristic feature of trauma—and of this *analagon* of genuine trauma, which shares some of its essential traits—is to be *forgotten as soon as it is suffered* and to give rise to no genuine temporalization of ex-per-ience (in contrast to upheaval, which arises from an event and is inseparable from its temporality). In face of the unceasing flow of information, the modern human being has no memory; he is skimmed over by events without being reached, without experience and without history. The only one who has a *memory*—that is, who is freed of the past—is an *advenant*, who can undergo events and can relate to them in the first person, who constantly makes an ex-per-ience of them, taking them over as such by relating not only to the past but to the future that is opened to him and that constantly ad-venes to him from the eventualities events make possible.

Thus, the "news" item—which is only apparently new—does not open to any genuine experience, in that it is addressed to everybody and nobody, or targets only impersonal groups: laborers, employees, unionists, citizens, consumers, etc. Information takes a historical event itself, offered and assigned to the public, and turns it into an object for current consumption. In contrast with a historical or novelistic narrative, it always implies a series of mediations inherent to what is today called "the media." It manifests only a second- or even third-hand experience, where the recipient of the information is not himself essentially in play in what is related and where journalists have the mission of generating a shock-"experience," at which they are more successful the less implicated they themselves are in what "comes to pass." Disengaged narrators (by contrast with novelists and historians), who are not themselves in play in what they relate: *intermediaries*, as pure mediators between those who undergo an event "in their flesh" and those who—the shapeless and anonymous public, the amorphous mass of spectators—through information, are the more struck by the sensational the less they are upended by it. The world's pulse is reduced here to a misprint in a press release. And since information also includes "testimonies," these cannot be the testimonies of a speech that gives assistance to itself, a speech of truth, for the sake of the truth itself; rather, they are testimonies that are already mediated, formatted, standardized, and adapted to ready-made rubrics, for which the journalist is a pure intermediary, a relay, orienting them by his questions and already recasting them through commentary. In this respect, there is no such thing as *unfiltered* information; the "filtering" does not happen *after the fact* but is contemporaneous with the journalistic process and is at constant risk of degenerating—in extreme but not chance cases, since they are inscribed in this form of transmission from the outset—into propaganda, whether disguised or overt.

A journalistic event, with its distinctive phenomenological characteristics of being novel, current, ephemeral, distant, spectacular, and anonymous (with the "anonymity" of a group or generic entity, which should in no way be confused with the original impersonal character of the adventure into which we are born, as analyzed above), gives rise to a shock "experience" for an *advenant*, which means the absence of any upheaval, a fundamental disengagement and disinterest in relation to what happens. A journalistic event does not concern me in my own ex-per-ience, where my selfhood would be at issue; rather it concerns the truncated, piecemeal, and collective "experience" of a social, economic, and political aggregate to which I am told I belong, the "experience" of an amorphous and anonymous group through which I am targeted and summoned under the regime of "*us.*" This "us" opens the space of the *social*, which is not the Greek *koinonia*, where equals (*homoioi*) meet in mutual independence and freedom, but a public domain in which differences are dissolved and subordinated to a common genus and in which a strictly interchangeable multiplicity of *advenant*s is invoked only as a "group," a collective, an association, etc. This degraded experience is neither a pure privation of experience, as in the case of genuine traumatism, nor a limit experience such as analyzed above; it is a simulacrum of experience, which in the end merely equates to the "distance" of a total detachment; with it comes a change in the meaning of events, which move closer to mere fiction and are hardly distinguished from it.

Believing that genuine events are those reported to us by information, we conform our understanding and behavior to them, by understanding in their light events *in general*. We do not take account of the artificial and normative character of these pseudoevents, because of the self-evident certitude, so strongly embedded in our historic situation, that the proper *meaning* of events is most directly open and accessible to us in the repeated shocks the press launches at us each day. But if information distills "events," they are events that no longer gather a world around them; their chaotic proliferation, with their acceleration and the shock they arouse, entails the world's diffraction and inexorable fragmentation. Indeed, far from bringing the world nearer, information's apparatus, by subordinating increasingly sophisticated technology to itself, by extending its broadcast and communication network ever further across the planet through satellites and cable networks, by ceaselessly accelerating the transmission and reception of "world news," makes both events and the world more distant: information is telescoped, events are blurred by hasty explanatory commentaries artificially imposed on them, information is cut up and adjusted to fit the norms and standards of a routine broadcast, only delivering debris from the world, a textureless dust of events, detached from any experience and straightaway forgotten. This shattering of the world is accompanied by a persistent ideology according to which, from the store of information, each viewer or reader can "choose" at whim the news that "touches" or "interests" him or her: they behave as consumers—the characteristic feature of consumption being precisely that it is concerned only with *products*, destined to be destroyed as soon as they have been used. Universal history itself becomes a "product" manufactured by information, in which the sensational competes with the "new," but where this borrowed novelty no longer has anything to teach us.

Thus, journalistic events are not characterized only by the *negative* trait of leaving both the world and ex-per-ience untouched; they *alter the world much more profoundly* than the phenomena of disinterest, distance, pseudonovelty, etc., would lead us to believe. An *advenant*'s entanglement in public events that are distant, ephemeral, de-worlded, and *without relation* to each other is inseparable from a profound *alteration* of the way he engages with ex-per-ience and with the world in all the fundamental dimensions of his adventure. Under the pressure of public events, the "world" itself appears as a mere *unconnected* summation of events and is thus stripped of its character as world: a shattered world, ruined from within, where events engage with one another according to a purely accidental "logic."

"The end of history" that Hegel spoke of is perhaps nothing other than this de-worlding of events and their anarchic proliferation.

b. The Recurrence of Time and Biography

Just as the world's phenomenality is fundamentally altered by the apparatus of information, so the intrinsic constitution of time undergoes a profound mutation under this constraint. The downgrading of original ex-per-ience into mere *empirie*, deprived of a world, is accompanied by an *evental* conception of the human adventure in which the latter is no longer grasped as anything other than a succession of de-worlded "events," which are simply added in a temporal sequence without any articulation between them. *Biography* no longer interprets the mortal adventure into which we are born as an unsubstitutable undergoing of events where an *advenant*'s singularity originates, but as a mere "life" (*bios*), whose unity is unproblematic. "Human life" is reduced here to an unlinked series of more or less "notable" facts, among which some can be marked out as "events." However, just as, eventially, the adventure into which we are born does not signify a collection of facts, no more can events be defined as facts that are singular or remarkable and thereby conceived in the light of other innerworldly facts, from which they are actually distinguished, but only so as to be identified more closely with them.

From a temporal perspective, the distinguishing feature of this *biographical* conception of human adventure is that a lifetime, extending from the fact of birth up to the fact of death, appears to be "full of events," from which nevertheless no world enworlds. Time is itself reduced to an empty structure that can be "filled": a linear and homogenous time that is no more than an indefinite extension of a single empty present, which is "filled" by pseudoevents, a time that unfolds and follows after itself without any real difference between times, without the radically diachronic triplicity of a past, future, and present that are nonsynchronizable, entirely carved off from each other, and that only arise in their opposition and polar disjunction in and through the inaugural event. *According to such a biographical conception, our human adventure becomes a mere* chronicle *of de-worlded events.* What is thereby obscured is the intrinsically temporal and temporalizing character of events: there is not first a lifetime that is then "filled" with events. Rather, events originally temporalize temporality, in that events themselves, in their constantly suspended occurring, are their own temporalization; any understanding or interpretation of them is always retrospective, because it is events themselves, and them alone, which are fundamentally *prospective*, originally making possible the possibilities in light of which I will be able to understand them. Since an *advenant* cannot be contemporaneous with an event that happens to him, this event can never occur in a present that is followed by another instance of itself, to which it bequeaths itself, according to the scheme of a linear and homogenous temporality. Instead, we must enquire more originally into temporality itself, so as to understand it in its evential-character.

If a human adventure cannot be conceived as a sequence of facts, or de-worlded "events," which succeed one another, how is original temporality to be described, in its bursting-forth from events themselves as pure temporalization? How is this original temporality related to the world, in its evential sense, if it is right that events always open a *new world* for an *advenant*? Henceforth, a purely *chronic* conception of "life" as a succession of "lived experiences" and "facts" must be opposed by a *chronological* conception of adventure, as an articulation of events that do not so much happen in a world as they open a world to an *advenant* and make this world the object of an ex-per-ience, the very traversing of which, at the risk of oneself, by undergoing the totally other, *is time*.

§26 Conclusion: The Task of a Hermeneutic of Temporality

How are we, then, to describe time as it gives itself to be understood and seen from the perspective of events? If events are precisely nothing other than their own taking time [*temporisation*] in the constitutive suspense with which they present themselves, if they always already overflow the present of their actualization and thus defer themselves, then it follows that they do not happen as such *in* time, but instead that they *open* time, or *temporalize* it. Here, "to temporalize" time means, strictly, *to make it appear as such*, to give it to be seen according to a phenomenological perspective that remains closed in principle to thinking that starts with the intrinsic constitution of a subject or with this subject's formal characteristics and only after this enquires into the way that specific "attitudes" of such a "subject" could deploy time. For perhaps time is not something "subjective," regardless of how the "subject's subjectivity" is conceived: psychologically (Saint Augustine, Bergson), transcendentally (Kant, Husserl), or ontologically (Heidegger). Time does not belong to an *advenant* like a feature of his essence—because an *advenant* in fact has neither "Being" nor "essence," he "is" nothing other than his capacity to advene to himself from what happens [*advient*] to him, that is, his ad-venture, which is arrayed as ex-per-ience. Conversely, an *advenant*'s adventure "is" solely the traversing and ex-per-ience of events, according to the temporality that is proper to them. In short, by leading into a hermeneutic of temporality, which is its complement, evential hermeneutics reframes the temporal problematic: it is no longer a matter of knowing whether time belongs to the subject, but in what way the "subject" belongs to time. Temporality is a characteristic of events in their transcendental neutrality and, *only under this condition* is it a determination of an *advenant* in the different guises of his adventure. For an *advenant* only advenes to himself because something happens [*advient*] to him, or because something "becomes" of him [*il en advient de lui quelque chose*]; he "is" only this capacity to undergo events, in being born into an exposure to them. Though time becomes manifest through an *advenant*, time is not something that ever belongs to him as a property or characteristic of his essence. Rather, an *advenant* only advenes to himself if time "takes place"; he "is" only the "place" where time takes place as such.

Thus, the temporal problematic that unfolds on the basis of evential hermeneutics completely inverts the traditional terms of the problem. Since events, in their suspended occurring, are solely their own temporalization, and since an *advenant* is nothing other than his own ad-venture, as it takes place starting from events, the issue is to understand how this adventure can itself be conceived starting from evential temporality. This approach replaces the "Cartesian" perspective, which still seems to prevail in *Being and Time*, and asks how temporality can be conceived from the features of a "proper ontological conception of the subject." For, as we have seen above, an *advenant* can only be characterized as a "subjectivity" when he is no longer himself: an *advenant*. Subjectivity is precisely that posture where he holds himself back from the possibility of being touched and upended by any event whatever. *Consequently, if temporality is indeed an original characteristic of the human adventure, this is true to the extent that this adventure is primordially arrayed as ex-per-ience, starting from events,* and obviously not in the sense where temporality would be a formal-transcendental characteristic of a "subject." But what is the more precise meaning of this thesis, that temporality, as a determination of the human adventure, must be interpreted phenomenologically starting from events and their own taking time? How is such an interpretation possible in light of this guiding concept? And, above all, what does the adoption of this new guiding concept fundamentally change for interpretation? In particular, what results for time itself if the suspended occurring of events foils any possible gathering into presence, according to the measure of a subject? Is it not in the first place the temporality of Being that should be set aside in favor of a more original one?

Our answers will never measure up to the questions that gave rise to them. But far from smothering all questions in advance, these answers are the fuel that regenerates their flame, incessant, insatiable. As long as this flame continues to absorb us, giving breath to our speech, perhaps we shall be able, in a light that is still low, and on furtive ways, to pursue our interrupted path, leaving the quiet blaze of the sun burning at its Orient, limpid and lucid as truth.

Notes

Introduction

1. Vladimir Jankélévitch, *Le je-ne-sais-quoi et le presque-rien*, vol. 3, *La volonté de vouloir* (Paris: Editions du Seuil, 1986, coll. Points Essais), 76.

2. [Both "*étance*" and "beingness" are literal translations of the Greek *ousia*, which is a substantivized form of the present participle of *einai*, to be. For background to this choice (rather than the conventional "substance"), see Part 1, n. 23, below.—Trans.]

3. Henri Bergson, "The Perception of Change," in *The Creative Mind: An Introduction to Metaphysics*, trans. Mabelle L. Andison (New York: Citadel, 2002), 147 (translation modified); *Duration and Simultaneity: Bergson and the Einsteinian Universe*, trans. Leon Jacobson (Manchester: Clinamen, 1999), 30.

4. Friedrich Nietzsche, *Writings from the Late Notebooks*, trans. Kate Sturge (Cambridge: Cambridge University Press, 2005), Notebook 2 (84), 75–76 (translation modified); Nietzsche, *Kritische Studienausgabe*, ed. Giorgio Colli and Massimo Montinari (Berlin: Walter de Gruyter, 1988), 12:104; hereafter KSA.

5. Ibid., Notebook 2 (83), 74; KSA 12:102.

6. Ibid., Notebook 2 (83), 74; KSA 12:101.

7. Ibid. Notebook 2 (84), 75 (translation modified); KSA 12:101.

8. Friedrich Nietzsche, *On the Genealogy of Morality*, trans. Carol Diethe (Cambridge: Cambridge University Press, 2005), first essay, §13, 28; KSA 5:279.

9. "And this is plain to us, that we always use the word 'something' [*ti*] of some being [*ep onti*], for to speak of 'something' in the abstract, naked, as it were, and disconnected from all beings is impossible, is it not?" Plato, *The Sophist*, trans. Harold North Fowler (Cambridge: Harvard University Press, 2006), 237d;

cf. also Plato, *Parmenides*, trans. Harold North Fowler (Cambridge: Harvard University Press, 2002), 132b–c.

10. This term, which is generally translated as "sayables," will not be translated here.

11. Seneca, Letter to Lucilius, *Letters*, 58.13–15; J. Von Arnim, ed., *Stoicorum Veterum Fragmenta* (Munich: Teubner, 1964; hereinafter *SVF*) 2.332, in A. A. Long and D. N. Sedley, eds. and trans., *The Hellenistic Philosophers*, 2 vols. (Cambridge: Cambridge University Press, 1987), text 27A. Cf. Jacques Brunschwig, "The Stoic Theory of the Supreme Genus and Platonic Ontology," in *Papers in Hellenistic Philosophy* (Cambridge: Cambridge University Press, 1994), 92–157.

12. Diogenes Laertius 7.63: "Sayables, the Stoics say, are divided into complete and incomplete, the latter being ones whose linguistic expression is unfinished, e.g. '[Someone] writes,' for we ask, 'Who?' In complete sayables the linguistic expression is finished, e.g. 'Socrates writes.' So incomplete sayables include predicates [*katēgorēmata*], whereas ones that are complete include propositions, syllogisms, questions and enquiries" (Long and Sedley, *Hellenistic Philosophers*, text 33F).

13. Emile Bréhier, *Chrysippe et l'ancien stoïcisme* (Paris: Presses Universitaires de France, 1951), 70.

14. Aristotle, *On the Soul*, III, chap. 6, 430a27: "En hois de kai to pheudos kai to alethes, sunthesis tis ēdē noēmatōn hōsper hen ontōn"; *De Interpretatione*, chap. 1, 16a12: "peri gar sunthesin kai diairesin esti to pheudos kai to alēthes."

15. Diogenes Laertius 7.55–56, in Long and Sedley, *Hellenistic Philosophers*, text 33H.

16. Indeed, although Aristotle specifies the grammatical distinction between nouns and verbs at the start of *De Interpretatione*, he has a tendency to cover over this distinction and *to think verbs themselves as a kind of noun*. (The distinction is based in particular on the asymmetry of negation: "The negation of 'to be a man' is 'not to be a man,' not 'to be a not-man'"; *De Interpretatione*, chap. 12, 21b1, in *Complete Works of Aristotle: Revised Oxford Translation*, ed. Jonathan Barnes [Princeton, N.J.: Princeton University Press, 1991].) Thus, Aristotle thinks about the inflection or case (*ptosis*) of nouns and verbs as being parallel: the case of a noun corresponds to its grammatical function (accusative, dative, etc.), while the case of a verb corresponds to its temporal inflection. Thus, "verbs in and by themselves are nouns" (*De Interpretatione*, chap. 3, 16b19; translation modified). From a logical perspective, this blurring of the grammatical difference between nouns and verbs corresponds to the analysis of predicates in terms of copula and attribute: the sentence "Socrates walks" would have the logical structure "Socrates is walking" (*Metaphysics*, IV, 1017a27–29). The consequence of this division of verbs (which the Stoics conceived as an indivisible whole: incomplete *lekton* or "predicate") into copula + attribute is *to conceal the logical asymmetry of the two parts of a proposition*. This asymmetry appears in Frege's analysis of phrases as function (or predicate) and propositional variable and constant, which "saturate"

this function, and which are always "a proper name, or . . . an expression that replaces a proper name" (Gottlob Frege, "Function and Logic," in *Translations from the Philosophical Writings of Gottlob Frege*, ed. Peter Geach [Oxford: Basil Blackwell, 1966], 31). According to such an asymmetry, nouns have a complete signification, while predicates have signification only in relation to a noun, to the extent that they possess an empty place that can be saturated by a subject. Aristotle thus loses from sight the heterogeneity of subject and predicate that is based on the asymmetry of negation. He conceives predication as a relation between one term (*horos*) and another. A term that functions as a predicate in one proposition can henceforward become a subject in another predication. This is what Peter Geach calls "the Aristotelian theory of interchangeability," which makes the transition from the noun-predicate theory to the "two-term theory": "Aristotle's going over to the two-term theory was a disaster, comparable only to the Fall of Adam," he writes. "He lost the Platonic insight that any predicative proposition splits up into two logically heterogenous parts; instead, he treats predication as an attachment of one term (*horos*) to another term" (Peter J. Geach, *Logic Matters* [Oxford: Basil Blackwell, 1972], 47). The Stoics, on the other hand, maintain a distinction in principle between naming and saying (*onomazein/legein*) and between a noun that alone possesses an inflection (*ptōsis*) and the predicate expressed by a verb: case is that which must be added to a predicate in order to obtain a proposition (Diogenes Laertius 7.64). This difference in principle is marked by the fact that nouns denote a *body*, for example Dion, in the expression "Dion walks," while predicates signify a state of affairs or a *nonbodily* event: "[The] two are bodies—the utterance and the name bearer [*to tugchanon*]; but one is incorporeal—the state of affairs signified and sayable [*to sēmainomenon pragma, kai lekton*], which is true or false" (Sextus Empiricus *Against the Professors* 8.11–12; *SVF* 2.166; in Long and Sedley, *Hellenistic Philosophers*, text 33B).

17. Cf. V. Goldschmidt, "*Huparkhein* et *huphistanai* dans la philosophie stoïcienne," *Revue des études grecques* 85 (1972): 331–44.

18. The Stoic "categories," catalogued by Simplicius in his commentary on Aristotle's *Categories*, are as follows: (1) substrate (*hupokeimenon*), which is nothing other than matter (*hulē*), entirely passive and stripped of qualities; (2) quality (*poion*), which determines the differences in matter, so that the substrate, determined by its own proper quality (*idiōs poion*), constitutes a body in its individuality, that is, constitutes a *being* in the fullest sense, since the Stoics admit only particular distinct beings and since their nominalism is opposed to the existence of universal entities; (3) way of being (*pōs echon*), for example, an act accomplished in relation to an agent; and (4) relation (*pros ti*). Simplicius *On Aristotle's "Categories"* 66.32–67.2; *SVF* 2.369; in Long and Sedley, *Hellenistic Philosophers*, text 27F.

19. Stobaeus 1.138.14–139.4; *SVF* 1.89 and 2.336; in Long and Sedley, *Hellenistic Philosophers*, text 55A, translation modified.

20. Sextus Empiricus *Against the Professors* 9.211; *SVF* 2.341; in Long and Sedley, *Hellenistic Philosophers*, text 55B, translation modified.

21. Seneca *Letters* 65.4: "The Stoics believe that there is only one cause, that which makes something [*facit*]."

22. Cicero *On Fate* 39–43; SVF 2.974; in Long and Sedley, *Hellenistic Philosophers*, text 62C.

23. Clement of Alexandria *Miscellanies* 8.9.26.3–4; in Long and Sedley, *Hellenistic Philosophers*, text 55C.

24. Clement, *Miscellanies*, 8.9.30.1–3; *SVF* 2.349; in Long and Sedley, *Hellenistic Philosophers*, text 55D, translation modified.

25. Quoted in Michael Frede, "The Original Notion of Cause," in *Doubt and Dogmatism: Studies in Hellenistic Epistemology*, ed. Malcolm Schofield, Myles Burnyeat, and Jonathan Barnes (Oxford: Clarendon Press, 1980), 231.

26. Clement *SVF* 2.121–24.

27. Emile Bréhier, *La théorie des incorporels dans l'ancien stoïcisme* (Paris: Vrin, 1928), 12–13. The consequences of this doctrine are fundamental. Thanks to it, the Stoics can take up and reformulate the fundamental problem of Platonic and Aristotelian ontology—the problem of becoming-other, alteration, change, in a word, the problem of the relation of being and time. For them, time is not first of all that in which beings go by and pass away, but that which determines events (cf. the text quoted by Stobaeus, *SVF* 2.509). Bréhier comments: "Moreover, as a text of Chrysippus makes clear, the Stoics must have come to an insight which started from grammar, but had more than grammatical import: time applies directly only to verbs; that is, to the predicates that they regarded as incorporeal events" (*La théorie des incorporels*, 59). It is time itself that is truly an event; that is, a predicate of all beings without exception ("every discrete thing moves and exists in accord with time" [same text of Stobaeus, *SVF* 2.509]). It is time itself that occurs to beings but that has itself no beingness (*ousia*). Thus, they disqualify from the outset the question with which Aristotle opens his treatise on time: "*poteron tōn ontōn estin ē tōn mē ontōn* [Is it a being or a non-being?]." Time *is* not; to speak of time, one can only say: the present "is encountered [*huparchein*]," while the past and the future "advene [*huphistanai*]." On the difficulties in translating these verbs, difficulties I make no claim to settle, see Goldschmidt, "*Huparkhein* et *huphistanai* dans la philosophie stoïcienne," and Malcolm Schofield, "The Retrenchable Present," in *Matter and Metaphysics*, ed. Barnes and Mignucci, 331ff. A study of the evental status of time according to the Stoics remains to be done; perhaps it should conclude, as P. Pasquino suggests, that "Platonic logic [is] a-temporal by its very object. Stoics, for their part, deal with events, their logic is a logic of temporality" ("Le statut ontologique des incorporels dans l'ancien stoïcisme," in *Les Stoïciens et leur logique*, ed. J. Brunschwig [Paris: Vrin, 1978], 383).

28. Emmanuel Levinas, *Unforeseen History*, trans. Nidra Poller (Urbana: University of Illinois Press, 2004), 68–69 (emphasis added).

29. Martin Heidegger, *Being and Time*, trans. John Macquarrie and Edward Robinson (New York: Harper-Collins, 1962), 67; *Sein und Zeit*, 7th ed. (Tübingen: Max Niemeyer, 1927), 42.

30. Emmanuel Levinas, "Martin Heidegger and Ontology," *Diacritics* 26 (1996): 17.

31. Martin Heidegger, *The Basic Problems of Phenomenology*, rev. ed., trans. Albert Hofstadter (Indianapolis: Indiana University Press, 1988), 120; *Die Grundprobleme der Phänomenologie, Gesamtausgabe* (Frankfurt am Main: Vittorio Klostermann, 1989) 24: 169; hereafter GA.

32. Martin Heidegger, *Introduction to Metaphysics*, trans. Gregory Fried and Richard Polt (New Haven, Conn.: Yale University Press, 2000), 31; *Einführung in die Metaphysik*, GA 40, 31.

33. Emmanuel Levinas, *En découvrant l'existence avec Husserl et Heidegger*, 3rd ed. (Paris: Vrin, 1982), 59; text omitted from English translation of this work.

34. Martin Heidegger, *The Onto-theo-logical Constitution of Metaphysics*, in *Identity and Difference*, trans. Joan Stambaugh (Chicago: University of Chicago Press, 2002), 65; *Identität und Differenz* (Stuttgart: Günther Neske, 1957), 56.

35. Ibid., 64; 56.

36. Ibid.

37. Ibid.

38. Ibid., 65; 57.

39. Ibid.

40. This is why Heidegger suggested substituting *Eignis* for this term: "Instead of *Ereignis*, I use *Eigen*, so as to keep its expressive force at a distance from the meaning of *Ereignis* in the sense of *eventus*." Letter to Roger Munier, 26 May 1973, *Discordance*, 1 (April–June, 1978).

41. Wolfgang Brokmeier, "*Heidegger und wir*," *Genos* (1992): 61–95; cited in François Fédier, *Regarder voir* (Paris: Belles Lettres, 1995), 116.

42. Fédier, *Regarder voir* 116.

43. Ibid., 117 (emphasis added).

44. Cf. §18, below.

45. Heidegger, *Being and Time*, 302; *Sein und Zeit*, 258.

46. Ibid., 301; 257.

47. Cf. also my two essays: "Le possible et l'événement," in *Il y a* (Paris: Presses Universitaires de France, 2003), 55–111; and "Mourir à autrui," *Critique* 51, no. 582 (November 1995): 803–24.

48. Heidegger, *Being and Time*, 297; *Sein und Zeit*, 253.

49. Ibid., 298; 254.

50. Ibid.

51. Ibid., 309; 265.

52. Ibid., 337; 291.

53. Ibid., 318; 273.

54. Ibid., 381; 332.

Part 1: Events

1. Friedrich Hölderlin, "The Rhine," in *Poems and Fragments*, trans. M. Hamburger (London: Anvil Press, 1994), 433.

2. Peter Frederick Strawson, *Individuals: An Essay in Descriptive Metaphysics* (London: Methuen, 1959), 46.

3. Leibniz uses *"simples phénomènes"* to describe *appearances* like a rainbow: the appearing of what shows itself from itself is thus no longer distinguished from *mere* appearance. Greek, by contrast, carefully distinguishes between two verbs: *phainomai*, to shine in itself, from its own light, from which is derived *phainomenon*, that which shines, appears, shows itself as itself; and *phantazomai*, from which is derived the noun *phantasma*, that which shows itself other than as it is, mere appearance (*Schein*), simulacra. Cf. Plato, *Sophist*, 234b, where *eidōlon* and *phantasma* are synonymous.

4. Paul Claudel, "Leaving the Land," in *Knowing the East*, trans. James Lawler (Princeton, N.J.: Princeton University Press, 2004), 99 (translation modified).

5. G. W. F. Hegel, *Phenomenology of Spirit*, trans. A. V. Miller (Oxford: Oxford University Press, 1977), 27; *Phänomenologie des Geistes* (Frankfurt: Suhrkamp Taschenbuch, 1986), 3:56.

6. [*"En propre"* refers to something that is done personally, as oneself, and will generally be translated as "first-hand."—Trans.]

7. Paul Claudel, "Rain," in *Knowing the East*, 48 (emphasis added; translation modified).

8. William Faulkner, *The Reivers: A Reminiscence* (New York: Random House, 1962), 24–25.

9. Cf. §11, below.

10. Guillaume Apollinaire, "It's Raining [*Il Pleut*]," in *Selected Writings of Guillaume Apollinaire*, trans. Roger Shattuck (New York: New Directions Books, 1971), 170–71.

11. Immanuel Kant, *Critique of Pure Reason*, trans. Paul Guyer and Allen W. Wood, The Cambridge Edition of the Works of Immanuel Kant (Cambridge: Cambridge University Press, 1998), A 444 / B 472.

12. Michel de Montaigne, "An Affective Relationship," book 1, 28, in *The Essays of Michel de Montaigne*, trans. M. A. Screech (London: Penguin, 1991), 212.

13. On the meaning of this "forever [*à jamais*]" and of "never again [*jamais plus*]"—that is, on temporality—see the second volume of this study, *Event and Time* (*L'événement et le temps* [Paris: Presses Universitaires de France, 1999]; forthcoming in English), and "Le possible et l'événement."

14. Cf. n. 13, above.

15. Marcel Proust, *The Captive*, in *Remembrance of Things Past*, trans. C. K. Scott et al. (London: Chatto and Windus, 1981), 3:408; *La prisonnière*, in *À la recherche du temps perdu* (Paris: Gallimard, 1988), 3:902.

16. Franz Kafka, Letter to Milena, 12 June 1920, in *Letters to Milena*, trans. Philip Boehm (New York: Schocken Books, 1990), 43.

17. Claude Simon, *The Grass*, trans. Richard Howard (New York: George Braziller, 1960), 127–28.

18. This impersonality appears clearly in Claude Simon's description of a separation between lovers: *Who*, in fact, wanted it? If one wanted it, does that make him or her responsible for it? The response is more difficult than it might appear, for I am responsible for what I *wanted* and therefore for the *state of affairs* when the decision *is announced*, but the genuine event, the decision as it has been building up for a long time, the impersonal reconfiguration of my possibilities in love—can I be "responsible" for that?

19. Friedrich Nietzsche, "The Stillest Hour," in *Thus Spoke Zarathustra: A Book For All and None*, trans. Adrian del Caro (Cambridge: Cambridge University Press, 2006), 117; KSA 4:189: "Thoughts that come on the feet of doves steer the world": a formula that applies first of all to events, since "the greatest thoughts are the greatest events"; Nietzsche, *Beyond Good and Evil*, trans. Judith Norman (Cambridge: Cambridge University Press, 2002), §285, p. 171; KSA 5:232.

20. Nietzsche, *Beyond Good and Evil*, §285, p. 171; KSA 5:232.

21. *Empirie* is used in both French and German to denote empirical experience. As it appears on only a few occasions and there is no obvious English equivalent, it is not translated.—Trans.

22. Henri Maldiney rightly gives this point strong emphasis in *Penser l'homme et la folie* (Grenoble: Jérôme Millon, 1991), 422.

23. On this translation of *ousia* as *substantia* by Boethius and his successors, see Jean-François Courtine, "Note complémentaire pour l'histoire du vocabulaire de l'être," in *Concepts et catégories dans la pensée antique*, ed. Pierre Aubenque (Paris: Vrin, 1980), 33–87.

24. Emmanuel Levinas, *Existence and Existents*, trans. Alphonso Lingis (Pittsburgh: Duquesne University Press, 2001), 42 (translation modified).

25. Ibid.

26. Levinas, *Unforeseen History*, 69.

27. Cf. §18, below.

28. Cf. part 1, n. 13, above.

Part 2. The *Advenant*

1. Maurice Merleau-Ponty, "*Egō* and *Outis*" (April 1960), in *The Visible and the Invisible*, trans. Alphonso Lingis (Evanston, Ill.: Northwestern University Press, 1997), 246; *Le visible et l'invisible* (Paris: Gallimard, 1964), 299.

2. Immanuel Kant, *Prolegomena to Any Future Metaphysic that Will Be Able to Present Itself as Science*, trans. Peter G. Lucas and Günter Zöller (Oxford: Oxford University Press, 2004), §17, p. 103; Akademie Auflage, 4:296.

3. Jean-Paul Sartre, *Being and Nothingness*, trans. Hazel E. Barnes (New York: Washington Square Press, 1966), 575–76; *L'Être et le néant* (Paris: Gallimard, 1943), 501 (translation modified).

4. Cf. §16, below.

5. When Freud writes, in a well-known formula, that "the theory of the instincts is so to say our mythology" (Sigmund Freud, *New Introductory Lectures*

on Psychoanalysis, trans. James Strachey [New York: W. W. Norton, 1989], 111), he clearly marks the gap that separates an anthropological understanding of the human being, which is entirely confined to the horizon of the world and takes the form of an explanatory arche-ology of his psyche, and evential hermeneutics, which endeavors to grasp the very *meaning* of the human being's adventure starting from those critical moments that events are. This latter cannot begin from a concept of the "human being" that is already given in advance and ready to use (in this case, Freudian anthropology, with its biologizing and psychologizing background); rather, it constructs this concept, or even draws it out—the two operations reducing to one and the same where interpretation must at the same time construct its concepts and aim at making these conform with phenomena—such that a properly evential interpretation of the human being's humanity becomes possible (cf. part 3, below).

6. Cf. §23, below.

7. Cf. §4, above.

8. Joseph Conrad, *The End of the Tether*, in *Youth and The End of the Tether* (London: Penguin Books, 1975), 57.

9. Hegel, *Phenomenology of Spirit*, 6–7; *Phänomenologie des Geistes*, Surkamp Taschenbuch, 3: 18–19 (translation modified).

10. Cf. §15, below.

11. Heidegger, *The Basic Problems of Phenomenology*, §5, 21; *Die Grundprobleme der Phänomenologie*, GA 24:29.

12. Cf. Martin Heidegger, *The Metaphysical Foundations of Logic*, trans. Michael Heim (Bloomington: Indiana University Press, 1984), 169; *Metaphysische Anfangsgründe der Logik*, GA 26, 217: "If I say of Dasein that its basic constitution is Being-in-the-world, I am then first of all asserting something that belongs to its essence [*Wesen*], and I thereby disregard whether the being of such a nature factually [*faktisch*] exists or not." Hence the distinction between facticity (*Faktizität*), as an ontological characteristic of Dasein, entirely *neutral* with respect to its factical (*faktisch*) existence, and factuality (*Tatsächlichkeit*: cf. *Being and Time*, 82; *Sein und Zeit*, 56) as the characteristic of *present-at-hand* [*vorhanden*] beings. What this distinction nevertheless obscures is the possibility of an ontology of birth, since there the question of Dasein's essence appears to be entirely separated from the question bearing on its existence in fact. The question of Being-in-the-world remains an entirely formal question, cut off from the question of knowing *how such a "world" can in fact happen to Dasein.* On the impossibility of an ontology of birth in *Being and Time*, see my essay "Le possible et l'événement," in *Il y a*.

13. [The play on words is untranslatable.—Trans.]

14. Heidegger, *Being and Time*, 331; *Sein und Zeit*, 285. The analysis of Being-guilty [*Schuldigsein*], which ontologically means "Being-the-basis of a nullity," where this nullity refers precisely to the fact that Dasein, in being born, has *not* posited his own basis for himself, concludes in fact by asserting that Being-in-the-world must *take over* this basis ("*das Grundsein zu übernehmen hat*"), that

is, must *exist it* by the making possible of its ontological projection: the basis "is never anything but the basis for an entity whose Being has to take over Being-a-basis [*Grund-sein*]." Cf. also: "When Dasein is resolute, it takes over authentically in its existence the fact that it *is* the null basis of its own nullity" (*Being and Time*, 354; *Sein und Zeit*, 306).

15. Heidegger, *Being and Time*, 443; *Sein und Zeit*, 391.

16. Cf. §15, below.

17. Cf. §14, below.

18. Whence there is another fundamental point of rupture with the ontology of Dasein: indeed, it is no longer the anticipation of the possibility that cannot be outstripped that opens within itself all factical possibility ("The possibility is disclosed because it is made possible in anticipation" [Heidegger, *Being and Time*, 309; *Sein und Zeit*, 264]), since it is the event of birth, and it alone, that opens possibility in general for an *advenant*. It follows that resolution is no longer the source of all meaning for existence; indeed, for Dasein all understanding is self-understanding as mortal (finite), and, as "meaning" is defined in *Being and Time* as "that wherein the understandability [*Verstehbarkeit*] of something maintains itself," "the 'upon which' [*das Woraufhin*] of a primary projection in terms of which something can be conceived in its possibility" (*Being and Time*, 370–71; *Sein und Zeit*, 324), it follows that there is not for Heidegger any meaning other than what Dasein projects as an essentially finite being—and this is why *the meaning of Being itself is finitude, which is to say temporality*: "*Only Dasein can be meaningful* [sinnvoll] *or meaningless* [sinnlos]" (*Being and Time*, 193; *Sein und Zeit*, 151). In other words, there is only meaning where understanding reigns, and all understanding is *self*-understanding in the projection of a finite potentiality-for-Being. But there is precisely a meaning that, because it does not come from the horizon of my death, precedes and exceeds such an understanding and, by delivering itself to this, hands it over to an inexhaustible task.

19. Gustave Flaubert, *Sentimental Education*, trans. Robert Baldick (London: Penguin, 2004), 451.

20. On this ab-soluteness of time, see *Event and Time*.

21. [Legal maxim: No one is obliged to do what is impossible.—Trans.]

22. Heidegger, *Being and Time*, §§46–53. Cf. note 17, above.

23. Paul Claudel, *Positions et propositions* (Paris: Gallimard, 1928), 166.

24. Conversations with Gasquez, in Michael Doran, ed., *Conversations with Cézanne: Documents of Twentieth-Century Art*, trans. Julie Lawrence Cochran (Berkeley: University of California Press, 2001), 114.

25. E. Straus, *Vom Sinn der Sinne* (Berlin: Springer, 1935), 372: "I become [myself] only insofar as something happens to me, and something happens to me only insofar as I become." This is precisely why an event cannot be conceived first as an innerworldly fact that, in a second moment, would "alter my lived experiences" and transform me; it is nothing other than this transformation of an *advenant* and of the world—transformation often as silent and discreet as a fact is loud and visible—that can only be understood after the fact when, the old

world having collapsed, I am called upon to understand myself otherwise. Thus, the inaugural character, the "first time" character (*Erstmaligkeit*), which E. Straus rightly makes a fundamental feature of events, does not concern innerworldly facts, which happen, but the transformation of an adventure that puts selfhood in play: "With the first time, the transformation [of an adventure] is accomplished, and at the same time, the first time is founded in the transformation." *Geschehnis und Erlebnis zugleich eine historiologische Deutung des psychischen Traumas und der Renten-Neurose* (Berlin: Julius Springer, 1930), 23.

26. Gilles Deleuze, *The Logic of Sense*, trans. Mark Lester (New York: Columbia University Press, 1990), 152.

27. Cf. §16(b), below.

28. Rainer Maria Rilke, Letter 148 of 22 November 1920, in *Letters of Rainer Maria Rilke*, vol. 2, *1910–1926*, trans. J. Bannard Greene and M. D. Herter Norton (New York: W. W. Norton, 1948), 230: "Art can proceed only from a purely anonymous center."

29. Rilke, Letter to Merline of 22 February 1921, in *Œuvres*, vol. 3, *Correspondance* (Paris: Seuil), 464.

30. Doran, *Conversations with Cézanne*, 111.

31. This point is taken up in *Event and Time*.

32. Heidegger, *Being and Time*, 381; *Sein und Zeit*, 332.

33. Of course, "metaphysical" here does not refer to the concept of "metaphysics" Heidegger sets out from *Being and Time* onward under the heading of "traditional ontology," whose derived character his 1927 work is concerned with showing in relation to Dasein's fundamental ontology. The sense in which I am using this concept will be clarified at a later point, when I turn to the interpretation of time.

34. In fact, this structure is more complex for Husserl, since three levels should be distinguished rather than two: (1) temporality of the living present, as absolute *nunc stans*; (2) temporality of the flux of consciousness, as gradation of phases in continuous modification; and (3) objective time, as a succession of unchanging temporal positions.

35. Heidegger, *Being and Time*, 292; *Sein und Zeit*, 248.

36. [The French *prime-saut* evokes the adjective *primesautier*, spontaneous, impulsive.—Trans.]

37. Schelling, *Philosophie der Offenbarung*, Sammelte Werke, 13:225.

38. Rainer Maria Rilke, Letter 8, of 12 August 1904, in *Letters to a Young Poet*, trans. M. D. Herter Norton (New York: Norton, 1962), 63.

39. Rilke, *Letters to a Young Poet*, 64.

40. Ibid., 65 (translation modified).

41. Heidegger, *Metaphysical Foundations of Logic*, 193; *Metaphysische Anfangsgründe der Logik*, GA 26, 248–49.

42. Flaubert, *Sentimental Education*, 85 (emphasis added).

43. *The Diaries of Franz Kafka: 1912–23*, ed. Max Brod (Harmondsworth: Penguin, 1964), 19 October 1921, p. 394.

44. Samuel Beckett, *Endgame*, in *The Complete Dramatic Works* (London: Faber and Faber, 1990), 126.

45. Friedrich Hölderlin, "Das Angenehme Dieser Welt . . . [The World's Agreeable Things]," in *Poems and Fragments*, trans. M. Hamburger (London: Anvil Press, 1994), 662–63.

46. The *impersonality* of despair, where selfhood itself collapses, ceding its place to an anonymous lucidity, should be carefully distinguished from states of *depersonalization*, such as are manifested in most psychoses and that literally mean an alienation, a becoming foreign to oneself, which is manifested particularly in delirium. Nevertheless, important structural analogies subsist between what is usually called "madness" and acute forms of despair, in particular the fact that in despair, as in states of psychotic depersonalization, the loss of self is accompanied by a modification in the relation to one's own body and to the world: de-realized corporality that has become "foreign" to the person, de-realization of the world and its ambience. In *Vivre en délirant* (Paris: Les empêcheurs de penser en rond, 1992), Sven Follin quotes the testimony of melancholic patients: it is "as if I was dead, as if I was floating in my skin, like the feeling of no longer having weight nor body" (301). Follin comments: "For these subjects being and non-being, death and life, are terms that no longer have meaning; the whole world is dead for them." Cf. also 65f: "he observes his own reactions like a spectator. The external world seems strange to him and has lost its character of reality." That despair is able to transform itself from this into "madness" is a possibility that belongs to it intimately. Tracing the border between these phenomena is a major phenomenological problem that we have to leave aside here.

47. Cf. §17, below.

48. In this respect, despair is fundamentally different from Heideggerian anxiety: while in anxiety, with the appearance of *Welt als Welt* [world as world] and the ultimate existential isolation, Dasein is revealed to itself as *solus ipse*, despair shows a more profound dimension of the human adventure, a prepersonal dimension that is inaccessible to existential analysis, since this adopts as its starting point the determination of existence as Dasein's Being-for-the-sake-of-oneself (*sich umwillen*) and the thesis of mineness (*Jemeinigkeit*) as constitutive for Being.

49. Samuel Beckett, *Fizzle 4*, in *Samuel Beckett: The Complete Short Prose, 1929–1989* (New York: Grove Press, 1995), 234.

50. Samuel Beckett, *Stories and Texts for Nothing* (New York: Grove Press, 1967), no. 9, p. 119.

51. This aspect will be developed in detail as part of the analyses of evential temporality and its relation to Dasein's temporality in *Event and Time*.

52. Beckett, *Stories and Texts for Nothing*, no. 10, p. 123.

53. Sigmund Freud and Joseph Breuer, *Studies on Hysteria*, trans. James Strachey and Alix Strachey (London: Penguin, 1991), 56.

54. In Greek, the first meaning of *trauma* is wounding, and more precisely wounding by breaking open: the noun derives from the verb *titrōskō:* to pierce.

55. "I went to the doctor [with my husband] and waited in the next room; trembling and crying, I heard his horrible groaning. The doctor told him that he

had a small sore in the bladder, but turning his back on him he looked at me with an expression that was so terrifying and devoid of hope that I remained frozen, with my mouth open in terror." Ludwig Binswanger, *Schizophrenie* (Pfullingen: Neske, 1957), 369; from the French translation *Le cas Suzanne Urban* (Paris: Gérard Monfort, 1988), 20.

56. Binswanger, *Le cas Suzanne Urban*, 41; cf. also H. Maldiney's notable commentary in *Penser l'homme et la folie*, 278–79.

57. Binswanger, *Le cas Suzanne Urban*, 44.

58. Cf. Le Congrès de psychiatrie et de neurologie de langue française, *Le traumatisme psychique: Rencontre et devenir* (Paris: Masson, 1994); and Claude Barrois, *Les névroses traumatiques* (Paris: Dunod, 1988).

59. Cf. §23(b), below.

60. *Le traumatisme psychique*, 95.

61. Ibid., 95.

62. The British Medical Association Guide, *Living with Risk* (London: Wiley Medical, 1987), quoted in *Le traumatisme psychique*, 63.

63. *Living with Risk*, quoted in *Le traumatisme psychique*, 109–10.

64. Psychiatry speaks willingly, in more psychological terms, of a "lowering of the threshold of general reactivity" (*Living with Risk*, quoted in *Le traumatisme psychique*, 120).

65. Ibid., 120.

66. Kafka, Letter to Milena of 12 June 1920, in *Letters to Milena*, 43.

67. [The unusual expression *mourir à* is used throughout this section to describe the way that bereavement is itself a kind of death. It has been translated literally, echoing English expressions such as "dead to the world" and "die to oneself."—Trans.]

68. Marcel Proust, *The Fugitive*, in *Remembrance of Things Past*, 3:494.

69. Ibid., 499.

70. Ibid., 470.

71. Ibid., 486.

72. "We have the faculty of making up stories to soothe our anguish" (ibid., 473).

73. Ibid., 473.

74. Even to the letter in certain expressions: a little later, we will find a literally Humean expression penned by the author of *Remembrance of Things Past*: "the easy slope of imagination" (ibid., 475)—an expression that refers in Hume's *Treatise on Human Nature* to the very process of association.

75. Proust, *The Fugitive*, 474.

76. Ibid., 475.

77. Ibid., 485 (emphasis added).

78. Ibid., 488.

79. Ibid., 493.

80. What does "incomparably" mean here? The other is not incomparable to me in being *other* (according to an absolute Otherness that, in Levinasian

terms, would be ab-solved of any relation to the Same) but in being *herself*, that is, *like myself*, radically singular. In this respect, therefore, there is a perfect *reciprocity* between me and the other: I am as incomparable to her as she is to me and to any other, and her otherness—if it is doubtless not a specific otherness subordinated to a common genus, a categorial difference, but genuinely an evential difference that is rooted in her history as it singularizes her—is a relational and *relative* otherness, which is said, consequently, *pros heteron*, like the determinate otherness of the *Sophist*. Moreover, selfhood is this way for an *advenant* to advene to himself as himself, this subjectivation starting from events that are in themselves *impersonal* and in no way the "subjection" of myself to the other such as Levinas conceives it.

81. On these reservations with respect to Heidegger's analysis of bereavement, cf. my essay "Mourir à autrui."

82. "If I am loved on account of my judgment or my memory is it *I* who am loved?" To which Pascal responds: "We never love a person but only qualities." Blaise Pascal, *Pensées: Notes on Religion and other Subjects*, ed. Louis Lafuma, trans. John Warrington (London: J. M. Dent & Sons, 1973), no. 167 (Br. 323), p. 47.

83. Proust, *The Fugitive*, 501.

84. We do not recover from a bereavement; at most, we only survive it. We survive a bereavement in that we make it ours. Phenomenological psychiatry describes, by contrast, those possibilities of a human adventure in which the melancholic, incapable of suffering, dispossessed of his sadness, is literally haunted by a grief that is not his: "The illness of the melancholic consists precisely in his 'inability-to-be-sad' (W. Schulte, 1961). The melancholic can suffer only in the form of obsession by a grief that is not his own" (Hubertus Tellenbach, *Melancholy: History of the Problem, Endogeneity, Typology, Pathogenesis, Clinical Considerations*, trans. Erling Eng [Pittsburgh: Duquesne University Press, 1980], 26; translation modified). But to survive bereavement—a "survival [*survie*]" that is a genuine "life [*vie*]," that is not the life on hold of the condemned—is never to abolish that lacuna of the world in which another's death plunges us by engulfing our compossibles. The Freudian idea of a "work of grief" through which, by means of introjection and idealization, the "me" would be "saved" by disinvesting itself of the "object," the idea of a work of the negative in which this lacuna would henceforth be filled by means of a sort of dialectical *Aufhebung*—are rigorously insufficient here; there is never a return to the *status quo ante*. For an event is precisely that which renders such a way back impossible in principle. It is of the event itself and of its temporality that an economy of drives cannot give an account.

85. Hugo von Hofmannsthal, "Encounters," *Yale French Studies* 9 (1965): 162.

86. Cf. Maldiney, *Penser l'homme et la folie*, 355.

87. Cesare Pavese, Letter to Constance Dowling of 17 April 1950, in *Selected Letters: 1924–1950*, trans. A. E. Murch (London: Peter Owen, 1969), 258; see also his Letter to Constance Dowling of 17 March 1950, in *Selected Letters*, 255.

88. Pavese, Letter to Constance Dowling of 17 April 1950, in *Selected Letters*, 258.

89. Kafka, Letter to Milena of 12 June 1920, in *Letters to Milena*, 43.

90. "I lament being born, I lament the light of the sun." Kafka, Letter to Milena of 12 June 1920, in *Letters to Milena*, 43.

91. Flaubert, *Sentimental Education*, 8 (emphasis added; translation modified).

92. Straus, *Vom Sinn der Sinne*, 408.

93. Cf. Jean-Louis Chrétien, *L'effroi du beau* (Paris: Cerf, 1987), 15.

94. Cf. §9, above.

95. René Descartes, *Meditations on First Philosophy*, trans. John Cottingham (Cambridge: Cambridge University Press, 1986), 3rd meditation, 30; A.T. 7: 44.

96. Rene Descartes, *Principles of Philosophy*, part 1, §51, in *Philosophical Writings*, trans. Elizabeth Anscombe and Peter Geach (Edinburgh: Nelson, 1954), 192; A.T. 8: 24.

97. Cf. part 3, below.

98. Descartes, *Meditations on First Philosophy*, 2nd meditation, 22–23; A.T. 7: 34.

99. Heidegger, *Being and Time*, 183; *Sein und Zeit*, 143.

100. Martin Heidegger, *The Phenomenology of Religious Life*, trans. Matthius Eritsch and Jennifer Anna Gosetti-Ferencei (Bloomington: Indiana University Press, 2004); "Phänomenologie des religiösen Lebens," in *Einleitung in die Phänomenologie der Religion*, GA 60. Cf. also Thomas Sheehan, "Heidegger's *Introduction to the Phenomenology of Religion*, 1920–1921," *The Personalist* 60, no. 3 (1979): 312–24.

101. Cf. my essay, "Le possible et l'événement."

102. Heidegger, *Being and Time*, 306; *Sein und Zeit*, 261.

103. Ibid., 302; 258.

104. Ibid., 301; 257.

105. Ibid, 310; 266.

106. Ibid., 309; 264.

107. Ibid., 357; 309.

108. Ibid., 308; 263.

109. Cf. "Le possible et l'événement."

110. Heidegger, *Being and Time*, 309; *Sein und Zeit*, 265.

111. Ibid., 416; 364.

112. Ibid., 418; 366.

113. On the evential determination of ex-per-ience and on transcendental empiricism, cf. Part 3, below.

114. Heidegger, *The Basic Problems of Phenomenology*, 277–78; *Die Grundprobleme der Phänomenologie*, GA 24, 393.

115. Heidegger, *Being and Time*, 439; *Sein und Zeit*, 387.

116. Ibid., 370–71; 324 (translation modified).

117. Ibid., 183; 143.

118. Ibid., 193; 151.
119. Ibid., 357; 309.
120. Ibid., 365; 317.
121. Ibid., 368; 322.
122. Ibid., 356; 309.
123. Ibid., 358; 310.
124. Sartre, *Being and Nothingness*, 654–55.
125. Heidegger, *Being and Time*, 355; *Sein und Zeit*, 307.
126. Ibid., 407; 355.
127. Ibid., 369; 322.
128. Ibid., 381; 332.
129. Ibid., 346; 299.
130. Cf. the excellent article by Yvonne Picard, "Le temps chez Husserl et Heidegger," *Deucalion* 1 (1946): 93.

Part 3. Experience
1. Martin Heidegger, *On the Way to Language*, trans. Peter D. Hertz (San Francisco: HarperSanFrancisco, 1982), 57; *Unterwegs zur Sprache*, GA 12:149.
2. I am following the indications given by Julius Pokorny, *Indogermanisches etymologisches Wörterbuch* (Berne: Francke, 1959).
3. Roger Munier, "Response to an Enquiry on Experience," *Mise en page* (May 1972): 37.
4. Cf. §23(b), below.
5. On the ontological sense of a priori, cf. Martin Heidegger, *History of the Concept of Time: Prologomena*, trans. Theodore Kisiel (Bloomington: Indiana University Press, 1992), 75; *Prolegomena zur Geschichte des Zeitbegriffs*, GA 20:102–3 (translation modified): the a priori is a "feature of the Being of entities and not a feature of entities themselves," such that "the discovery of the a priori is really connected or actually identical with the discovery of the concept of Being in Parmenides or in Plato." This is why a-priorism is the method of all ontology as such (*Being and Time*, 490, n. 10; *Sein und Zeit*, 50, n. 1).
6. Heidegger, *Being and Time*, §6.
7. Hans-Georg Gadamer, *Truth and Method* (London: Sheed & Ward, 1975), 265–66; *Wahrheit und Methode* (Tübingen: J. C. B. Mohr, 1960), 282.
8. "Non-sense" is not used here in its usual sense of nonsense or absurdity. Rather, it refers to meaning's original opacity for any understanding—an opacity that nevertheless remains a modality of meaning, in that meaning is first given only to a primary and basic *incomprehension*.
9. ["*Connaître une expérience*," literally "be acquainted with an experience," is a common French expression for "having an experience."—Trans.]
10. Cf. §10, above.
11. Aeschylus, *Agamemnon*, line 177. Cf. also *Prometheus Bound*, lines 10–11: for Kratos, it is the suffering of being chained to a rock that will teach Prometheus wisdom, or at least acceptance of the new regime. This tragic apprenticeship at the price of pain, summed up as "passional learning," where "passion"

must be understood in the primary sense of the Latin verb *patire*, to suffer, will be weakened by Aristotle, thereby implying a degradation of the concept of exper-ience into an "empiricist" sense, when the Stagirite conceives of passion as a psychological "affect," a passion that arouses the compassion of spectators called "purification [*katharsis*]." In Aristotle's *Poetics*, as Karl Reinhardt states, "*pathos* in itself, taken in a pedagogico-psychological sense, just like purification, refers to nothing other than a psychic or ethico-aesthetic phenomenon" (*Eschyle, Euripide*, French translation by E. Martineau [Paris: Éditions de Minuit, 1972], 85). We will see how this degradation of the original sense of experience is expressed philosophically at the beginning of the *Metaphysics*.

12. Friedrich Hölderlin, "On the Operations of the Poetic Spirit," in *Essays and Letters on Theory*, trans. Thomas Pfau (Albany: State University of New York Press, 1988), 81.

13. It is not on the basis of a classification of literary genres that we call a particular speech "poetic," but conversely, on the basis of the inaugural-eventual character of a particular speech that we call a determinate genre "poetry": this implies that prose can be "poetic," and even more "poetic" than poetry, and that "poetry" (or at least what is reputed to be such) can be prosaic. On the possibility of a phenomenological approach to poetic genres, cf. Emil Staiger, *Basic Concepts of Poetics*, trans. Janette C. Hudson and Luanne T. Frank (University Park: Pennsylvania State University Press, 1991).

14. Ferdinand de Saussure, *Course in General Linguistics*, trans. Roy Harris (London: Duckworth, 1983), 13–14.

15. Rainer Maria Rilke, *The Notebooks of Malte Laurids Brigge*, cited in Maurice Blanchot, *The Space of Literature*, trans. Ann Smock (Lincoln: University of Nebraska Press, 1982), 87.

16. T. S. Eliot, "East Coker," in *Four Quartets* (London: Faber and Faber, 1999), 19.

17. André Malraux, cited in Blanchot, *The Space of Literature*, 228.

18. Rilke, Letter of 28 February 1921, in *Letters to Merline*, 89.

19. Rilke, Letter to Marie de la Tour et Taxis of 6 September 1915, in *Correspondance*, 380.

20. Rilke, "The Letter of the Young Worker," in *Symbolism: An Anthology*, trans. T. G. West (London: Methuen, 1980), 88.

21. Boris Pasternak, *Safe Conduct: An Early Autobiography and Other Works*, trans. Alec Brown (London: Elek Books, 1959), 213.

22. Edmund Husserl, *Ideas Pertaining to a Pure Phenomenology and to a Phenomenological Philosophy. First Book: General Introduction to a Pure Phenomenology*, trans. F. Kersten, *Collected Works*, vol. 2 (London: Kluwer Academic Publishers, 1998), §124, p. 296; *Ideen zu einer reinen Phänomenologie und phänomenolgischen Philosophie. Erstes Buch: Allgemeine Einführung in die reine Phänomenologie*, ed. Walter Biemel (The Hague: Martinus Nijhoff, 1950), Hua III/1, 284ff.

23. Hugo von Hofmannsthal, "*Das Gespräch über Gedichte* [Dialogue on Poetry]," *Neue Rundschau* 1, no. 2 (February 1904): 132 (emphasis added).

24. Christian Friedrich Hebbel, *Sie seh'n sich nicht wieder* [*They see one another no longer*].

25. Hofmannsthal, "*Das Gespräch über Gedichte*," 133.

26. Ibid. (emphasis added).

27. Ibid., 135.

28. "Making sense happen" is not *creating* it, nor is it simply *reactivating* significations that are passively "sedimented" in language (Husserl, Merleau-Ponty): the event of saying is prior in this respect, like all events, to the distinction between "active" and "passive."

29. Hegel, *Phenomenology of Spirit*, 21; *Phänomenologie des Geistes*, Surkamp Taschenbuch, 3:39.

30. Ibid., 19; 3:36.

31. Ibid., 49; 3:72.

32. Aeschylus, *Agamemnon*, line 177.

33. [*En souffrance* has two senses: "to be suffering" and "to be waiting."—Trans.]

34. Hegel, *Phenomenology of Spirit*, 51; *Phänomenologie des Geistes*, Surkamp Taschenbuch, 3:74.

35. Martin Heidegger, *Hegel*, GA 68:103; cf. also 134–35.

36. Franz Kafka, quoted in Gustav Janouch, *Conversations with Kafka*, trans. Goronwy Rees (London: André Deutsch, 1971), 13.

37. Leo Tolstoy, "The Death of Ivan Ilyich," in *The Death of Ivan Ilyich and Other Stories*, trans. Aylmer Maude (New York: New American Library, 1960), 139.

38. Tolstoy, "The Death of Ivan Ilyich," 154.

39. Cesare Pavese, *This Business of Living: Diary 1935–1950*, trans. Alma E. Murch (London: Peter Owen, 1961), 146–47.

40. Tolstoy, "The Death of Ivan Ilyich," 152.

41. Ibid., 119.

42. Schelling, *Textes esthétiques*, French translation by A. Pernet (Paris: Klincksieck, 1978), 133.

43. Ovid, *Metamorphoses I–IV*, trans. D. E. Hill (Warminster: Arisa Phillips, 1985), book I, lines 85–86, pp. 14–15.

44. Rainer Maria Rilke, "*Komm du, letzer* . . . [Come, then, you the last thing]," in *Uncollected Poems*, trans. Edward Snow (New York: North Point Press, 1996), 250–51.

45. Rainer Maria Rilke, "Death Experienced," in *Selected Works*, vol. 2, *Poetry*, trans. J. B. Leisham (London: Hogarth Press, 1980), 165.

46. Hegel, *Phenomenology of Spirit*, 76; *Phänomenologie des Geistes*, Surkamp Taschenbuch, 3:103 (translation modified).

47. [*Changement du tout au tout* is a common French expression for a complete and radical change, a change "through and through."—Trans.]

48. Cf. *Event and Time*.

49. Rilke, *Duino Elegies*, "The Eighth Elegy," in *Selected Works*, 2:242.

50. Heidegger, *Being and Time*, 302; *Sein und Zeit*, 258.

51. Blanchot, *The Space of Literature*, 155.

52. Heidegger, *Being and Time*, 357; *Sein und Zeit*, 309.

53. [As well as its primary meaning of "escape," "*échappée*" also refers to an opening, especially one through which something can escape, for instance a gap that allows a view to break through.—Trans.]

54. Alterity primary in itself and original, since the other depends on it just as much as I do, as soon as her revelation is suspended in an *encounter*.

55. Blanchot, *The Space of Literature*, 122.

56. Ibid., 241.

57. Heidegger, *Being and Time*, 235; *Sein und Zeit*, 191.

58. Ibid., 295; 251.

59. Ibid., 310; 266.

60. Ibid., 289; 245.

61. Rainer Maria Rilke, *The Book of Hours*, in *Selected Works*, vol. 2, *Poetry*, third book, no. 7, p. 91.

62. By endeavoring to remove death from the factuality of an event (*Ereignis*), by conceiving it as a future possibility of myself, a possibility that is merely possible, Heidegger still *represents* it as a quasi-fact, the fact of "the loss of Being-in-the-world" (*Being and Time*, 280; *Sein und Zeit*, 236), and this is why Dasein can still be *afraid* of it, even if this fear no longer has anything "empirical" about it; what Heidegger thereby misses is precisely the difference between fact and event: death is not a possibility, *the* absolute and not to be outstripped possibility of existence, but an impersonal *making-possible*—strictly, an *event*.

63. The phenomenon of despair, which has served thus far as the guiding thread for bringing this anonymity to light, has for this reason a particular privilege: *such privileging does not imply, however, that it is the sole possible attitude that, in the face of death*, leaves to death its incommensurable otherness; in peaceful renunciation, in tranquil abandonment to death, from which the tragedy of despair is excluded, we are not resolute, there is no will opting toward a future possibility of ourselves, and nevertheless we *prepare* ourselves for the unpreparable, we still *answer* for death by answering for our impossibility to answer for it, we recommit ourselves to it by abandoning ourselves to it.

64. Hugo von Hofmannsthal, *Die Briefe des Zurückgekehrten* [*Letters from a Voyager upon his Return*] (1907–8), second letter, in *Sämtliche Werke: Kritsche Ausgabe*, vol. 31, *Erfundene Gespräche und Briefe*, ed. Ellen Ritter (Frankfurt am Main: Fischer, 1991).

65. Aristotle, *Poetics*, chap. 6, 1449b24–28, in *The Complete Works of Aristotle* (translation modified).

66. Cf. §16(a), above.

67. Aristotle, *Metaphysics*, I, chap. 1, 980b29.

68. Ibid., 981a15.

69. Ibid., 981a16–17.

70. David Hume, *A Treatise of Human Nature* (Harmondsworth: Penguin, 1987), book 1, part 4, §6, p. 301.

71. Aristotle, *Metaphysics*, I, chap. 1, 981a4–5.

72. Ibid., 981a27–28.

73. Ibid., 981a14.

74. Ibid., 980b29–981a1 (emphasis added).

75. Aristotle, *Posterior Analytics*, II, chap. 19, 100a3–6, in *The Complete Works of Aristotle*.

76. This is why animals "have but little of connected experience [*empeiria*]; but the human race lives also by art and reasonings [*technē, logismos*]" (Aristotle, *Metaphysics*, I, chap. 1, 980b26–28); animals only have recollections and not a true memory able to identify regularities in what is repeated. While all animals are endowed with sensory perception, it is only in the higher animals that there is also a persistence of a sensory impression beyond the act of perceiving: "And when many such things come about, then a difference comes about, so that some come to have an account from the retention of such things, and others do not. So from perception there comes memory, as we call it, and from memory (when it occurs often in connection with the same thing), experience" (Aristotle, *Posterior Analytics*, II, chap. 19, 99b39–100a5); this text shows well the inextricable intertwining in the human being of what Aristotle nevertheless endeavors to distinguish: experience, knowledge of the particular, on the one hand, knowledge of what happens *most often*, that which, without achieving constancy, approaches it (Aristotle, *Metaphysics*, XI, chap. 8, 1065a4–6; and *Posterior Analytics*, I, chap. 30, 87b22–25), and, on the other hand, the formation of a universal notion, by means of an inductive process, which is not required by the former. Consequently, the human being alone, insofar as he is able to arrive at notions, can have a genuine experience, being capable of grasping, in what repeats, the *identity* of the similar.

77. Hume, *A Treatise of Human Nature*, book 1, part 4, §6, p. 301.

78. Ibid., §7, p. 312.

79. Ibid.

80. Cf. Gilles Deleuze, *Empiricism and Subjectivity: An Essay on Hume's Theory of Human Nature*, trans. Constantin V. Boundas (New York: Columbia University Press, 1991), 68: "We could even say that habit is experience."

81. David Hume, *Enquiry Concerning Human Understanding*, §5.1, in *Enquiries Concerning Human Understanding and Concerning the Principles of Morals* (Oxford: Oxford University Press, 1975), 44.

82. Hume, *Enquiry Concerning Human Understanding*, §5.1, 44 (emphasis added).

83. Hume, *A Treatise of Human Nature*, book 1, part 4, §7, 312 (emphasis added).

84. Ibid., book 1, part 1, §1, p. 66. Hume's nominalism excludes, in his philosophy, any recourse to general ideas: on the contrary, individual ideas can be grouped and brought together under a general term of language only "with a view to that resemblance, which they bear to each other, this relation [which] must facilitate their entrance in the imagination, and make them be suggested

more readily upon occasion" (ibid., §7, p. 71). To hold that the difference between impressions and ideas is only a difference of degree in "vivacity" is to pre-
clude thinking about the way in which the transition comes about from the
merely "similar" to the "same" and from observation to anticipation: for each
sensation of flame to be able to awaken the idea of heat and, by association, that
of burning, it is necessary that this idea, even if it is not "abstract," nevertheless
be *the same* for all given sensations of flame. For a definitive critique of Hume's
theory of ideas, cf. Edmund Husserl, *Logical Investigations*, trans. J. N. Findlay
(London: Routledge & Kegan Paul, 1970), II, chaps. 1 and 5. Cf. in particular
Logical Investigations, II, chap. 1, §3, 342–43; Hua XIX, 112, where the crux of
Husserl's entire critique of Hume's empiricism is set out: "*We find in fact that
wherever things are 'alike,' an identity in the strict and true sense is also present.* We
cannot predicate exact likeness of two things, without stating the respect in which
they are thus alike. Each exact likeness relates to a Species, under which the objects compared, are subsumed: this Species is not, and cannot be, merely 'alike'
in the two cases, if the worst of infinite regresses is not to become inevitable."
Identity cannot be derived from likeness, as Hume believes, but instead the inverse alone is possible: "'Alikeness' is the relation of objects falling under one
and the same Species" (Husserl, *Logical Investigations*, II, chap. 1, §3, 343; Hua
XIX, 113).

85. Hume, *A Treatise of Human Nature*, book 1, part 4, §6, 303.

86. Ibid., book 1, part 1, §7, 70.

87. Cf. §24(c), below.

88. Kant, *Prolegomena to Any Future Metaphysic*, §18, 104; Akademie
Auflage, 4: 298.

89. This difficulty is confirmed in the example given by Kant, which I am
going to analyze: "When the sun shines on the stone, it grows warm" (Kant,
Prolegomena to Any Future Metaphysic, §20, 107n; Akademie Auflage, 4: 301n).
For this judgment of perception to be formulated, must not at least two categories be introduced already, that of substance ("the sun," "the stone") and that of
quantity, since it is a matter of a *quantum* of warmth?

90. Kant, *Prolegomena to Any Future Metaphysic*, §20, 107n; Akademie
Auflage, 4: 301n.

91. Kant, *Prolegomena to Any Future Metaphysic*, §20, 106; Akademie
Auflage, 4: 300 (translation modified).

92. Kant, *Critique of Pure Reason*, B218.

93. Husserl, Letter to Hocking, 25 January 1903; quoted in Walter Biemel,
"Les phases décisives dans le développement de la pensée de Husserl," in *Husserl*
(Paris: Cahiers de Royaumon, 1959), 46.

94. Husserl, *Ideas I*, §47, 106; Hua III/1, 89.

95. Edmund Husserl, *Formal and Transcendental Logic*, trans. Dorion Cairns
(The Hague: Martinus Nijhoff, 1969), § 99, 251–52; Hua XVII, 222.

96. Paul Ricoeur, *From Text to Action: Essays in Hermeneutics, II*, trans. Kath-
leen Blamey and John B. Thompson (Evanston, Ill.: Northwestern University
Press, 1991), 50.

97. Husserl, Manuscript B IV, 1 (1903), Hua VII (translated from French).

98. Indeed, it seemed that the "discovery" of intentionality should have freed phenomenology from all theory of representations, as a substitute for things actually present "in" consciousness: every intentional lived experience is ostensive of the thing itself, without it being possible to interpose between the thing and consciousness the useless double of a "representation." Nevertheless, Husserl maintains, at the heart of lived experience, a fundamental difference between its real and intentional components: the noesis and the *hylè* belong to the former, the noemata to the latter. Accordingly, for example, color as an objective noematic property of the thing is distinguished from "color" as an impressional *datum* really immanent to consciousness: "Now *this* color, put into parentheses, belongs to the noema. But it does not belong to the mental process of perception as a really [*reelles*] inherent component piece, although we can find in it 'something like color': namely, the 'sensed color [*Empfindungsfarbe*],' that hyletic moment of the concrete mental process by which the noematic, or 'objective [*objektive*],' color is 'adumbrated'" (Husserl, *Ideas I*, §97, 237; Hua III/1, 226). The color of the object, in the noematic sense, is therefore distinguished from what must be called, in an unavoidable homonymy, "sensed color." But this "second color," in which the first is sketched, *does not appear*. What, then, are these sensed adumbrations, these hyletic "colors" that seem to float within consciousness and that must be distinguished, under reduction, from noematic colors, if not a pure "impressional manifold" little different from the empiricists' *sensualia*? Of course, they are still distinguished from them insofar as they are descriptive givens determined by an internal characteristic of a lived experience and not by the external characteristic of their provenance in the senses (*Logical Investigations*, II, chap. 1). But there remains a homonymy in principle, from which intentional analysis cannot free itself, between impressional "color," improperly called "color," which is the intermediary through which the object is aimed at, and its objective color, present in the noema, itself given *originaliter*. Sometimes color is an attribute of the thing, sometimes it qualifies sensations. Henceforth, as Levinas comments, "sensation becomes the *analogon* of the object" (*En découvrant l'existence avec Husserl et Heidegger*, 149) and seems to take on a quasi-autonomy: we fall back into the abstraction that intentionality alone can combat, thanks to the structural solidarity between the two moments of lived experience, hyletic and morphological (*Ideas I*, §85, 204; Hua III/1, 192). Husserl, in an unpublished manuscript, himself addresses this objection: "*Ist nicht meine ursprüngliche Auffassung von der immanenten Sphäre mit den immanenten Daten, die am Ende erst durch die passive Leistung der Assoziation zu 'Auffassung kommen,' noch ein Rest der alten Psychologie, und ihres sensualistischen Empirismus?* [Is not my original apprehension of the immanent sphere with immanent data, which in the end first 'come to apprehension' through the passive production of association, still a residue of the old psychology, and its sensory empiricism?]" (Manuscript B I, II, p. 8, quoted in G. Brand, *Welt, Ich und Zeit*, 27, n. 2).

99. Walter Benjamin, "On Some Motifs in Baudelaire," trans. Harry Zohn, in *The Writer of Modern Life: Essays on Charles Baudelaire*, ed. Michael W. Jennings (Cambridge: Harvard University Press, 2006), 173–74.

100. Walter Benjamin, "Central Park," trans. Howard Eiland, in *The Writer of Modern Life*, 140.

101. Walter Benjamin, "The Storyteller," in *Illuminations*, trans. Harry Zohn (New York: Brace and World, 1968), 89.

102. Charles Baudelaire, "Fusées," in *Œuvres complètes* (Paris: Gallimard, 1976), 2: 641.

Index

Perspectives in Continental Philosophy Series

John D. Caputo, series editor

Karl Jaspers, *The Question of German Guilt*. Introduction by Joseph W. Koterski, S.J.

Jean-Luc Marion, *The Idol and Distance: Five Studies*. Translated with an introduction by Thomas A. Carlson.

Jeffrey Dudiak, *The Intrigue of Ethics: A Reading of the Idea of Discourse in the Thought of Emmanuel Levinas*.

Robyn Horner, *Rethinking God as Gift: Marion, Derrida, and the Limits of Phenomenology*.

Mark Dooley, *The Politics of Exodus: Søren Kierkegaard's Ethics of Responsibility*.

Merold Westphal, *Overcoming Onto-Theology: Toward a Postmodern Christian Faith*.

Edith Wyschogrod, Jean-Joseph Goux and Eric Boynton, eds., *The Enigma of Gift and Sacrifice*.

Stanislas Breton, *The Word and the Cross*. Translated with an introduction by Jacquelyn Porter.

Jean-Luc Marion, *Prolegomena to Charity*. Translated by Stephen E. Lewis.

Peter H. Spader, *Scheler's Ethical Personalism: Its Logic, Development, and Promise*.

Jean-Louis Chrétien, *The Unforgettable and the Unhoped For*. Translated by Jeffrey Bloechl.

Don Cupitt, *Is Nothing Sacred? The Non-Realist Philosophy of Religion: Selected Essays*.

Jean-Luc Marion, *In Excess: Studies of Saturated Phenomena*. Translated by Robyn Horner and Vincent Berraud.

Phillip Goodchild, *Rethinking Philosophy of Religion: Approaches from Continental Philosophy*.

William J. Richardson, S.J., *Heidegger: Through Phenomenology to Thought*.

Jeffrey Andrew Barash, *Martin Heidegger and the Problem of Historical Meaning*.

Jean-Louis Chrétien, *Hand to Hand: Listening to the Work of Art*. Translated by Stephen E. Lewis.

Jean-Louis Chrétien, *The Call and the Response*. Translated with an introduction by Anne Davenport.

D. C. Schindler, *Han Urs von Balthasar and the Dramatic Structure of Truth: A Philosophical Investigation*.

Julian Wolfreys, ed., *Thinking Difference: Critics in Conversation*.

Allen Scult, *Being Jewish/Reading Heidegger: An Ontological Encounter*.

Richard Kearney, *Debates in Continental Philosophy: Conversations with Contemporary Thinkers*.

Jennifer Anna Gosetti-Ferencei, *Heidegger, Hölderlin, and the Subject of Poetic Language: Towards a New Poetics of Dasein*.

Jolita Pons, *Stealing a Gift: Kirkegaard's Pseudonyms and the Bible*.

Jean-Yves Lacoste, *Experience and the Absolute: Disputed Questions on the Humanity of Man*. Translated by Mark Raftery-Skehan.

Charles P. Bigger, *Between Chora and the Good: Metaphor's Metaphysical Neighborhood*.

Dominique Janicaud, *Phenomenology "Wide Open": After the French Debate.* Translated by Charles N. Cabral.

Ian Leask and Eoin Cassidy, eds., *Givenness and God: Questions of Jean-Luc Marion.*

Jacques Derrida, *Sovereignties in Question: The Poetics of Paul Celan.* Edited by Thomas Dutoit and Outi Pasanen.

William Desmond, *Is There a Sabbath for Thought? Between Religion and Philosophy.*

Bruce Ellis Benson and Norman Wirzba, eds. *The Phenomoenology of Prayer.*

S. Clark Buckner and Matthew Statler, eds. *Styles of Piety: Practicing Philosophy after the Death of God.*

Kevin Hart and Barbara Wall, eds. *The Experience of God: A Postmodern Response.*

John Panteleimon Manoussakis, *After God: Richard Kearney and the Religious Turn in Continental Philosophy.*

John Martis, *Philippe Lacoue-Labarthe: Representation and the Loss of the Subject.*

Jean-Luc Nancy, *The Ground of the Image.*

Edith Wyschogrod, *Crossover Queries: Dwelling with Negatives, Embodying Philosophy's Others.*

Gerald Bruns, *On the Anarchy of Poetry and Philosophy: A Guide for the Unruly.*

Brian Treanor, *Aspects of Alterity: Levinas, Marcel, and the Contemporary Debate.*

Simon Morgan Wortham, *Counter-Institutions: Jacques Derrida and the Question of the University.*

Leonard Lawlor, *The Implications of Immanence: Toward a New Concept of Life.*

Clayton Crockett, *Interstices of the Sublime: Theology and Psychoanalytic Theory.*

Bettina Bergo, Joseph Cohen, and Raphael Zagury-Orly, eds., *Judeities: Questions for Jacques Derrida.* Translated by Bettina Bergo, and Michael B. Smith.

Jean-Luc Marion, *On the Ego and on God: Further Cartesian Questions.* Translated by Christina M. Gschwandtner.

Jean-Luc Nancy, *Philosophical Chronicles.* Translated by Franson Manjali.

Jean-Luc Nancy, *Dis-Enclosure: The Deconstruction of Christianity.* Translated by Bettina Bergo, Gabriel Malenfant, and Michael B. Smith.

Andrea Hurst, *Derrida Vis-à-vis Lacan: Interweaving Deconstruction and Psychoanalysis.*

Jean-Luc Nancy, *Noli me tangere: On the Raising of the Body.* Translated by Sarah Clift, Pascale-Anne Brault, and Michael Naas.

Jacques Derrida, *The Animal That Therefore I Am.* Edited by Marie-Louise Mallet, translated by David Wills.

Jean-Luc Marion, *The Visible and the Revealed.* Translated by Christina M. Gschwandtner and others.

Michel Henry, *Material Phenomenology.* Translated by Scott Davidson.

Jean-Luc Nancy, *Corpus.* Translated by Richard A. Rand.

Joshua Kates, *Fielding Derrida.*

Michael Naas, *Derrida From Now On.*

Shannon Sullivan and Dennis J. Schmidt, eds., *Difficulties of Ethical Life.*

Catherine Malabou, *What Should We Do with Our Brain?* translated by Sebastian Rand, Introduction by Marc Jeannerod.